the
Other Side
of the
Frontier

HENRY REYNOLDS is one of Australia's best-known and most widely
read historians. He is an adjunct Professor at the University of
Tasmania. His sustained and meticulous research has played a major
part in the political and legal milestones: the Mabo and Wik
judgements. Professor Reynolds' books include *With the White People*,
Fate of a Free People, *This Whispering in Our Hearts*, *Why Weren't
We Told?*, *Fate of a Free People* and *Nowhere People*.

Other Books by Henry Reynolds

Aborigines and Settlers
Race Relations in North Queensland
Frontier
The Law of the Land
Dispossession
With the White People
Fate of a Free People

the
Other Side
of the
Frontier

Aboriginal resistance to the
European invasion of Australia

HENRY REYNOLDS

UNSW PRESS

A UNSW Press book

Published by
University of New South Wales Press Ltd
University of New South Wales
Sydney NSW 2052
AUSTRALIA
www.unswpress.com.au

First published by James Cook University of North Queensland, 1981
Published by Penguin Books, Ringwood, 1982
This UNSW Press edition 2006

National Library of Australia
Cataloguing-in-Publication entry

Reynolds, Henry, 1938- .
The other side of the frontier : Aboriginal resistance to
the European invasion of Australia.

Rev. ed.
Bibliography.
Includes index.
ISBN 0 86840 892 1.

1. Aboriginal Australians – History. 2. Aboriginal Australians – Wars.
3. Government, Resistance to – Australia. 4. Australia – Colonization – History.
5. Australia – Race relations – History. I. University of New South Wales.
II. Title.

Typeset Thomson Digital
Cover design and illustration Di Quick (after J Macfarlane, *Aboriginals
surprised by a camel team*, 1893)
Printer Griffin Press

For Isabelle Alice Reynolds

CONTENTS

NEW INTRODUCTION

I wrote *The Other Side of the Frontier* 25 years ago and with some anxiety asked a handful of colleagues to read the manuscript. Their encouragement prompted me to send it to several publishers whose negative responses were deeply disappointing. One publisher observed that there were already too many books about the Aborigines; the other that my manuscript had left out many significant themes and that it would need substantial revision. Feeling that the readers had not appreciated how innovative the work was, I received the support of my head of department at James Cook University, the late B.J. Dalton, and we published the book ourselves and sold it entirely by post. The venture was far more successful than we could have imagined. For weeks the departmental office was overwhelmed with orders from all around the country. The secretaries spent much of their time packing and dispatching books. A year later Penguin was keen to take the book on and over 20 years it was reprinted numerous times.

The manuscript was the fruit of ten years' intense, if intermittent, research – of the kind that was possible for a busy tertiary teacher. By the end of that time I had worked in the major archives and research libraries all over Australia and in London as well. In 1972 I published a collection of documents entitled *Aborigines and Settlers: The Australian Experience, 1788–1939*, and assorted articles in academic and literary journals. It was an exciting time to be working on Aboriginal history. There was much international interest in race relations and I had taken several honours courses which looked at a number of settler societies and their relations with indigenous people. Young scholars all over Australia were beginning to research hitherto neglected aspects of the country's past. But living in Townsville, in a time before email, I only had limited contact with them. My most important professional associations were with an increasing number of honours and post-graduate students in my own department in Townsville.

By the end of the 1970s I had gathered together a great deal of material and had begun to feel a sense of urgency about the need to write a substantial book. My plans changed a number of times. Originally it was to be about Queensland in the nineteenth century, then eastern Australia and finally the continent as a whole from 1788 to the early twentieth century. It began to take shape as a study of the European settlers – as much as, or more than, the Aborigines – and of what they did to, planned for and thought of the blacks.

It was only when I sat down to write with several free months in front of me that I was forced to confront the stylistic problems involved in shifting the focus from settler to indigene and back again. Suddenly, and quite impulsively, I made a decision to write two books and begin with one about the Aboriginal side of the frontier and to put aside by far the larger part of my research for a subsequent book, which eventually appeared in 1987 as *Frontier: Aborigines, Settlers and Land*.[1] Even then there seemed to be more that needed to be said. In neither frontier books had there been much about the Aborigines – and there were many of them – who worked for and associated with the pioneer settlers. This required a third book, *With the White People*, which was published in 1990.[2] The three books in the trilogy were, then, closely related and rested on research material quarried at much the same time from the same sources.

When I decided to begin with a book about the Aboriginal experience I was not sure that there was enough evidence to support the story. Much of what was available to me had been found by

chance and for at least the first five years of research had been collected more out of curiosity than with the idea of producing a book
of the kind that eventuated. When writing an introduction to the
1981 James Cook edition I observed:

> The decision to concentrate attention on the other side of the
> frontier was quite a recent one. Initially, I was convinced, like
> many previous Australian scholars, that such a study would be
> impossible to consummate, that the evidence was too fragmen-
> tary to sustain serious scholarship, or that the Aboriginal psyche
> was so different that it was uniquely resistant to the historical
> imagination. I became convinced that both propositions were
> awry and in fact they gave way together as the evidence piled up
> as slowly and inexorably as a sand-drift.[3]

I am sure that much of the momentum of the narrative derived
from the sheer excitement of piecing together the small fragments of
information and eventually finding that they made a plausible mosaic. Oral history carried out in and around Townsville provided
some of the most compelling evidence, although the resulting material was probably less important in itself than the stimulation provided to the imagination and the concurrent growth of empathy.

I recalled one occasion in particular. I was visiting a Murray
Islander elder with my friends Noel Loos and Eddie Mabo. The old
man orated in characteristic Island style with a loud commanding
voice. He retold the stories that he had heard as a child: tales of
European castaways, shipwrecks, pearl-diving and the arrival of the
London Missionary Society's teachers in 1871. One of the stories
was about the appearance of a sailing ship off Murray Island. The
old man vividly described the scene. His ancestors were scrutinising
the ship and its occupants. They had seen Europeans at the rail just
as interested in them. Indeed they were looking through telescopes
or what our informant called 'white men's eyes'. I think that may
have been the moment when the idea of *The Other Side of the
Frontier* first took root.

The book was clearly a product of north Australia and the experiences of life there in the 1960s and 1970s, which I was later to
outline in *Why Weren't We Told*.[4] But equally there were academic

origins. I had been very impressed with the new social history and the work of English scholar E.P. Thompson with his commitment to see working-class history from below. But to write about Aborigines and their experience of white Australia was quite a different task. I attempted to explain the situation when I argued in the conclusion that the book sought to turn Australian history not upside down, but inside out.

It was only much later that I realised that what I was trying to do closely paralleled the contemporaneous work of the historians of south Asia who launched the school of subaltern studies. A month or two after *The Other Side of the Frontier* was published in Townsville, in Canberra Ranajit Guha wrote the preface to the first volume of *Subaltern Studies*, which he explained would deal with those who were subject to subordination whether expressed in terms of class, caste, age, gender or office or in any other way.[5] In Volume III of *Subaltern Studies*, which appeared in 1984, Guha emphasised his opposition to elitisms and the failure of traditional history to acknowledge the subaltern as the maker of his own destiny.[6]

In Australia the impact of European colonisation was so varied and so powerful that it would be fanciful to claim that the Aborigines were ever in a position to make their own destiny. But what *The Other Side of the Frontier* showed was that by reading mainly European texts against the grain, as it is often called, it was possible to create a picture of an indigenous response that was far more varied and creative than had hitherto been supposed.

In a preface to the 1982 edition I argued that the book was a major challenge to conventional ideas about Aborigines and therefore to the way most Australians viewed important aspects of their past. Even sympathetic whites, I argued, spoke as though there was a single mode of black behaviour. I believed that I had shown that there was always diversity, contradiction, competing objectives; that Aborigines behaved politically even in the most unpromising and challenging circumstances. Previously European writers had depicted a rigid, unchanging Aboriginal society unable to cope with new challenges, which had collapsed suddenly and completely.

What I thought I had been able to show was that the Aborigines were curious about white society and endeavoured to incorporate new experiences within the resilient bonds of traditional culture. They reacted creatively to European ideas, techniques, language and commodities. Nor, I argued, were they a particularly peaceful or passive people as conventional studies often suggested. Frontier conflict was apparent in almost every part of Australia, though it varied in duration and intensity. While suffering disproportionately, Aboriginal clans levied a considerable toll on pioneer communities – not just in death and injury but in property loss and prolonged anxiety as well. The cost of colonisation, I argued, was much higher than traditional historical accounts had suggested.

While seeking to make Aboriginal behaviour understandable to white readers I hoped to draw parallels with the well-known experience of pioneer settlers. I wrote:

> Many themes link the pioneers who looked inward to Aboriginal Australia and the tribesmen who looked outward towards the encroaching wave of European settlement. Like the white colonists the blacks were pioneers, struggling to adjust to a new world of experience and one even stranger and more threatening than the Australian environment was to the Europeans.[7]

In my enthusiasm I hoped that my readers would find the other side of the frontier a new and exciting province providing fresh insights and forcing a radical reinterpretation of old themes. Aborigines who experienced the massive impact of European invasion with fortitude and courage were, I argued, people who demanded our attention and respect. I wondered if they might eventually earn as much, or even more, admiration than explorers, pioneers and other traditional heroes of nationalist mythology.

The response to my book was more positive than I could have hoped for. Even our small first edition was soon sold out, while the Penguin edition of 1982 was reprinted several times over the next few years. Over 20 years total sales have amounted to about 35 000 copies. There were many favourable reviews and several literary prizes. But in that time it has been the chance conversations with readers that have given me most encouragement. They have often said that the book allowed them to see Australian history through new eyes. Over the years, singers, composers, painters, poets and film makers have told me how they have drawn on material they found in *The Other Side of the Frontier*. Beyond a limited number of contacts of that kind an author can only speculate about how their book has been read and received. Certainly the most moving experience I can remember was when visiting Yarrabah, the Aboriginal community near Cairns, an old man showed me his copy of *The Other Side of the Frontier*. I had never seen a book so worn and so used. It had been passed around the whole community. Almost everyone had read it or had it read to them.

It is an interesting experience returning to a book written more than 20 years before. One immediate question is whether it should be rewritten or amended or left as an artefact of its time. It would have been tempting to add new evidence turned up in more recent years. But much of it would have merely added to and embellished existing interpretations. One thing that has happened since 1981 is the great expansion of oral history and the placing on the record of large amounts of Aboriginal testimony associated with land claims. There is now a significant body of evidence about the experiences and reactions of those Aboriginal people who had their first sustained experience of Europeans in the twentieth century. There is clearly another, important book to be written that would complement the nineteenth-century material that makes up the great bulk of the text of this book.

Since it first appeared I have often referred to *The Other Side of the Frontier*, have quoted from it in many lectures, but I had not, until very recently, read it from beginning to end. What immediately struck me was just how much detail the nineteenth-century sources actually provided about the Aboriginal response to the European invasion. But what unfolds is not a simple story at all. On almost every page there is evidence of complexity. It is far from being a facile moral tale of black virtue and white turpitude. It just does not fit into that category stigmatised in the 1990s as black armband history – if indeed such a phenomenon actually exists outside the imagination of conservative commentators.

But, in retrospect, some of the criticisms of the book do have currency. As any reader will be aware the evidence I used comes from all over Australia and is drawn from every period from the late eighteenth century to the early twentieth century. Underpinning the narrative is an assumption about an Aboriginal homogeneity that was never there – and a tendency to treat European settlement as an unchanging presence. These points have to be conceded. They were always there in the back of my mind. But such is the scarcity and the fragmentary nature of much of the evidence that it always seemed to be a case of doing it in the way that I did or not doing it at all.

The sad fact about Australia is that there are only a few places, and a couple of moments, when much more detailed, specific studies are possible. There was no 'middle ground' in Australia – that long era of American history described by Richard White when Indians, whites and mestizos mixed on terms of equality and left abundant documentary evidence behind.[8] The early years at Sydney were a time when a group of capable Europeans both related closely with resident Aborigines and wrote and thought about the experience. Inga Clendinnen's book *Dancing with Strangers* illustrates how creatively such documentation can be used.[9] But there were few other moments like that. The early years at Perth offer another example. The Van Diemen's Land journals and letters of George Augustus Robinson are a source still waiting for the researcher of the other side of the frontier, as are the journals and diaries of numerous nineteenth-century missionaries. But over much of the continent we are never likely to uncover more than small shards of evidence – of the kind swept up to help construct the mosaic presented here.

Another criticism voiced now and then over the last 20 years is that the history of indigenous society is written with modern anthropology in mind; that ideas taken from that discipline are then projected backwards to provide an interpretive framework. It is a practice known as upstreaming. I was always aware of this problem but I'm not sure there is any easy solution to it. It would be unthinkable to approach Aboriginal history without at least a grounding in the principal anthropological works. Having absorbed that material, it cannot be rinsed from the mind before turning to the historical record and trying to interpret the past.

Another recurring question is that of the role of the historian in writing Aboriginal history. In both editions of the book I declared my position. The work, I explained, was a white man's interpretation, aimed primarily at white Australians. What I now presume about my family's Aboriginal ancestry – as outlined in my recent book *Nowhere People*[10] – does not significantly change my view on the matter. I have long believed that, while there are aspects of traditional society that are off limits to anyone without specific permission from elders and custodians, history since 1788 is the story of the interaction of indigenous people and the new settler society; and that the available and relevant records are overwhelmingly written by white men – even when they were reporting and commenting on what Aboriginal informants told them.

Over the years I have heard conflicting opinions from indigenous Australians. Indeed, some have told me in no uncertain terms that I have trespassed on their intellectual territory. Others have spoken up in my defence and many Aboriginal people have supported my work. In Townsville my friends found a different way to deal with the question. They insisted that, although I might not know it, I was actually a Murri – an observation that returned to me with great force when my family began to uncover ancestral secrets.

The intellectual criticism of the book has long been overshadowed by attacks that are political in motivation. In fact many of them come from people who give the impression of not having actually read the text, yet don't like the idea of it. Some of the antagonism stems from my open avowal that the book could not escape the fate that awaits a political document. In the opening paragraph of both editions I nailed my colours to the mast observing that it was not 'conceived, researched or written in a mood of detached scholarship. It is inescapably political, dealing as it must with issues that have aroused deep passions since 1788 and will continue to do so into the foreseeable future'.

It is a declaration that may need a little exegesis. The book came out of Townsville, a place where race relations were a matter of everyday concern and discussion. As a lecturer in Australian history, I found that even to raise the subject created consternation – whether expressed vociferously or in deep, thoughtful silence. Almost no-one seemed detached or dispassionate when race was considered, not even in everyday conversation. To talk openly about Aboriginal history was, in itself, a political act and was seen to be so. It would have seemed a complete misrepresentation to fail to mention the fraught context in which the book was conceived, re-searched and written. And no matter how the book was addressed to an Australian audience in the early 1980s it would inevitably be received politically. This seems to be even more the case today than it was 25 years ago.

The most common criticism of my work is that I make too much of frontier violence. I have never conceded this point. I think it plays a relatively small part in the text of *The Other Side of the Frontier* and for that matter in my work as a whole. And the conflict I refer to in chapters three and four is always placed in context in an at-tempt not to condemn anyone but to explain the circumstances in which violence arose. On re-reading this material I fail to find any tendency at all to moralise about specific violent incidents or to de-liberately aggravate a tender white conscience.

But the section of the book that has acted like a lightning rod for continuing criticism is the one where I sought to determine how many people had died in frontier conflict. I began by mentioning the work of other scholars who had attempted to assess the death rate in specific regions of the country and then wrote:

> For the continent as a whole it is reasonable to suppose that at least 20 000 Aborigines were killed as a direct result of conflict with the settlers. Secondary effects of the invasion – disease,

deprivation, disruption – were responsible for the premature
deaths of many more although it is almost impossible to arrive
at a realistic figure.[11]

It was the figure of 20000 that has caused the greatest contro-
versy. Several points need to be made. I debated with myself
whether I should attempt to arrive at an estimate of the Aboriginal
death toll. I had, after all, spent ten years researching all over
Australia. I decided it was incumbent on me to report what conclusion I had arrived at as a result of that research. I thought it would
be evasive to do anything else. I could scarcely pretend that I hadn't
thought about the question. So it was an estimate and could not
have been anything more than that. I did not think 20000 was an
excessive figure for a conflict that occurred continent-wide over a
period of close to 150 years. It was a much smaller figure than other
writers have suggested given the dramatic decline of the Aboriginal
population after 1788. I still think it is reasonable to suppose that
the death rate was somewhere near that figure. None of the detailed
scholarly work over the last 20 years in books, articles and theses
has persuaded me to change my mind on the matter. What still
surprises me is that many Australians so clearly resist such a conclusion, despite our national obsession with our war dead in every
conflict from the Boer War to the present.

I thought in 1981, as I do now, that there are far more interesting questions than the actual number who died in frontier conflict, which will always have to be a matter of speculation. There
is the abiding matter of the politics of the dead or, as I asked in the
conclusion, How, then, do we deal with the Aboriginal dead? Are
they best forgotten or should they be celebrated and memori-
alised? Should they receive as much attention and reverence as
white Australian soldiers who fell in battle? Should they be celebrated as warriors who died defending their way of life against an
all-powerful invader? I certainly thought 25 years ago that we
would have made some progress in answering these questions. But
they lie there still, quite unresolved. It is time, I believe, they were
faced again. Such issues were often discussed during the 1990s,

the decade of the Reconciliation movement, but they seem to have disappeared from public discourse.

The most severe criticism of my estimate of Aboriginal deaths has come from Keith Windschuttle, particularly in his book *The Fabrication of Aboriginal History*,[12] which while focussed on early Tasmania has implications for Australia as a whole. Central to his argument is the proposition that, like many other historians, I had deliberately exaggerated the number of people killed in frontier conflict. He concluded that only about 120 Tasmanians died violently. He also reduced the conventional estimate for the pre-contact population from 5000 to 2000, the better to explain the rapid demographic decline after 1803. There is scarcely anyone familiar with Tasmanian history in the recent past who would agree with either of these figures. In his defence of his low estimate of frontier deaths, Windschuttle turned to already well-known features of the Black War. The rugged and forested terrain favoured the Aborigines, giving them advantages in both attack and escape. Convicts working in the bush were often denied guns and rarely had horses. Even when firearms were available they were cumbersome, inefficient and inaccurate.

Given these particular features of the conflict of the 1820s we would reasonably expect that the Aboriginal death toll would be greater in later decades in mainland Australia where frontiersmen were invariably mounted and armed with far better weapons. But, even if we leave these considerations aside and project Windschuttle's Tasmanian figures across Bass Strait and into the later years of the nineteenth century, we arrive at what, for many people, may be an unexpected result. Even if we take the lowest estimate of the pre-contact population of 300 000, the presumed death rate – using Tasmania as our model for conflict – would amount to between 18 000 and 19 000: a figure not far short of my estimate of 20 000. However the contemporary view is that 300 000 is much too low a figure, and that the original population might have been twice as large, suggesting further that my contentious estimate of frontier deaths was modest indeed.

With the assistance of the University of New South Wales Press we relaunch *The Other Side of the Frontier*. The climate of opinion and the general knowledge of the Australian community is quite different from that in 1981. I am as curious now as I was 25 years ago to discover how a new generation of readers responds to the book.

Chapter 1

EXPLORERS AND BEFORE

FIRST SIGHTINGS

They never seen a white man in their lives – this is in the early time. There was one white man must've got lost and he followed the Murray River down and there was a big camp and a few dark ladies went out to pick the wild-bean – they go out daily to get this wild food every day. When they went out and they looked up the river and they saw somebody moving and they got up and look again and someone was moving alright and they take it for – they call it the witchcraft man – the witchcraft man must be moving about. They left all their bean trees and they ran home to tell all the people back home in the camp – '*We saw something strange up there – It's like a white man! – a white man!!*'[1]

This is one of a number of traditional Aboriginal stories recorded in North Queensland a few years ago. It probably dates from the 1860s or 1870s but it has not been possible to relate it to a known historical event and the detail may have been significantly altered during a hundred years of currency. Similar stories were no doubt told in many parts of Australia during the nineteenth century, but when clans were dispersed and languages lost much of the Aboriginal record of their experience with Europeans was lost. Fragments survive; some in the written accounts of early settlers others embodied in Aboriginal oral tradition. The nineteenth century South Australian missionary George Taplin knew several men who remembered the arrival in 1830 of Sturt's expedition at the mouth of the Murray and the terror experienced as they watched the whale-boat cross Lake Alexandrina. Coastal tribes told European confidants about the awesome appearance of the first sailing ships off hitherto desolate coasts. In 1831 G. A. Robinson noted down in his diary the childhood recollections of a Tasmanian Aborigine who as a boy had first seen a ship anchored off Maria Island (probably the Baudin-Peron expedition of 1802). His perplexed kinsmen thought it looked like a small island but were left bewildered and ran fearfully away from the sea. Swan River Aborigines described with 'great vividness' their impressions on seeing the first ship approach the shore. They imagined it to be some 'huge winged monster' and there was 'a universal consternation'. One man ran fourteen miles inland breathlessly spreading the alarming news. Apprehension was general and women hid their children in the bush.[2] A similar story was related by Port Fairy blacks who recalled that they thought sailing ships were either huge birds or trees growing in the sea. Old men in North Queensland still tell a story about the arrival of a sailing ship at Rockingham Bay:

> In this Cardwell district there was many natives camped along that beach. And one morning they got up and looked out in the sea and they saw this ship was sailing out in the sea. And they wondering what this coming. *It was so big!!* And they watched it and watched it and watched it and gradually the ship came to the shore.[3]

For coastal tribes the sudden and unexpected appearance of Europeans was often an awesome event but away from the sea white men did not arrive unannounced. News of them travelled inland well in advance of the encroaching wave of settlement while straying domestic animals and an assortment of European commodities long preceded the bullock drays into the interior.

EUROPEAN COMMODITIES

Trade routes criss-crossed Aboriginal Australia. Shells, ochre, stone artifacts, spears, woven bags, gum, pituri and many other items were ceremonially exchanged at regular meetings, often hundreds of miles from their point of origin. European commodities gradually infiltrated traditional trade routes beginning within months of earliest contact. At the first settlement on the Tamar in 1804 local blacks gave a necklace to one of the soldiers who found to his surprise a white button threaded among the shells. Robert Dawson witnessed the trade of goods on the central coast of New South Wales in the 1820s. Tribes in the interior exchanged animal skins and fur artifacts with coastal blacks who through contact with Europeans were able to reciprocate with iron axes and pieces of glass along with such traditional objects as sea shells. Late nineteenth-century explorers of the remoter areas of the continent found exotic artifacts in isolated Aboriginal camps illustrating both the importance of traditional trading networks and the increasing use of European commodities. Carnegie found pearl shells in camps 500 miles in the interior of the Western Desert along with assorted European bric-a-brac – an old iron tent peg, the lid of a tin matchbox and small pieces of glass carefully wrapped in covers of woven feathers. Warburton found a large sea-shell and an old butcher's knife in one camp and in another two shells, a steel axe and part of an iron dray tyre. Mulligan's Cape York expedition of 1876 came across a camp where traditional items mingled with an empty sardine box, a jam pot and a sharpened piece of inch-iron. A pioneer pearler on the northwest of Western Australia came across a small cannon in a deserted camp on an island in Vansittart Bay.

The random discoveries of explorers and pioneers illustrated a more general phenomenon. All over Australia at varying times traditional tool kits were augmented with bottles, glass, strips of cloth, pieces of greenhide, articles of clothing. Iron was particularly attractive. Aborigines were given, found, or scavenged scraps of iron and finished steel tools from camps, stations and homesteads in every district in Australia and traded them back beyond the frontier. Traditional stone artifacts were being rapidly supplanted among most Aboriginal communities even before the arrival of the first permanent white settlers. Aborigines from the far south-west of

Queensland told a local pioneer that a few iron tomahawks had preceded the squatters into the district by a good thirty years. Explorers found abundant evidence of Aboriginal use of iron and steel in places well beyond the reach of European settlement. Near the farthest point of his 1846 expedition into central Queensland Mitchell saw a steel axe. 'Even here', he mused, in the heart of the interior 'on a river utterly unheard of by white men, an iron tomahawk glittered on high in the hands of a chief'.[4] Knowledge of axes may have spread even more widely than the desired objects themselves. While on his voyage around Australia in the 1820s P. P. King saw Aborigines on several parts of the coast who came down to the shore making chopping signs with their hands as if asking for European axes. Hovell met a group of blacks in central Victoria in the mid-1820s who pointed in the direction of Port Phillip indicating that they had seen white men fell trees there. Taking an axe they illustrated the way in which the Europeans had used it, 'not forgetting the grunt or hiss which the men invariably do when they are striking anything with force'.[5]

Late in 1847 Edmund Kennedy was returning from an expedition along the lower, unexplored reaches of the Barcoo. As he advanced towards the outer fringes of white settlement he began to notice the increasing evidence of the European presence – at one camp a bundle of spears tied up with a piece of cotton handkerchief, then at succeeding ones a pint pot, a fragment of a blue knitted Guernsey shirt, rags, a broken hobble strap and a buckle. But as well as such material objects Aborigines often had experience of domestic animals – cattle, horses, dogs, cats, donkeys, camels and rabbits – which strayed away from centres of European settlement.

STRAYING ANIMALS

Cattle escaped from the struggling community at Sydney cove within a few weeks of the first landing and many animals subsequently followed the example of these bovine pioneers. Explorers often found their tracks and dung far out beyond the nearest

European settlement. Oxley saw tracks 80 to 90 miles west of Bathurst in 1817. During an expedition of 1831 from the infant Swan River settlement over the Darling Range G. F. Moore reported finding what he coyly termed 'symptoms of Cows' which had already ventured into the interior.[6] When deep in the central desert in 1873 Warburton met a group of Aborigines who, he concluded, had heard of cattle both by the signs they made and their 'tolerably good imitation of lowing when they saw the camels'.[7]

The sudden appearance of cattle must have been a terrifying experience. A few traditional stories that have been preserved refer to the large size of the new animals, their fearsome looking horns, their bellowing and often aggressive behaviour. Davis and Bracefield, convict escapees from Moreton Bay, related that the Aborigines of the upper Brisbane Valley and Wide Bay were terrified of two stray bullocks that rampaged through their country and they clambered up nearby trees at the sound of their approach. South Australian Aborigines told the missionary George Taplin of the fear experienced when a couple of bullocks wandered into their tribal territories. They dubbed the exotic animals *'windwityere'*, or beings with spears on the head. In the south-east corner of South Australia local blacks told a story about their first sight of European animals. They were terrified by strange sounds in the night that could not be accounted for. At daylight one of the men crept out to investigate the source of the noise but came back deeply perplexed saying that he did not know what the creatures were for they could not be compared with anything seen before in their country. The whole party cautiously approached the strange creatures. 'We had a peep through the bushes', they later recalled:

> and saw what we now know to have been sheep, cattle, and horses and a dray. The bullock's bellowing was a terror to us. We saw the tracks of the cattle, sheep and horses, and could not imagine what it could be that made them.[8]

Cattle were probably the most common intruders into Aboriginal territory and consciousness but rabbits, cats, camels, donkeys and horses found their way out beyond the fringes of settlement in various parts of the continent. Both the Elder expedition of 1891–92 and that of Carnegie five years later discovered domestic cats in remote parts of the western desert. Horne and Aiston reported that a middle aged Aborigine from central Australia told them of his first meeting with a rabbit thirty years earlier. On leaving his camp one morning he saw the strange animal under a bush. He ran back to get his father and several other men and they decided to kill the exotic creature. It was knocked down with boomerangs and then speared and the carcase was carried into the nearest point of European settlement to be identified.

Horses ventured out beyond European settlement as well. Leichhardt's party saw one on the Dawson River in 1844 several hundred miles beyond the nearest stations as did McKinlay at Coopers Creek in 1861. North Queensland blacks tell a story about their forebears' first meeting with a stray horse. The story may date back to the release of several horses by Kennedy's expedition in 1848:

> Somebody lost a horse - first time they ever saw a horse ... and they got their spears and boomerangs and nulla-nullas and they chased this horse and they speared the horse and they put so many spears in the horse that the old horse fell down. And they walked up and had a look at him and they lift his head up and said, 'What sort of creature is this?' They never see an animal so big. They said, 'I wonder where this animal has come from, it's so big'.[9]

It is clear then that pioneers were preceded into the interior by feral animals and a range of European commodities. But what about information? How much had Aborigines learnt about the white invaders before they were caught in the onrushing tide of settlement?

INFORMATION

There was widespread cultural exchange over large areas of Aboriginal Australia. Ceremonies, songs, dances, words and ideas all flowed back and forth along the traditional trade routes. In his

late nineteenth-century study of Aboriginal life in Queensland Roth
described how ideas were interchanged:

> superstitions and traditions [are] handed on from district to dis-
> trict, and more or less modified in transit ... new words and
> terms are picked up, and ... corroborees are learnt and ex-
> changed just like any other commodities.[10]

The large ceremonial gatherings of neighbouring tribes provided the
venue for gossip, trade and cultural interchange. The anthropologist
W. E. H. Stanner observed such a meeting while studying the Daly
River tribes in the early 1930s. He noted that diffusion of ideas took
place most propitiously in quiet moments punctuating the large,
dramatic ceremonies, while little knots of men and women were
resting under the trees or around campfires at night and the songs
were chanted, 'the myths retold, the dances rehearsed, the little
technological tricks explained.[11]

Tribal messengers were widely used in traditional society. These
'living newsmongers'[12] travelled quickly over long distances conveying information from clan to clan. Early European observers of
Aboriginal life were impressed with the speed and spread of
Aboriginal communications. G. A. Robinson concluded that songs
and corroborees current around Melbourne in the 1840s had arrived 'with amazing celerity' from as far north as the Hunter
River.[13] At much the same time on the far side of the continent a
member of the Port Essington settlement noted that information
passed so rapidly from tribe to tribe that 'an event of any importance is known over a large extent of country in the course of a very
few months'.[14] Howitt made similar observations while camped
near Coopers Creek in 1861. He discovered that messengers were
continually coming in from up to 150 miles away with news for the
local clans about the movements of McKinlay's contemporaneous
expedition. Howitt was later able to confirm the accuracy of reports
that his fellow explorer had been caught in flood waters and had
consequently abandoned his dray.

Castaways and convict escapees provided additional evidence
about the passage of information. Davis and Bracefield reported

that news of Europeans frequently passed back from the outer fringes of European settlement while James Morrell confirmed that news soon spread from tribe to tribe. Barbara Thompson found that information about white activities in the Cape York area 'went at once throughout the islands',[15] a judgement supported by John Jardine the Government Resident at Somerset who wrote that:

> the communication between the islanders and the natives of the mainland is frequent, and the rapid manner in which news is carried from tribe to tribe to great distances is astonishing. I was informed of the approach of HMS 'Salamander' on her last visit two days before her arrival here. Intelligence is conveyed by means of fires made to throw smoke up in different forms, or by messengers who perform long and rapid journeys.[16]

Did news of Europeans travel as far as their artifacts? Was the meaning and significance of information significantly altered as it passed from tribe to tribe? If shells could pass right across the continent from north to south could information do likewise? We may never have enough evidence to answer these questions satisfactorily but an interesting event was reported by Windsor-Earl in relation to the Port Essington settlement in the Northern Territory. To the surprise of the Europeans Aborigines visiting the encampment from the interior spoke of 'white people who dwelt in the country to the south, and who built houses of stone',[17] referring, it was assumed, to the new colony in South Australia on the far side of the continent.

LINGUISTIC DIFFUSION

Explorers were often convinced that previously uncontacted Aborigines had heard of Europeans. Oxley thought it evident from the behaviour of blacks he met that they had 'previously heard of white people'.[18] Early Western Australian exploring parties used black guides to communicate with more remote tribes whose members confirmed that they had been told of the settlers, their behaviour and possessions. As news of Europeans spread a few words of pidgin English were probably carried back beyond the frontier – notably *yarraman* for horse, *jumbuk* for sheep, *bula or bulloki* for cattle, *wheelbarrow* for dray. These words and one or two others found their way into Aboriginal vocabularies from Bass Strait to Cape York and west into central Australia. *Yarraman* for instance, which came from the Batemans Bay dialect, was used in a large number of Aboriginal languages all over eastern Australia. In the areas around Adelaide the term *pindi nanto* or literally the newcomer's or European's kangaroo was coined as a term for horse. The diffusion of these two words – one from New South Wales, the other from South Australia – is a fascinating study. *Yarraman* reached central Australia from the east to be ultimately borrowed by the Walbri from their neighbours in that direction the Warramanga. But they also used the term *nantu* which they had borrowed from the Aranda to the south. It would seem therefore, that two currents of linguistic borrowing met and merged in the centre of the continent.

There is a little evidence from the Aboriginal side of the frontier which helps establish a link in the chain of linguistic diffusion from the Adelaide region to central Australia and beyond. In the 1920s a South Australian pioneer published an account of a series of contact stories he had collected from an old Aborigine who had grown up in the region bounded by the Flinders Ranges and Lake Frome. The old man related how:

> some of the tribe lower down south had seen these strange peo-
> ple, and they had sent a messenger on with news that these peo-
> ple were making up towards their camp, and to be on the look-
> out for them and their wonderful nantoes[19]

In the early 1860s Howitt used the word nantoe when conversing with Dieri tribesmen on the shores of Lake Hope near Coopers Creek and was immediately understood. At some stage the term passed on beyond central Australia and eventually reached the far side of the continent entering the vocabulary of the Wagaidj clans around Darwin.

Europeans typically collected Aboriginal vocabularies after considerable contact, when numerous English and pidgin terms had

been adopted directly from the settlers or acculturated blacks from districts of earlier settlement. This frontier pidgin has been studied by a number of writers since 1834 when L. E. Threlkeld published his pioneering work *An Australian Grammar* which listed over twenty 'barbarisms introduced by sailors and stockmen'.[20] But there is some evidence which suggests that prior borrowing took place from Aboriginal contacts before the arrival of Europeans. In 1846 Mitchell met a group of Aborigines on the Belyando, a locality remote from the nearest white settlement. He was amazed when the blacks exclaimed *Yarraman* on coming up to the expeditions' horses. McKinlay had a similar experience in the far north-east corner of South Australia in 1861 where there was perhaps slightly more chance of prior European contact. Explorers and pioneer squatters came across Aborigines with no apparent previous contact who used the term *white-fellow* when speaking of the Europeans. This happened to Mitchell, Alan Macpherson and Leichhardt in different parts of Queensland in the 1840s and to Carnegie in the western desert in 1896. Mitchell commented on this phenomenon in his account of his first expedition in northern New South Wales in 1831–32:

> We heard calls in various directions, and 'whitefellow' pronounced very loudly and distinctly. 'Whitefellow', or 'white-ma' appears to be their name ... for our race, and this appellation probably accompanies the first intelligence of such strangers, to the most remote, interior region.[21]

Howitt provided the most substantial evidence of the diffusion of information about Europeans and of new terms to express it. He discovered that Aborigines over a wide area of central Australia were aware of the northward progress of McKinlay's expedition of 1861. McKinlay himself was called *whilprapinnaru* by the blacks living on the outlying cattle stations in South Australia, an expression which meant the old-man, or leader, of the dray, or wheelbarrow as it was termed in pidgin English. Howitt discovered that the word followed McKinlay 'on from tribe to tribe' certainly as far as the south-west corner of Queensland along with assorted information about the expedition's possessions and behaviour.[22]

FIREARMS

News of the danger and mysterious power of firearms was almost certainly passed on to Aborigines before they came into physical contact with Europeans. Explorers often found that blacks were highly apprehensive of guns even before they had been fired. While surveying Port Phillip in 1803 Tuckey met local Aborigines who 'signified their knowledge and fear of the effect of firearms'.[23] Oxley found that blacks immediately ran off if anyone picked up a musket and would only return when it was put down 'showing by every simple means in their power their dread of its appearance'.[24] McKinlay, Stuart and Giles all reported similar reactions in remote parts of the interior. Tribesmen who met Stuart pointed meaningfully to the expeditions' guns making loud noises with their mouths; Searcey reported that when he met a group of blacks on a remote beach in the Northern Territory one man came up, touched his revolver and said 'Boom!, Boom!, Boom!'[25] Oral history from Mornington Island confirms this picture. Roughsey related that his father heard about guns long before he had seen white men. Mainland Aborigines told him how the Europeans could kill a man 'with thunder that sent down invisible spears to tear a hole in his body and spill his blood in the sand'.[26]

Linguistic evidence supports the proposition of an early diffusion of knowledge about guns. Numerous Eastern Australian languages contained terms for gun which derived from the English word musket. This suggests that the word passed from tribe to tribe quite early in the history of settlement possibly before muskets became obsolete. None of the variations of the word in question appear in lists of frontier pidgin suggesting that they evolved on the Aboriginal rather than the European side of the frontier. The geographical dispersal of musket words is impressive. They appeared in several Victorian languages – *Madjgad* in Wergaia and *Matjkat* in

Wemba-Wemba – but were more common in Queensland and the Northern Territory. *Marrkin* was used by the Budjara around Charleville and the Gugu-Badhun five hundred kilometres away on the upper-Burdekin. *Marrgin* was employed by the Gugu-Yalanji on Cape York, *Makini* by the Kalkatungu around Cloncurry, *Mugadi* by the Djingili at Tennant Creek and Daly Waters, *Makati* by the Walbri and *Mukuta* by the Aranda. Variations of the same word were used by Aboriginal tribes living 1500 kilometres apart scattered over an area almost half the size of the continent.

Thus while the evidence is fragmentary and widely scattered we can gain some impression of the impact of European settlement on Aboriginal society before face to face contact had occurred. Most clans would have already been using an array of European commodities when pioneer settlers appeared even if they did not always know precisely where the new articles had come from. Feral animals would also have entered their territories – cattle, horses, dogs, cats and pigs from the earliest period; camels, rabbits and donkeys during the second half of the nineteenth century. Information about the Europeans would probably have filtered through from distant tribes especially about the power and danger of their weapons. Along with news of the whiteman a handful of new words would also have entered ancient vocabularies all over the continent.

A CASTAWAY

Many of the themes discussed to this point were illustrated by the experiences of the English sailor James Morrell (there are various spellings of his name) of the ship 'Peruvian', wrecked on Horseshoe Reef in 1846, who lived with the Jurn and Bindal tribes of the Townsville-Bowen region for seventeen years. Morrell's reminiscences are sketchy and he was not as sharply observant as the contemporaneous castaway Barbara Thompson, but his tribal sojourn was much longer than hers spanning the period of early contact with sea-borne visitors, the first land expeditions, the appearance of feral animals and the eventual arrival of pioneer pastoralists and native police troopers which was a prelude to Morrell giving himself up to two frontier stockmen.

Morrell's tribesmen did not see any of the land expeditions of the 1840s – those of Leichhardt, Mitchell, Gregory – which all travelled inland along the valleys of the Burdekin and its tributaries. However, news of the European parties filtered through to Morrell as he recalled in a letter published in the *Rockhampton Bulletin* in 1865. But his account presents the historian with some difficulties. He maintained that two reports of European parties were received by his kinsmen in 1855 although it is by no means certain that Morrell had been able to keep track of time during his seventeen years in the bush. Nor do we know how fresh the stories were, or how altered in transit, although it is clear that some information about Europeans did come in from distant tribes.

One of the reports referred to a party of Europeans seen to the north-west, accompanied by a large number of horses and cattle. The position tallies very well with the southward route travelled by A. C. Gregory's North Australia Expedition of 1855–56. The party set out with 50 horses and 200 sheep although the flock would have been much depleted by the time it reached Queensland. But apart from the absence of cattle the Aboriginal report measures up very well with the known facts. Morrell's second story is much harder to pin down. The white party was said to be to the north but that eventually all but one member had grown thin and died. There does not appear to be any obvious source for this story though it may have become significantly changed in its passage down the coast. It could have referred to survivors from shipwreck for there must have been many such unrecorded misadventures; it may have related to the fate of the members of Kennedy's disastrous 1848 expedition who starved to death at Weymouth Bay. There is a scrap of evidence suggesting that news of Kennedy's party passed down the coast at least as far as Townsville making it likely that Morrell would have picked the story up. In the 1880s an old Aboriginal man from the Townsville district told Archibald Meston that as a young man he remembered news of an expedition coming down the coast from the north (Meston assumed it was Kennedy's) and was able to relate considerable details about the party and its assortment of animals and equipment.

From the late 1850s news began to filter through to Morrell about the pastoral occupation of central Queensland and the violence accompanying it. A distant tribe reported that they had seen a white man with two horses who shot at a funeral party killing one of the chief mourners. But the European was subsequently caught off-guard, was set upon and killed. A short time later four cattle strayed into Morrell's district and while he did not see them himself his tribal relatives showed him the tracks and carefully described the exotic animals mentioning their horns, teats and big ears. Morrell questioned his kinsmen closely and they said that:

> three had teats and one had none; thus I understood three were cows and one was a bull. I told them they were what we ate, and they chaffed me about their great size, long tails, big ears and horns.[27]

With the next report the intruders were closer and even more threatening. A party of both black and white men on horseback – presumably the Native Mounted Police – had shot down a group of the Cape Upstart people with whom Morrell had previously lived. His informants had closely observed the violent newcomers, telling him about the saddles, stirrups, bridles and other accoutrements as well as the noise and smoke when the guns were fired. From this time on Morrell received almost daily reports about the Europeans till eventually stockmen arrived in his neighbourhood with a large herd of cattle. Two old women were sent out to watch the white men and report on their activities. They did the job very well for they:

> brought word back that there was a large hut, and that they had seen red and white blankets hanging on the stockyard fences and heard a dog bark, and an old sheep bleating tied to a tree; they also heard the report of a gun twice; but could not see where it came from.[28]

A few days later Morrell approached the stockmen bringing to an end his involuntary seventeen year exile. For his Aboriginal kinsmen the events were even more portentous; many thousands of years of freedom from outside interference were coming to an abrupt and bloody end.

Morrell was one of the few Europeans who witnessed, from the other side of the frontier, the climactic moment as Aboriginal society felt the shock of the arrival of the first permanent settlers. Amongst the small group of Europeans who lived with the Aborigines only a few left any record of their experiences. But the voluminous writing of explorers contains a large amount of material useful to the scholar seeking to understand the Aboriginal response to the European invasion of their homelands.

MEETING EXPLORERS

Explorers with wide experience beyond the frontiers of European settlement were impressed by the diversity of Aboriginal reactions they encountered. Mitchell found that the 'difference in disposition' between tribes 'not very remote from each other was very striking'[29] while Stokes after circumnavigating the continent remarked that whereas some groups he met were 'most kindly disposed' to the white travellers, others manifested the 'greatest hostility and aversion'.[30] European and Aborigine met in such a wide variety of circumstances that the historian may never be able to reduce the diversity to simple patterns of behaviour. For the foreseeable future description may have to take precedence over analysis.

It is probable that a majority of Aborigines had about as much prior notice of the European approach as Morrell's tribesmen. Yet despite forewarning early meetings were still fraught with tension. So much about the whites – their appearance, behaviour, possessions, accompanying animals – were radically new; awesome; unexpected. News of the Europeans' weapons and their apparent control of powerful magic compounded the fear and anxiety. Horses were a further source of anguished curiosity, with their noise and size and speed. Aborigines often asked if horses bit. Gippsland blacks told Alexander McMillan that they had originally thought that the noise of gunfire came from the horses' nostrils. Morrell remarked that neighbouring blacks who had not had the advantage of his advice thought that horses as well as their riders could 'speak and do mischief to them.[31] Elsewhere it was thought that horse and rider were one.

Meetings with Europeans were often terrifying experiences even when violence was absent. Screaming, perspiring, shaking, involuntary urination and defecation – all the normal human reactions to extreme fear were reported at one time or another by white observers. Eyre recalled coming upon an Aboriginal camp at night and provoking a 'wild exclamation of dismay' accompanied by a 'look of indescribable horror and affright'.[32] P. P. King wrote of a party all members of which trembled with fright at the approach of the Europeans. Oxley met Aborigines who 'trembled excessively' being 'absolutely intoxicated with fear'.[33] In the western desert Carnegie thought the 'trembling fear' of local blacks 'painful to witness'.[34]

But perhaps the most notable feature of such meetings was less the terror induced than the courage displayed by people placed in situations of extraordinary tension. This was surely the hidden, perhaps the larger part, of the heroism of Australian exploration. Explorers often recognized the psychological strength of the blacks they came into contact with. Mitchell met an old man in central Queensland who, though perspiring profusely from terror; allowed no hint of anxiety to cloud his demeanour. Austin noted in Western Australia that although the Aborigines he came across were aware of the superiority of European arms their bearing was always fearless and manly. Sturt made similar observations about blacks he fell in with in central Australia. One man in particular called forth his admiration. 'His composure and apparent self possession', he wrote, 'were very remarkable':

> his whole demeanour was that of a calm and courageous man, who finding himself placed in unusual jeopardy, had determined not to be betrayed into the slightest display of fear or timidity.[35]

But while the courage of the men who went forward to meet the Europeans was clear it was probably surpassed by that of the young women who were frequently dispatched by their male relatives to appease the sexual appetite of the strange and threatening white men.

Attacks on exploring parties varied considerably in tactics, size and seriousness. Sometimes spears were thrown from cover – of the forest when Kennedy was transfixed, of darkness when Gilbert died. Occasionally large, well organized attacks were mounted like the one reported by Giles on his fourth expedition. But armed resistance to the explorers was less common than might have been expected owing no doubt to a prudent weighing of costs and benefits. The belief that Europeans possessed powerful and malignant magic may have been a crucial factor in limiting Aboriginal aggression. Clans were much more likely to carefully watch the Europeans than openly confront them. Indeed overlanding parties were rarely able to move across country without being seen by resident blacks and news of their movements was carried forward either by messenger or smoke signal. There are many examples of Aboriginal use of smoke signals. When Sturt's party was crossing Lake Alexandrina blacks on a headland lit a large fire as soon as the Europeans noticed them. It was answered from every point of the compass and in less than ten minutes the party counted fourteen different fires. Mitchell reported a similar experience. A fire lit close to the party was a sequel to a whole series of others, extending in 'telegraphic line far to the south'.[36] A party which landed on the Yarrabah Peninsula in 1882 found that as they began to move back from the beach signal fires flared on every hill as far as the eye could reach. J. S. Roe reported that as his party passed across country smoke signals would suddenly rise up within a mile and a half of their line of march. Explorers may have never been out of sight, even of earshot, of local Aborigines even at times when they imagined themselves alone in the wilderness. Some sensed the ubiquitous black presence. Writing after his expedition into north-west Queensland W. O. Hodgkinson observed that the blacks were so expert at hiding that it was unsafe to 'accept their absence from view as proof of non-existence'.[37] Oxley, the leader of one of the earliest inland expeditions, remarked that:

> it is probable that they may see us without discovering themselves, as it is much more likely for us to pass unobserved the little family of the wandering native, than that our party ... should escape their sight, quickened as it is by constant exercise in procuring their daily bread.[38]

Europeans sensitive to their surroundings felt they were being constantly watched. When landing on apparently deserted coasts Stokes believed that the eyes of the Aborigines were always upon him and that his 'every movement was watched'.[39] Jukes cautioned that no matter how uninhabited a place might appear 'even for days together' the white man should always walk in the expectation that 'a native has his eye upon you'.[40] Gilbert made a similar note in his diary shortly before he was to die from a spear thrown into the camp from the encompassing and apparently unpeopled darkness. The bushman, he fatefully wrote, must never forget that although no blacks could be seen 'they may be within a few yards of his camp closely observing every action'.[41]

Explorers occasionally stumbled on blacks who had been sent to watch them. Young women sentries kept up a constant surveillance of G. A. Robinson during his first expedition in Western Tasmania. Mitchell found that two women had sat in the bush throughout a cold, wet night without fire or water in order to observe his party. While on sentry duty one dark night Jukes nearly trod on an old man who with two or three others was crouching in the grass observing the camp. Expedition members who backtracked for one reason or another found clear evidence that vacated camping sites had been minutely examined and tracks followed for long distances. John Mann, a member of Leichhardt's party of 1844–45, observed that the Aborigines 'overturned'[42] the camp sites as soon as they were vacated. Writing of the same expedition Gilbert noted the rush of blacks to search abandoned camps where they were to be seen 'busily engaged in searching about picking up any little thing which attracted their attention'.[43] Aboriginal attraction to deserted European camp sites was emphasised in the contact stories of the Flinders Range-Lake Frome clans. They referred to the arrival of an expedition which entered their country from the south – it was probably Eyre's abortive attempt to push up into central Australia in 1840. The local blacks carefully watched the Europeans from the security of the hills but as soon as the explorers set off in the early morning they rushed into the deserted camp:

> one of the chief treasures found were parts of a bottle that had got broken ... every scrap of bottle was picked up and handed over to the head 'doctor'. These same pieces were afterwards used in their rites in place of flint ... Empty tins, a couple of horseshoe nails, bits of rope and twine – every scrap was picked up and taken to camp.[44]

Contact between explorers and Aborigines was often friendly and mutually satisfactory. The French navigator Labillardiere, for instance, wrote in praise of hospitable Tasmanians. The attentions, he observed:

> lavished on us by these savages astonished us. If our paths were interrupted by heaps of dry branches, some of them walked before, and removed them to either side; they even broke off such as stretched across our way ... We could not walk on the dry grass without slipping every moment ... but these good savages, to prevent our falling, took hold of us by the arm, and thus supported us.[45]

Explorers have left accounts of many meetings when both whites and blacks behaved with decorum and sensitivity thereby reducing the tension of contact. Flinders wrote of such an occasion on the Tasmanian coast. He gave a local Aborigine a ship's biscuit and in return accepted an old piece of whale flesh. Both parties politely put their presents in their mouths but surreptitiously spat them out when they thought the action would not be noticed.

Aborigines afforded significant assistance to white explorers in every corner of the continent supplying valuable, and at times life saving, information about waterholes and springs; fords and paths; mountain passes, easy gradients, short cuts. The West Australian

explorer Austin noted the value of such intelligence when recount-
ing his meeting with a local clan whose members gave him the name
and position of all the significant places on his line of march as far
as the boundaries of their country. He noted down the information
and then enquired about the water, rocks, timber and feed to be
found at each site. While summing up his extensive experience of
Aboriginal Australia, Eyre wrote in appreciation of the hospitality
so often afforded:

> I have been received by them in the kindest and most friendly
> manner, had presents made to me of fish, kangaroo, fruit; had
> them accompany me for miles to point out where water was to
> be procured, or been assisted by them in getting at it, if from the
> nature of the soil or my own inexperience, I had any difficulty in
> doing so myself.[46]

How can we account for such hospitality? We may never know for
certain although glimpses of the Aborigines provided by the explorers allow us to make tentative assessments of their motivation. It
seems reasonable to assume that the clans themselves were often divided over the question of an appropriate policy to adopt towards
travelling Europeans. On many, perhaps a majority, of occasions the
decision was obviously made to watch carefully but avoid contact
though this strategy was less likely to be noticed by the explorers.
But the attraction of European goods provided a powerful incentive
to establish friendly contact and awareness of firearms dampened
enthusiasm for confrontation. The provision of guides was probably a deliberate policy to resolve the contradictory objectives of
seeking access to the white men's possessions while hastening the
departure of potentially dangerous sojourners. Guides may have
been additionally motivated to take Europeans on guided tours
through their country thereby avoiding sites of spiritual significance. Exploring parties were aware that they were often taken on
circuitous routes and usually assumed that detours were made to
circumvent unseen geographical hazards. But the objectives of their
hosts may have been more religious than topographical. Interest in
the strangers; even the simple desire to be hospitable may have

encouraged the establishment of friendly contact. From their response to white visitors it is clear that clans were proud of their country, happy to recite its deeply understood amenity and to display their profound knowledge of the environment.

ABORIGINAL CURIOSITY

How curious were the Aborigines about the European invaders? Such a question would hardly arise if Australian scholars had not so often asserted that the blacks were a uniquely passive and incurious people, an assessment recently given new authority by Blainey who argued that Aborigines reacted to the sudden appearance of whites with the 'calm apathy' of a people who had lived so long in isolation 'that intruders were inconceivable'.[47] But the historical record provides scant evidence for this view. While we lack detailed information about the social customs of many tribes from districts settled in the nineteenth century it is reasonable to conclude that across wide areas of Australia displays of overt curiosity were considered the height of rudeness. Among many tribes it was customary to totally ignore visitors when they first arrived in camp. Drawing on his experience at Port Phillip in the 1840s E. S. Parker observed that when:

> individuals of other tribes thus arrived on a visit, the etiquette, if I may so term it, was remarkable! The visitor sat down at a little distance, but never spoke. He scarcely looked, indeed, at the parties he came to see.[48]

Decorum not apathy determined Aboriginal behaviour as the more perceptive explorers and settlers realized. Writing of desert Aborigines Giles remarked that 'of course they saw us, but they most perseveringly shunned us'.[49] Eyre noted the 'innate propriety of behaviour' exhibited by blacks in their 'natural state' especially in the 'modest unassuming manner' in which they positioned themselves to watch the Europeans and the total absence of anything that was 'rude or offensive'.[50] Sturt came across a desert Aborigine whose composure and self-possession were 'very remarkable' for despite the awesomeness of the meeting he was clearly determined to exhibit neither 'astonishment nor curiosity'.[51]

But there were many occasions when curiosity became the over-mastering passion breaking through traditional restraint, overlaying fear and anxiety. Mitchell wrote of a group of Queensland Aborigines for whom 'intense curiosity' overcame 'all the fears of such strangers'.[52] Leichhardt met some old men far in the interior who:

> observed with curious eye, everything we did, and made long explanations to each other of the various objects presented to their gaze. Our eating, drinking, dress, skin, combing, boiling, our blankets, straps, horses, everything in short, was new to them, and was earnestly discussed.[53]

Sturt found on his expedition down the Murray and Murrumbidgee that the party was obliged to submit anew to close examination by every group of Aborigines they met. They were pulled about and touched all over; their faces were felt; their fingers counted and their hands and feet measured against those of the investigators. Even the old and decrepit came down to the river to see them. 'The lame', Sturt wrote:

> had managed to hobble along, and the blind were equally anxious to touch us. There were two or three old men stretched upon the bank, from who the last sigh seemed about to depart; yet these poor creatures evinced an anxiety to see us, and to listen to descriptions of our appearance.[54]

In the early years of settlement the Aborigines were often intensely interested in determining the newcomer's gender. Clothing cloaked their sexual identity and clean shaven faces compounded the uncertainty. While surveying the coastline in 1819–20 P. P. King found blacks both curious and importunate demanding that one of his party undress and expose his genitals. Writing of the foundation of the Swan River Settlement, C. H. Fremantle noted that 'they think young men are women and so they want them to take their trousers off'.[55] G. B. Worgan, a first fleet surgeon, described another such encounter:

> I must not omit mentioning a very singular Curiosity among the
> Men here, arising from a Doubt of what Sex we are, for from
> our not having, like themselves long Beards, and not seeing
> when they open our Shirt-Bosoms (which they do very roughly
> and without any Ceremony) the usual distinguishing
> Characteristics of Women, they start Back with Amazement,
> and give a Hum! with a significant look, implying. What kind
> of Creatures are these?! – As it was not possible for Us to sat-
> isfy their Inquisitiveness in this Particular, by the simple Words.
> Yes or No. We had Recourse to the Evidence of Ocular
> Demonstration, which made them laugh, jump and Skip in an
> Extravagant Manner.[56]

The desire to determine the sex of the Europeans may have had
more important reasons than idle curiosity. Establishing the sex of
a party could help explain its objectives; an all male group might
presage conflict, one with women and children a more peaceful mission. Baldwin Spencer noted that in central Australia the fact that a
party:

> is travelling with women and children is prima-facie evidence
> that their intentions are not hostile, but a party of men trav-
> elling without their women-folk is always looked upon with
> suspicion.[57]

Aborigines with little previous experience of Europeans were
often perplexed by their clothes and hats and footwear. It may not
have been immediately apparent where the covering ended and the
flesh began. Writing of his life while pioneering the Champion Bay
district in Western Australia F. F. Wittenoom recalled that one wet
night he pulled off his pyjama coat to dry it. A local black watching
the procedure let out a shout on seeing the white skin and soon a
crowd came round to witness the spectacle. Daniel Brock, a member of Sturt's central Australian expedition of 1844 noted the interest aroused by his clothes among a group of blacks camped close to
the exploration party. A curious clansman was inspecting his boots
when Brock drew up his trousers exposing the white skin to the
amazement of those watching, a reaction which was intensified
when he drew off both his boot and his sock. The Aborigines' reaction to European clothing was graphically related in a traditional

story about the arrival of Europeans on the beach at Cardwell. The whites came ashore and offered various presents to the assembled clans. They threw clothes and blankets towards the blacks whose reactions of fears and wonder are still remembered:

> and they got a big long stick and they picked it up with the stick and they couldn't make out what that was. They thought this man was changing his skin. They said this man left his skin there. All the natives thought this man was taking his skin. They said this man has been peel himself like a snake and they got the stick and they picked it up with a stick and they looked and looked at this shirt and trousers. You know they couldn't make out and they pick up a blanket and have a look, some pretty colours, they couldn't make out and this fellow took his shirt out and threw it down on the ground. They see him how he took his shirt. Don't know what colour was the shirt. But when he took his shirt and he was white they thought he change his colour when he took his shirt off. They pick up that shirt with the stick because they was too frightened to pick it up with a hand because in our custom might be something very dangerous, witchcraft.[58]

As they cautiously picked up the articles of clothing on the end of a long stick the Cardwell blacks illustrated the ambivalence which characterized the Aboriginal response to Europeans all over the continent, the amalgam of curiosity and fear, attraction to the new yet the resistance to change inherent in the ancient cultures of Aboriginal Australia.

Chapter 2

CONTINUITY AND CHANGE

GHOSTS

The sudden arrival of Europeans provoked more than fear and curiosity. It sparked intense and often prolonged debate as to the true nature of the white men, their origin and objectives. During the early years of settlement many blacks believed that Europeans were beings returned from the dead, an assessment confirmed by the testimony of the small group of Europeans who gained some insight into tribal attitudes and behaviour. Moorhouse, the Protector of Aborigines in South Australia, believed it was the 'universal impression' among blacks of that colony.[1] Eyre thought the 'general belief' was that Europeans were 'resuscitated natives'[2] while Stokes considered the view 'universally diffused'[3] among the tribes. Writing of his experience at Port Essington Windsor-Earl noted that local clans recognized the spirits of the dead in all the strangers who visited their country. Castaways and escapees concurred, Buckley reporting that Port Phillip Aborigines were convinced that white men were Aborigines who 'had returned to life in a different colour'.[4] Thompson found on Cape York that all the local blacks thought that white men were the 'spirits of black men come again in a new form'.[5] When Davis, the Moreton Bay escapee, was 'rescued' by an exploring party his relatives said he was going back to join the dead. Linguistic evidence provides further confirmation. All over the continent in areas of early settlement the Aborigines applied to Europeans traditional terms meaning variously, ghost, spirit, eternal, departed, the dead. In north Queensland, settled in the second half of the nineteenth century, the same rule applied. The celebrated ethnographer W. E. Roth observed that in the many local dialects which he had recorded the same word was 'found to do duty for a European and a deceased aboriginal's spirit, ghost'.[6]

Why was this idea so pervasive? To begin with it is important to stress that far from being an example of childlike fancy or primitive irrationality this view of the European was a logical conclusion premised on important and widely shared beliefs. What were they, then? The Aboriginal cosmos was geographically limited. Most, if not all people, of the known world were kin or potentially so. Outside the circle of known, and at least partially intelligible clans, was the 'cosmological periphery' which had little geographical definition. A contemporary scholar has written that:

> Owing to the Australian kinship system everybody is – or can be – related to everybody else. If a friendly stranger approaches a camp, he is always finally recognized as being related to someone of the group. Consequently, for the Australians, only one 'world' and only one 'human society' exist. The unknown regions outside familiar lands do not belong to the 'world' – just as unfriendly or mysterious foreigners do not belong to the community of men, for they may be ghosts, demonic beings, or monsters.[7]

While the secular world was circumscribed and populated by a few hundred, or even a few thousand individuals, the realm of the spirits was wide and vibrant with life. At death the spirit left the body, and unless correct ceremonial was followed it might remain moving about tribal territory, but in the normal course of events it would return to the land of spirits which was variously in the sky, beyond the horizon, or more portentously for many coastal people, beyond the sea. The spirit world was real, tangible and ever present. It was a much more likely starting point for the white strangers than unknown, even unsuspected, countries beyond the horizon.

COUNTRYMEN AND RELATIVES

In many cases whites were thought to be not merely re-incarnated blacks but actually returned countrymen. This conclusion was also a perfectly logical one given acceptance of a few basic assumptions. In Aboriginal Australia individuals were thought to belong to their country by powerful spiritual bonds. The unexpected arrival of Europeans caused many to conclude that they too must have belonged to the land in question, or at least know of it, in a previous life. The West Australian pioneer G. F. Moore reported that local blacks had decided that none but those who were 'already acquainted with the country could find their way to it'.[8] Another early settler was asked if Europeans had not known of the country in an earlier existence: 'why should you come here with your wives, your ships, your flour, your cattle? How did you know there was plenty of water?[9] George Grey sensed the logic implicit in the Aboriginal viewpoint. They themselves, he wrote:

> never having an idea of quitting their own land, cannot imagine others doing it; – and thus, when they see white people suddenly appear in their country, and settling themselves down in particular spots, they imagine that they must have formed an attachment for this land in some other state of existence, and hence conclude the settlers were at one period black men, and their own relations.[10]

Other available evidence appeared to support the view that Europeans had returned from the dead. White was a colour widely associated with death; pipe-clay was used extensively in mourning. When Daniel Brock displayed his white feet to inquisitive desert Aborigines they immediately associated the sight with death and sang a lament over him. In parts of the country corpses were peeled of the outer skin leaving them a pinkish colour reminiscent of northern European complexions. South Australian Aborigines in fact called white men *grinkai* the term for a peeled, pink corpse. A legend told to W. E. Roth on the Pennefeather River in north Queensland confirms the perceived link between the white complexion and the loss of the outer skin. The story concerned a boy who was playing in a lagoon and was swallowed by a big brown snake. The reptile expelled the boy in three or four days but by then he had lost his outer skin and had become a white fellow.

Coastal clans in many parts of the continent believed that at death the spirit travelled across or through the sea to offshore islands or places far over the horizon. An early West Australian settler noted that local blacks 'inform us that the spirits of their departed traverse the great waters and then become white'.[11] Aborigines from Cape Bedford on the far north-Queensland coast believed that spirits travelled east where they entered the bodies of white people. They actually called Europeans *ganggal-naka-waraigo* or babies coming from the east. West Australian Aborigines explained to the official Aboriginal interpreter that they attributed the pale colour of the Europeans to the influence of saltwater during the long marine journey to the land of spirits.

With apparently sound reasons for regarding Europeans as reincarnated countrymen it needed only the recognition of characteristics of appearance, mannerisms or gait to claim them as returned relatives. 'Likeness', Grey observed, 'either real or imagined completed the illusion'.[12] Aborigines from around Perth were said to be able to recognize several hundred colonists by their 'countenance, voices and scars of former wounds'.[13] G. W. Moore confirmed this picture. West Australian pioneers were, he wrote, frequently claimed as relatives by old people who treated them 'according to the love they formerly bore to the individuals supposed to be recognized'.[14] Stokes referred to the case of a settler who was visited by his supposed kin twice a year though it necessitated a journey of sixty miles. Dr S. W. Viveash noted in his diary in February 1840 that the Aborigine Mignet had told him that his real name was *Muswite* 'a York native who had died and jumped up a white fellow'.[15] Mrs Edward Shenton recalled that Perth Aborigines had called her grandmother *Budgera* saying she was a 'black woman jumped up white woman' and they always wanted to make friends with her.[16] An early settler at Port Phillip noted that local blacks informed him that they recognized long lost relatives in the persons of white neighbours. A South Australian woman recalled that she was actually given the name of a deceased member of the local clan and nothing that she said would convince the blacks to do otherwise. Grey wrote of his experiences when claimed as the re-incarnated son of an old Aboriginal woman:

> A sort of procession came up, headed by two women, down whose cheeks tears were streaming. The eldest of these came up to me, and looking for a moment at me said ... 'Yes, yes, in truth it is him'; and then throwing her arms around me, cried bitterly, her head resting on my breast; and although I was totally ignorant of what their meaning was, from mere motives of compassion, I offered no resistance to her caresses ... At last the old lady, emboldened by my submission, deliberately kissed me on each cheek ... she then cried a little more, and at length relieving me, assured me that I was the ghost of her son, who had sometime before been killed by a spear wound in his breast ... My new mother expressed almost as much delight at my return to my family, as my real mother would have done, had I been unexpectedly restored to her.[17]

But while the belief in re-incarnated relatives appeared to fit some of the objective circumstances problems constantly arose which required further explanation. Eyre remarked that South Australian Aborigines of his acquaintance could not understand why the settlers did not recognize their former relatives and friends. He had, he said, often been asked why the 'dead were so ignorant, or so forgetful so as not to know their friends'.[18] Similar complaints were reported from other parts of the continent. A West Australian woman wrote in 1839 that the local blacks thought Europeans 'fools and blockheads to have forgotten everything that happened while we were sojourning with them'.[19] Fifty years later Roth found that Cape Bedford blacks wondered how and why the Europeans had 'forgotten all about their aboriginal ancestors'.[20]

The same problem arose with castaways like Buckley and Thompson who on introduction to tribal society were unable to speak a word of the local languages and were totally ignorant of their hosts' customs and manners. But with enough resilience this too could be explained. It was assumed in both cases that the traumatic experience of death and unexpected return to life had impaired the intelligence and expunged the memory. Thompson was treated with the slightly amused compassion reserved for the simple minded. Her gradual mastery of the local language was taken as a slow restoration of lost linguistic skills. Buckley was humoured and shielded in a similar way being kept out of quarrels and away from recurrent skirmishing. His kinsmen were highly amused when he was unable to eat a dog's leg. 'No doubt', he later reminisced:

> they thought my having died and been made white had strangely altered my taste. My not being able to talk with them they did not seem to think at all surprising – my having been made white after death, in their opinion, having made me foolish; however, they took considerable pains to teach me their language, and expressed great delight when I got hold of a sentence or even a word, so as to pronounce it somewhat correctly, they then would chuckle, and laugh and give me great praise.[21]

'NOTHING BUT MEN'

For how long did this view of the European prevail? Unfortunately, the evidence is so meagre that we must speculate. However, it is realistic to assume that the nature of the white man was a major question of debate within Aboriginal society and that the emergence of a more 'secular' view of the newcomers took place unevenly both between and within tribal groups. A writer in the *Perth Gazette* remarked in 1836 that it was impossible to dissuade the old people from their original view of the Europeans but the younger ones were beginning 'to have their faith shaken on this point'.[22] Moorhouse, the Protector of Aborigines in South Australia, sensed the shift of Aboriginal opinion. Local blacks, he wrote, were concluding that white people were 'nothing but men'.[23] There is some linguistic evidence which illustrates the changing view of the Europeans. In Miriam, the language of the Eastern Torres Strait, the original term for white-men which meant ghost or spirit was replaced by a word meaning 'bow-men' referring to the position characteristically taken up by white men in dinghies and luggers. Blacks from the Pennefeather River in north

Queensland originally thought Europeans were spirits and called them *kai-worda-ngai* or bark-sap-spirits, white complexions being compared to the light colour found on the inside of bark on local trees. Eventually they concluded that the white men had nothing to do with the spirits so they dropped the relevant word *Ngai* and simply used the term *Kai-worda* on its own.

In other places attitudes to Europeans altered but ghost words survived while undergoing a subtle pejorative change to eventually mean devil, malignant spirit or simply evil doer. Having been applied to whites in one place ghost words were sometimes adopted elsewhere while the original connotations of spirituality were left behind. This seems to have taken place in central and north Queensland. The word *miggloo* (there are many variations) appears to have come from central Queensland where it meant both ghost and white man. But it spread throughout the north as the most common word for Europeans while losing its original meaning on the way. It is still widely used today as a derisory, even contemptuous, term for white Australian.

In areas of later settlement the illusion that Europeans were spirits may never have taken root. The 'secular' view probably arrived 'ready-made' from the other side of the frontier along with diverse information about the Europeans. This is strongly suggested by the linguistic evidence. In more remote areas there was a greater tendency for the blacks to use terms for Europeans which lacked any spiritual connotation. The widespread adoption of variants of 'white fellow' or 'white man' was symptomatic of the change in attitude. These were, after all, new words with no weight of traditional meaning, stemming from European rather than Aboriginal society. Many examples spring to mind – *walpala* as used around Cloncurry, *white-pella* on the Georgina, *weilbulea* along the upper Darling, *waelbela* among the Aranda and *wapala* among the Walbri. Other terms were used, sometimes conjointly with 'white-fella' words, referring to physical or cultural attributes of the Europeans. The Walbri had one term meaning 'dusty coloured' and another which meant literally a 'house person'; the Djingili from the central Northern Territory used the generic word for red (sunburn perhaps); some Tasmanian tribes coined the term 'ugly head' for the white intruders.

The belief that Europeans were relatives returned from the dead had important consequences for the Aboriginal response to the invasion of their territory. It was clearly crucial in determining the fate of castaway mariners and convict bolters. Recognition meant acceptance and security, lack of it ensured death. The unexpected visitor had to be either kinsman re-incarnate or a dangerous spirit from the cosmological periphery. Davis, Morrell, Buckley and Thompson were all accepted and taken in; many others forgotten to history were no doubt killed. Davis observed perceptively that there was always considerable danger when first meeting a new tribe for 'should no-one recognize you as a relative returned to life you are sure to be speared'.[24] When he appeared before a Parliamentary Select Committee he was questioned on this point:

> Mr. Watts: How did the blacks receive and treat you in the first instance?
> Davis: First rate, nothing could be better.
> Chairman: Knowing you to be a white man?
> Davis: Yes, they took me to be the ghost of a black fellow.[25]

Buckley noted that when whites had been killed it was due to the fact that the blacks 'imagined them to have been originally enemies, or belonging to tribes with whom they were hostile'.[26] A traditional story from north Queensland about the first meeting with a white man details the reaction to a person who was considered a malignant spirit:

> and all the boys went down and took their spears and their swords and nulla-nulla and they went up to the river and they see this white man was coming down and he was putting his hands up – was surrendering himself to them – but these natives never seen a white man in their life and they run up to him – and the blackfellows speared him because they didn't know he was a white man. They'd never seen a white man. They speared him and they killed him there and then they left him there and they run away for their life. They said this is a witch-craft man come to destroy us and they ran away ...[27]

Initially many Aborigines endeavoured to absorb the experience of European invasion within the framework of traditional thought. They were successful to a surprising degree. The sudden appearance of white men could be explained although something had clearly altered the familiar cosmic processes with spirits re-entering the world of men in a radically new guise. But even this could be accommodated by minds made flexible, or gullible if you will, through intimate acquaintance with, and everyday acceptance of, magic. Some followed the apparent line of logic even further assuming that they too would henceforth follow the newly established cycle of death, spirit journey and return as a white man. How widespread this belief was is difficult to say although there were numerous reports of it from pioneer settlers. The *Perth Gazette* for instance, noted in 1838 that it was a superstition which was 'very general' among local black communities.[28] Another observer believed that many Aborigines were actually looking forward to death in order to 'return with guns, arms and provisions'.[29] At much the same time in Victoria the Aboriginal Protector James Dredge remarked that many local blacks thought that when they died they would 'jump up white men'.[30]

One consequence of seeing Europeans as returned relatives was that they could be readily absorbed into kinship networks. This had potential advantages for Aboriginal society by defining the appropriate behaviour both by and towards the white people. It also created expectations concerning the Europeans' obligation to share their material abundance. A Western Australian pioneer observed that the blacks had concluded that as the whites were 'their relatives restored to them with plenty of bread and good things' they should 'have a right to share with us, as their law compels them to divide whatever they have'.[31] Once the illusion of re-incarnation had been shattered other mechanisms were used in an endeavour to encompass settlers within the reciprocal sway of kinship. From being resurrected relatives the whites could be regarded as 'de-facto' kin through place of residence, sexual intimacy or mutual gift giving.

Aboriginal misconceptions about the white invader had important consequences for the early development of the Australian colonies, shielding infant and insecure settlements from latent black hostility. Perth Aborigines were asked why they speared the settlers if they genuinely looked upon them as ancestors and friends. Their answer was interesting. They said that in their view they had treated the whites with much greater consideration than would have been shown to strange blacks. If unknown Aborigines had attempted to intrude in the way the Europeans had done the local clans would 'have done all in their power to destroy them'.[32] In South Australia Moorhouse noted that as long as the Aboriginal illusions about Europeans survived they 'seldom attacked the whites'. Consequently he wanted to preserve black misconceptions as long as possible otherwise they would come to realize that Europeans could be 'beaten, overcome and murdered by the same means as the natives themselves'.[33] Similar views were expressed in north Queensland a generation later. The editor of the *Port Denison Times* remarked in 1866 that local blacks were rapidly losing a portion of the 'awe of the white man, which is so great a safeguard to us'. He was concerned that they would 'very soon lose ... their superstitious dread' of the Europeans, that:

> the less insight the blackfellows are allowed to get into the white man's habits the more awe they will have of him, and the more easy they will be to manage.[34]

Thus the Aboriginal debate about the true nature of the white invaders, mirroring similar discussions on the European side of the frontier, had important consequences for both the settlers and the blacks themselves. But there were also many other ways in which Aboriginal society adjusted to the presence of the whites. Developments in language, music, dancing, painting and practically all aspects of material culture illustrated the linked themes of continuity and change, accommodation and resistance.

LINGUISTIC CHANGE

It was more common for Aborigines to learn English than for settlers to pick up indigenous dialects although there were notable exceptions. Edward Curr observed in 1880 that most blacks were accustomed from childhood to hear and often speak languages other than their own and consequently learnt new ones more readily than the average colonist. They were, he wrote, usually able to 'quickly pick up sufficient broken English to understand what is necessary, and to make themselves understood'.[35] Communication was facilitated by the use of an Australian pidgin – a melange of words from English, from Pacific creole and more especially from the dialects in use around the earliest settlements. A list of such words includes well known 'Aboriginal' terms like *nulla-nulla, woomera, warrigal, coolamon, mia-mia, waddy, boomerang, gibber, gin, kangaroo, carbon, bail, boogery*. A few dozen words like these became the linguistic core around which an Australian frontier pidgin was built with variations according to place and period. The origin of many of the words was soon forgotten and in the use of pidgin both blacks and whites laboured under 'the mistaken idea' that each was conversing in the other's language as the missionary Threlkeld perceptively observed.[36]

Modern linguistic studies combined with Aboriginal vocabularies collected in the nineteenth century make it possible to chart some of the intellectual currents generated by contact with European society. Three basic developments can be observed – the direct adoption of European words, the creation of new ones and the expansion of old to encompass novel circumstances, objects and concepts. The adoption of English words involved more than a simple linguistic transfer. Foreign terms had to be significantly modified to assimilate to local pronunciation and orthography often producing sufficient alteration to disguise the borrowing to all but the expert ear. In some cases words were borrowed while meanings changed. Thus the Jodajoda called sheep *wulubua* deriving from the English word wool. Elsewhere words continued to be used in Aboriginal society after they had become archaic in English. The widespread use of musket words in the late nineteenth century and twentieth has been documented above. There are numerous examples of the expansion of traditional words to encompass new meanings. In

Kalkatunga sugar was given the traditional name for honey, coins were called pebbles and writing called patterns. In Yidin the word *dama* which meant anything dangerous like a snake or centipede was extended to include alcohol, opium and medicines. Nineteenth century word lists contain many similar examples. Compasses were called circles in South Australia; in the Burdekin Valley watches were given the same word as the sun. In South Australia pots and kettles, through identification by shape, were given the traditional word for bottle-tree, in Victoria bottles were referred to as being emushaped. Introduced animals were sometimes given traditional names. In Gippsland European cats were given the same name as native ones, in Tasmania pigs were called wombats.

The various new formations were even more interesting. A simple device was to preface a traditional word with an expression meaning whiteman's as in white man's kangaroo for horse and white man's maggots for rice. Perhaps the greatest variety was shown in the various words coined for policemen – *knot maker* or *tier* in Kalkatunga, *tie up hands* in Wergaren, *chainman* in Wade-wade, *tier* or *binder* in Yutilda, *with stripes* in Yidin, *jumping ant* in Gugu-Yalanji, *octopus* in Gippsland, *hatturned-up* in Wandwurril, the *bitter ones* among clans around Boroloola, and in Walbri two words expressive of a significant emotional dichotomy, *angry person* and *elder brother*.

European animals called forth a variety of new words. Rabbits were called *stand up ears* and *white bottom* in Wembaweba and *long ears* in Wergaga. In various other Victorian languages sheep were called *soft feet* and *feed on ground*, pigs were termed *turn ground* and roosters *call for day*. There were several examples of onomatopoeic words – *boo.oo* for cattle and *ba.ba* for sheep in Tasmania, *gump-gump* and *neight-neight* for horse in the Western District. A few other words illustrate the diversity of the Aboriginal linguistic response. In Kalkatunga wind-mills were called *turn-turn water-fetchers* while boots were termed *foot-stinkers* in Ngalooma. Clans around Newcastle called peaches *tah-rah-kul* or literally 'to set the teeth on edge'.

PAINTING

Change and continuity in Aboriginal languages were paralleled by post-contact development of painting on both rock and bark. In many parts of Australia references to Europeans, their artifacts and animals can be found amid the vast assortment of traditional figures which cluster and overlap at rock-art sites. Around the northern coasts ships, recognizably rigged as schooners, praus or luggers sail incongruously through seas of alien iconography. Feral cats appear among massed marsupials on Hammersly Station; horse and bullock tracks are engraved on the walls at Goat Rock Site in Central Queensland; four horses appear on painted walls on the Cobar Pedeplain. At Laura a giant horse eleven feet long and seven-feet high bestrides the rock shelter. Rifles, revolvers and axes appear at a number of sites and here and there Europeans are depicted – on horseback, with hats and clothes. In the rock shelter near Ingaladdi waterhole in the Northern Territory a nameless drover has been immortalized driving his horses and cattle across the sandstone wall. Painting on trees or bark have generally not survived but nineteenth-century reports leave a few valuable references like the tree painting of a ship in full sail seen on the Darling Downs or the charcoal sketches of a large party of natives spearing a white man seen by G. A. Robinson in Central Victoria. A Tasmanian settler discovered that inland Aborigines were in the habit of 'representing events by drawing on the bark of trees'. He reported that:

> the march of a certain party over a country before unfrequented by us was found a short time afterwards drawn with charcoal on a piece of bark, by a tribe of natives who [had] been observed attentively watching their movements. The carts, the bullocks, the men, were distinctly represented, according to the exact numbers that really existed.[37]

MUSIC AND DANCE

European tunes, words and themes were gradually introduced into secular songs and corroborees. In the early 1840s G. A. Robinson discovered that 'Italian melodies' were being adopted by Victorian blacks; were sung by the young people with considerable ability and were passing quickly from clan to clan while J. Mathew noted a little later in Queensland that English popular songs were often woven into corroborees. A settler from the Hume River told a government inquiry in 1849 that local blacks punctuated their songs with calls of 'Halleluyah' and 'Oh be Joyful'. Threlkeld heard groups around Newcastle singing and some had 'attempted with no bad effect to imitate the sacred music of the church'.[38] When out in the bush Eyre frequently lay awake to listen to Aboriginal singing. A sentence or two of English, was, he wrote, often introduced by way of direct quotation while 'Europeans, their property, presence, and habits, are frequently the subject of these songs'.[39] Corroborees were composed featuring dramatic events of settler society. Moreton Bay blacks created one about the wreck of the S.S. *Sovereign* in 1847. Murray River clans created one about the first steamship which sailed the inland waterway. The Rockhampton camp performed a train dance when the railway reached central Queensland; South Australian Aborigines were likewise inspired by the sight of the steam train and sang:

> You see the smoke at Kapunda
> The steam puffs regularly
> Showing quickly, it looks like frost
> It runs like running water
> It blows like a spouting whale[40]

Barbara Thompson described a white man, or 'ghost ship' dance created by the Mount Ernest Islanders in Torres Strait. Two men were dressed up as Europeans with masks made from light coloured bark and rind from coconut trees. She explained that:

> they don't whiten the mask but put red on the cheeks and leave the other part their natural light yellowish colour ... they rubbed white on their legs and wore shirts the white men had given them ... they sing songs about ships, that they are gone away to their own land and will come again with biscuits, tobacco and knives and shirts[41]

Aboriginal interest in and acute observation of European animals found expression in horse and cattle dances witnessed by

Europeans in a number of places during the nineteenth century. There are several accounts of the horse dance of the Tasmanians. Robinson explained how the participants crawled around the fire upon hands and knees, shook their heads, stopped and then imitated horses feeding. A second account detailed how the dancers took hold of each other's loins, followed one another, and then simulated the prancing of the animals while a woman played the part of the driver gently tapping them with a stick as they passed. Several writers left accounts of Queensland cattle dances. The squatter G. S. Lang was most impressed with the accuracy of the imitation; the action and attitude of every individual member of the entire herd being 'ludicrously exact' – some lay down chewing the cud, others stood scratching themselves with hind feet or horns, licking themselves or their calves while several rubbed against each other 'in bucolic friendliness'.[42]

DOMESTIC ANIMALS

Aboriginal reactions to introduced animals is an important aspect of contact history although available evidence is scattered and inadequate. It seems appropriate to distinguish between the response to cattle and sheep, which will be discussed below, and to horses and dogs. One of the most impressive examples of successful adaption was the Tasmanian's utilization of dogs which in a few years became important in tribal society, both for hunting and a variety of other purposes. In a remarkably short time Island blacks had learnt how to control and employ large dog packs. Robinson found that 'the tact these people have in quieting their dogs' was 'truly surprising'.[43] Some lessons were undoubtedly learned from the settlers, the *Launceston Advertiser* reporting the discovery of several pieces of bullock-hide rope to which were attached little collars which Island blacks used for the purpose 'of securing their dogs'.[44] But there was evidence of independent adaption as well. Hunting techniques were modified, huts were sometimes enlarged to accommodate the dogs and in southern Tasmania large bark catamarans were built to enable them to be transported across estuaries and out to off-shore islands. Rhys Jones observed that the Tasmanians sought dogs avidly:

> incorporating them into their culture with extraordinary rapidity. In so doing they adapted their hunting methods, and managed to make the profound social and psychological adjustments necessary in setting up an affectionate relationship with the new animal, a relationship radically different from anything that they had had with other animals.[45]

It was much easier for blacks to acquire European dogs than horses which were many times more valuable and therefore closely guarded. Wild horses were hard to catch and domesticate and their size and speed made them objects of awe and fear. The rapidity of pastoral expansion precluded the possibility of a gradual acquisition of the techniques of horsemanship. Yet clearly Aborigines did sometimes succeed in taking horses from the settlers or catching stray ones and then experimenting in their use. In 1883 Edward Curr published a translation of an Aboriginal song relating to such a case although it is impossible to date the piece. Yet it clearly deals with a tentative approach to horse riding:

> Halloo! (a)-horse, (canst) thou wild ride?
> No! of -horses I (am) afraid.
> Thou why afraid?
> (The) -horse (might) -throw -(me)
>   (my) bones (Might) -break.
> Try thou, mount, (to see) whether
>   (he will) -buck.
> Thou-indeed for-the-horses-go, we
>   (shall) -lie in-the-scrub, i.e., camp out.
> In-a-little-while (we shall) -go, (the)
>   ground (is) damp at-present.[46]

A native police officer in Central Queensland reported seeing a group of young Aborigines experimentally riding fat wethers round a bush clearing. There are accounts from north Queensland of horses being taken and used by blacks before they had 'come in' to European settlement. A Flinders River squatter complained to the Queensland Government that local clans took his horses and rode

them sometimes three at once, while an early Cloncurry settler remarked that 'as an instance of their advancement by contact with
the whites, the natives have discovered the adaptability of a sheet of
bark as a substitute for a saddle'.[47] Yet another outback squatter
wrote in anguish to the Brisbane papers complaining that the blacks
not only killed cattle and attacked stations but also stole the horses:

> to drive the cattle to wherever they may think fit to slaughter
> them; a thing probably not on record before. It is well known
> that the blacks in this district have now in their possession five
> saddle horses which they put to this use.[48]

In 1884 a police constable found a stockyard in the bush containing two horses which were being regularly fed and ridden by the
local Aborigines. A few years earlier a Queensland Native Police detachment followed a group of Aborigines who had speared a
European and taken his horse. They led the animal through miles of
broken country, hobbled it at night when they camped and practised
riding during the day. The catching and corralling of European animals will be considered more fully below. But what of the impact
of new commodities on Aboriginal material culture?

EUROPEAN ARTIFACTS

The early and widespread adoption of iron has been already men-
tioned. Its advantages were quickly apparent – it was hard, durable,
pliable and easily sharpened and maintained in that condition. It
was used for a whole range of implements and weapons – for spearheads, axes, knives and even for boomerangs. Blacks on the west
coast of Tasmania collected rust from a shipwreck and after grinding and mixing with water used it as a substitute for ochre. Iron was
absorbed into traditional technology and was usually hafted and secured with gum and sinews in the customary manner. It must have
often been shaped and sharpened by many hours of grinding and
hammering with stone tools. The Queensland explorer R. L. Jack
observed that Cape York Aborigines fashioned 'with infinite pains'
such 'unconsidered trifles' of old iron as shovels, broken pick heads,

scraps of iron hoops, ship's bolts, telegraph wires, nails, cartwheel tyres into weapons and implements.[49] The anthropologist Donald Thomson observed that by the 1920s iron had replaced wood or bone headed harpoons in the armoury of the dugong hunters on the coast of Cape York. 'When it is remembered', he wrote:

> that the only iron available to the native is in the form of odds and ends discarded by the white man, and that his only tools are an unlimited quantity of pumice stone or coral limestone, and perhaps an old discarded file or two, the results he achieves are often remarkable. The bush Aborigine, even after he has learned to use iron for his weapons, has no knowledge of the working of iron hot ... if an iron rod, or a piece of wire is to be straightened out, this is always done cold. For the rest he depends upon his natural deftness in technological matters, and an inexhaustible patience.[50]

Did Aborigines elsewhere learn how to use heat when working with iron? Cape York blacks had no direct contact with European settlements. Whites arrived, if at all, by boat. It is just possible that on the vast land frontier knowledge of metal technology passed back beyond the edges of white settlement. Clans in contact with European townships or stations would have soon become aware of the importance of the blacksmith and we can assume were curious about his function and methods. But the Wiradjuri of central New South Wales seem to have been the only people to coin their own term for the blacksmith whom they called *burguin mudil* or literally the beater out of tomahawks. Beyond that the evidence is very scarce. Europeans occasionally found iron weapons in Aboriginal camps which they assumed had been shaped while the metal was hot but their testimony is far from conclusive.

After iron, glass was probably the most important addition to the traditional tool kit. Initially it may have been confused with quartz crystals and therefore assumed to possess magical powers, but its utilitarian properties were ultimately much more important. Glass was even more amenable than iron to the various stone-working techniques – either chipping of flakes or the grinding and sharpening of solid spearheads from thick bottle glass. But successful working in glass could only come with a great deal of ex-perimentation with the medium and accumulation of expertise about its unique properties. Despite the widespread adoption of iron and glass in Aboriginal society there seem to have been some who refused to accept innovation, persevering with traditional stone technology. Horne and Aiston reported that in Central Australia in the early twentieth century there were a few 'strictly conservative workers' who used stone even for the 'rough hewing of the boomerang' and who refused to use bottle glass for 'smooth-ing down the ridges'.[51]

The Aborigines were intensely interested in European goods and they expertly pilfered from explorers and pioneers. Mitchell greatly admired their deftness, explaining one technique which involved treading softly on a desired article, seizing it with the toes, passing it up the back or between the arm and side to conceal it in the arm pit or between the beard and throat. Aboriginal camps often be-came curiosity shops of collected European artifacts. One in Gippsland in 1841 for instance was found to contain a large variety of clothing including shirts, trousers, frocks and a Mackintosh cloak; dress material, thread, thimble, blankets, tools, bottles, the tube of a thermometer, one seal-skin hat, muskets, tomahawks, a pewter two gallon measure, pewter hand basin, camp kettle, two children's copy books, one bible, London, Glasgow and Aberdeen newspapers.

Perhaps few clans were as successful at collecting European goods as this one. Yet contact with the settlers often led to a rapid increase in the number of possessions in any one camp, creating novel problems of transport and storage. Often the newly acquired objects were simply left behind, being too heavy and cumbersome to be carried about from camp to camp. But the unique problem seems to have called forth creative attempts to provide permanent storage of a kind probably unknown in traditional society. Three European observers provided accounts of such structures. Robinson found that Tasmanian blacks had dug a hole to secure their new possessions, had laid grass and bark at the bottom, stones and bark around the stores and a wooden structure above-ground to mark the spot. In central Queensland a generation later a squatter came across a 'plant' of stolen goods. Logs had been placed on the ground to provide a platform for food of all sorts as well as clothes and tools and the whole cache – a drayload and more – had been carefully roofed with bark stripped from nearby trees. An even more interesting case was discussed by William Thomas the Assistant-Protector of Aborigines at Port Phillip. In 1840 he followed up a party of Gippsland blacks who had attacked a station on the eastern fringes of European settlement. They had taken everything from the station that was moveable and on their return to their own country had constructed what Thomas termed, 'two devices'. At the ford of a river they had cut down trees and saplings and made a bridge 'to enable them to more rapidly convey their booty to yonder side'. On the far bank was another structure. Thomas' description is far from clear but he called it an 'artificial grove of saplings and tea tree' which extended for some yards and which had been used as a depot for storing the stolen goods.[52]

There are two other references to modified building techniques during the period of early contact, one contemporaneous, the other resulting from recent archaeological work. Jorgenson observed in the 1820s that as the Tasmanians were increasingly forced out of the river valleys and into the mountains they began building 'stone structures, not the least resembling the usual wigwams'.[53] In western Victoria scholars have found examples of stone houses with central fireplaces which it is assumed date from the period after contact as the sites yielded such traditional relics as stone flakes admixed with broken glass and clay pipes.

WHITE MEN'S FOOD

Traditional patterns of cooking and eating underwent a change as well. In most parts of Australia mutton, beef and rabbit meat were added to diets diminished by the impact of settlement. Culinary practices were modified accordingly. There are numerous reports of

the evacuation of large earth ovens to accommodate bullock carcases. Thomas Mitchell claimed that in the 1840s in one district of
northern New South Wales ovens had been used for the consumption of up to twenty head of cattle a day. Some settlers thought that
the blacks had adopted these methods after observing European
boiling down works but it seems more probable that they simply
adapted existing techniques for cooking the larger marsupials.

Chronic insecurity following the European invasion apparently
increased the desire to preserve and stock-pile food. As old certainties vanished clans sought new ways to maintain their food supply.
Beef and mutton fat was stored and carried in small bark bags or in
the knotted legs and arms of European trousers and shirts. Central
Australian blacks collected pieces of cow-hide which they soaked,
cooked and then ground up before eating. Legs of lamb and mutton
were preserved by smoking and apparently carried on walkabout
for future use. A Western District pioneer reported that on raiding
a local camp he found the remains of many sheep and 'a quantity
cut up in hams, which had been smoked and hung up to dry'.[54] In
1865 a central Queensland squatter came across what he called 'a
perfect meat curing establishment'[55] hidden in coastal mangroves.
The meat had been cut up and portions of it were being smoked.

European flour rapidly won approval over the laboriously collected and prepared indigenous cereals and became one of the
favoured targets for Aboriginal raids on stations, tents and drays.
Traditional methods of cooking cereals merged with damper making
techniques used by Europeans all over frontier Australia. In various
parts of the continent blacks attempted to preserve and stockpile
supplies of flour. In 1805 a European party was shown forty bushels
of wheat 'secreted in a single cavity'[56] on the fringes of white settlement. The hoarders were apparently blacks and not renegade
Europeans. In 1830 Tasmanian settlers found a hundredweight of
flour baked into dampers in an Aboriginal camp. Queensland police
came upon a camp in the rainforest near Maryborough in 1867 and
discovered a three hundredweight store of sweet potatoes and a two
foot pile of damper and there were similar reports from other parts

of Australia. Tea and sugar were also found in Aboriginal camps. In Tasmania the frequent discovery of tea-pots would suggest that the local clans had begun to brew the beverage in the approved European manner. Tobacco was also widely disseminated on the other side of the frontier; its addictive appeal was one of the more powerful forces attracting Aborigines to European settlement. Lumholtz reported that in north Queensland tobacco was bartered, wrapped up in leaves, and was consequently 'known among remote tribes who have never themselves come into contact with Europeans'.[57] There seems no doubt that the desire to obtain tobacco drove many blacks in towards the nearest source of supply. A woman on the Etheridge gold field reported a typical incident. Two strange Aborigines suddenly appeared before her tent. They kept pointing to their mouths saying 'toomback' 'toomback'. When given a supply they quickly disappeared. At much the same time in central Australia Chewings observed that 'the craving for tobacco, in both sexes, is intense'.[58]

European artifacts eventually affected almost every aspect of Aboriginal life. Even the practices and possessions of the 'clever men' or 'doctors' were influenced and the new commodities joined the stones and bones which they seemingly drew from injured or diseased bodies of ailing patients. In his memoirs Simpson Newland recalled that he had seen clever men in South Australia and western New South Wales produce, as the cause of sickness, a bullock's tooth, the bottom of a tumbler, a piece of the jawbone of a sheep, fragments of pottery. Horne and Aiston reported the case of a 'clever man' from central Australia who drew nails and wire out of a patient's chest while Howitt referred to a man who attributed acute rheumatism to the fact that an enemy had put a bottle into his foot. Blacks around Echuca were said to prepare powerful magic by mixing the dried and powdered flesh of a dead man with tobacco which was then given to the unsuspecting victim to smoke. It was a common practice in traditional society to apply heat to an object belonging to an intended victim thereby causing intense pain and even death. Howitt observed that blacks on the Wimmera River successfully adjusted their methods to the new circumstances which followed white settlement. They found the kitchen chimneys of the sheep stations unrivalled places where the object in question could be subjected to prolonged heat.

Because the Aborigines sought European possessions the settlers assumed they were full of admiration for the skill of white craftsmen and the ingenuity of their manufactures. Such beliefs were central to the European presumption that Aborigines were overawed in face of settler power and material abundance. But it may not have been like that at all. Manufactured goods were not intrinsically more complex or impressive than those occurring naturally. With no experience of European methods of production Aborigines assumed that the newcomers' possessions were organic products of an exotic natural environment. The tribal father of Davis, the Moreton Bay escapee, was given a pocket watch taken from a frontier shepherd. While it ticked he thought it was alive: when it stopped he 'took it for a stone'.[59] Thompson noted similar reactions among her Cape York hosts. Having been on board the *Rattlesnake* they asked her if the cups and saucers they had seen walked about like shellfish. As she told her chronicler, O. W. Brierly, the Aborigines thought:

> our bottles are shells and ask what kind of fish live in them and where they are found and wonder that there are none of them on their own beaches.[60]

Continuity and change thus ran like an intricate plait through the history of early contact. Aborigines were curious about Europeans, sought their artifacts and were innovative in a wide range of situations. Yet traditional beliefs and assumptions continue to display a strength and resilience resistant to even the most traumatic consequences of the invasion like firearms and epidemic diseases.

GUNS

Guns were alarming weapons – they made a noise that could be equated only with thunder, could kill and injure at great distance with an unseen missile that often left a wound apparently incommensurate with the resulting injury. Running parallel with the development of tactics to avoid exposure to the lethal firepower was the endeavour to understand the secret of the new weapons. The initial assumption seems to have been that guns were magic. The oral tradition of the Flinders Range-Lake Frome people contained reference to their first experience of firearms. While they were watching the progress of an early exploration party the Europeans shot two crows and a kangaroo, all at considerable distance:

> This was the most startling thing they had seen. Just the bang and there were the things dead ... there was much discussion again that night as to how the kangaroo and crows were killed and what killed them. Some suggested it was *muldarpie* [devil] that did it; it was some years before they could solve that problem.[61]

The idea that guns were magical at least brought them onto familiar ground for the 'clever men' were almost universally thought to be able to kill at a distance by projecting missiles – quartz crystals, pebbles and the like – through the air and into the bodies of intended victims. In her study of the Euahlayi tribe Mrs K. L. Parker referred to the *moolee* or death dealing stone which was said to knock a person insensible or even 'strike him dead as lightning would by an instantaneous flash'.[62] R. M. Berndt described the process more precisely while discussing the survival of magical practices in the twentieth century. The clever man, he explained:

> concentrated upon the victim, and moving his chest and shoulders forced the crystal up so that it passed out of his mouth and, travelling at such a velocity that it escaped the notice of other men, entering the victim.[63]

A related belief was that it was possible for clever men to load spears, clubs and boomerangs so that they sped straight to the chosen victim, were unavoidable, and produced paralysis on contact.

European weapons were manifestly dangerous, but not necessarily more so, or more mysterious, than the magic of powerful clever men. Perhaps the most surprising thing about guns for those with little experience of the invaders was that every white man seemed to be able to activate the magic rather than a few select 'men of high degree'. The suggestion that European ballistics were seen in terms of traditional magic received some confirmation from the reminiscences of two elderly Aborigines recorded recently in southern inland Queensland. Both old people recalled the importance of corroborees in the camp life of the late nineteenth and early twentieth centuries and the discipline imposed on women and children by the 'clever men' who had become the 'doctors' in the narrative. The old man recalled that 'no-one was ever to laugh or speak at the corroboree, or the doctor there'd give them the bullit'. The old lady confirmed that 'they'd say bullit hit you'[64] if there was any defiance of taboos. Thus the ability of the clever men to kill those defying tribal lore had become closely related to the power of European firearms even down to the creation of the verb 'to bullit' to describe the process.

Yet the need to understand the mechanism of guns continued if only to allow the Aborigines to co-opt the European firepower. Knowledge of the range of firearms and frequency of fire was quickly learnt and may even have passed back beyond the frontier. Guns were stolen both to deny them to Europeans and to examine them more closely. Eventually some Aborigines learnt how to use and maintain stolen weapons even experimenting with local flints to provide the spark and with stones as projectiles. By the late 1820s the Tasmanian clans had mastered the mysterious weapons and their success was mirrored elsewhere. Robinson discovered that island Aborigines had hidden caches of well maintained guns which they could handle proficiently and shoot accurately. In 1832 he was shown a hollow tree armoury containing muskets which were primed, loaded and in 'good condition with a piece of blanket thrust into the muzzle'. One of the last island blacks to be brought in from the bush had in his possession:

> a very excellent carbine for the preservation of which he had made a case from the skin of the kangaroo – he stated further that numerous firearms were concealed in the woods.[65]

The linguistic evidence concerning guns is of limited use because the widespread adoption of 'musket' words concealed rather than illuminated Aboriginal thinking on the subject. But in some languages there was an obvious attempt to relate gunfire to familiar experiences or objects. Port Lincoln clans used a word for gun meaning also club or stick; those around Perth coined the term *winji-bandi*. G. F. Moore explained that it meant:

> literally an emu leg or shank, perhaps from the thin handle part of a gun resembling in its carving the rough grains of the skin of an emu's leg. A double-barrelled gun is described as having two mouths. A gun with a bayonet, as the gun with the spear at its nose.[66]

Elsewhere words were used which related gunfire to making fire by friction or to banging, rattling or echoing noises. Teichelmann reported that South Australian Aborigines called guns *pandapure* which appears to have been formed by joining two other words – *parndendi* meaning to crackle and sparkle and *pure* meaning a stone. James Gunther recorded that the Wiradjuri of northern New South Wales called muskets *barrima* from the word *barrimarra* which meant to get fire by rubbing. In the Gidabal dialect of northern New South Wales and southern Queensland guns were termed *dululbi* which derived from a word meaning rattling and echoing noises. The Aranda called bullets *mukuta anna* or the fruits or kernels of muskets while the Kalkatunga coined an even more graphic term for rifle which meant literally holemaker.

INTRODUCED DISEASE

Aborigines clung to their own theory of illness despite the traumatic impact of introduced disease. E. S. Parker, the Assistant-Protector of Aborigines at Port Phillip, reported that the Loddon River blacks rejected the medical advice of the Government doctor despite the serious health problems facing them. They remained convinced that disease was caused by the malignant magic of distant tribes. The one exception which they would allow was venereal disease which they associated directly with sexual contact with the Europeans. More of this interesting case will be made later. G. A. Robinson met a group of Western District Aborigines in 1845 who were apprehensive about a dispute with a neighbouring tribe who, they said, had the power of inflicting a plague. They were in daily expectation of such a visitation. What little evidence we have suggests that the tribes of south-eastern Australia believed malevolent sorcery was the cause of the epidemic – probably of smallpox – which ravaged large areas of the continent in the early decades of the nineteenth century. The Wiradjuri attributed the disease to a malignant deity who lived in the south-west, down the river systems. The Euahlayi people of northern New South Wales believed that their enemies sent it in the winds 'which hung it on the trees, over the camps, whence it dropped onto its victims'.[67] In Victoria the source of the disease was believed to be the unleashing by distant tribes of the devastating power of Mindye the Rainbow Serpent. Smallpox was actually called *moo-noole mindye*, or *monola-mindi*, the dust of serpent, the skin eruptions *lillipe-mindije* or *lillipook-mindi*, the scales of the serpent. The missionary Teichelmann reported that South Australian Aborigines had a song called *Nguyapalti*, a smallpox song which they said was the only means of stopping the disease. They had learnt it from tribes in the east from whence the disease itself had come.

The implications of these attitudes are important. Epidemic disease – perhaps the most dramatic consequence of European invasion – was interpreted in traditional ways as being due to human agency and amenable to curative magic. The powerful sorcery of distant tribes was more awesome and devastating than anything the Europeans could do. The Aboriginal way still held the key to the great forces of the universe. These were things which few Europeans even guessed at. Belief in the power of the 'clever men', in their ability to impart and cure disease, to foretell the future, to embark on spirit journeys; all of these survived the invasion. The anthropologists Elkin, Berndt and Reay discovered the amazing vitality of the Aboriginal view of the world while working with fringe and mission-dwelling blacks in New South Wales and Queensland in the 1930s and 1940s one hundred years or more after the initial dispossession.

SELF-CONFIDENCE

The intimate relationship with the land was a factor of great importance. On one level this was a matter of practical bush skills and profound knowledge of the environment. Aboriginal self-confidence was noted by Europeans from the earliest years of settlement. While writing about one of the first expeditions inland from Sydney Tench observed that the 'perplexities' of the Europeans afforded accompanying Aborigines 'an inexhaustible fund of merriment'.[68] Robinson found that his black companions were continually testing his ability to find his way in the bush because they entertained 'but a mean opinion of the white people's knowledge'.[69] The Brisbane pioneer Tom Petrie remarked that Aborigines laughed at the inability of the whites to match them in bush skills but perhaps an even more interesting observer was Schmidt the German missionary at Moreton Bay. When giving evidence before the 1845 New South Wales Select Committee on the Condition of the Aborigines he was asked if in his experience the Aborigines were 'conscious of inferiority' to the Europeans or did they think their own mode of life 'most pleasant and best'. From some of their own expressions, Schmidt remarked, 'I judged that they consider themselves superior to us'. The exchange continued:

> Do you mean that they consider themselves superior to the whole of the white race ... or only convicts?
> To the whole; they preferred their mode of living to ours ...[70]

Aboriginal self-confidence was not based solely on the mastery of practical skills but on the spiritual relationship with the land, the sense of belonging and responsibility for performing the increase ceremonies which ensured the proper ordering of nature, the coming of the rain and the renewal of plant and animal life. Belief in the necessity and the efficacy of increase ceremonies continued on well into the period of European settlement. Europeans brought change and damage to many local ecologies but the larger rhythms of nature remained constant and predictable to those who had learnt the signs. It remained possible despite the European presence to go on believing in the causal link between tribal ceremony and the turn of the seasons. In June 1899 W. E. Roth met a celebrated rainmaker called Ngamumarko on the McIvor River who it was widely assumed had caused the devastating cyclone of the previous March which destroyed the pearling fleet in Princess Charlotte Bay. Darling River Aborigines told Simpson Newland that 'rain never fell without the exercise of aboriginal power, and but for them, the white man, his cattle and sheep, would perish miserably'.[71] While that faith remained even the arrogant white man appeared to be the unwitting beneficiary of Aboriginal wisdom and power. That most Europeans were ignorant of the 'secret life' of the Aborigines merely confirmed their seemingly unquenchable faith in their own moral worth even in the midst of desperate post-contact poverty.

Aborigines were neither apathetic in face of the European invasion nor incurious about the newcomer's lifestyle. The historical record indicates that they were not locked into a rigid unchanging culture. They showed themselves just as capable of adapting to altered circumstances as the European pioneers who were learning to strike their own balance between continuity and innovation in the new world. Yet there were aspects of Aboriginal culture and philosophy which proved remarkably resistant to change. Traditional society was, therefore, both more conservative and more innovative than standard accounts have suggested with their picture of a culture too rigid to bend collapsing suddenly and completely under the pressure of European invasion.

There may be an important clue to Aboriginal behaviour in the attitude of the Loddon River clans to the ravages of venereal infection. While continuing to believe unshakeably in the traditional theories of disease they regarded V.D. as a post-contact phenomenon due to physical contact with Europeans and, unlike other illness, amenable to white medicine. Implicit in this reaction was the acceptance of a realm of experience new to Aboriginal society outside the sway of customary belief and practice. It may have been such judgements that broke the seal of custom and opened the way for innovation, creating in the process the complex pattern of continuity and change discussed to this point. But emphasis on cultural change and adaption should not obscure the overwhelming importance of the violent conflict accompanying the invasion of the continent.

Chapter 3

RESISTANCE: MOTIVES AND OBJECTIVES

Australian historians have only recently rediscovered the violence used to secure the conquest and effect the pioneering of the continent. Yet almost every district settled during the nineteenth century had a history of conflict between local clans and encroaching settlers. Many of the Europeans who lived through the time of confrontation were quite realistic about the human cost of colonisation. A small town pioneer wrote in 1869 that his community 'had its foundations cemented in blood'.[1] 'I believe I am not wrong in stating', observed another, that 'every acre of land in these districts was won from the Aborigines by bloodshed and warfare'.[2] Black resistance in its many forms was an inescapable feature of life on the fringes of European settlement from the first months at Sydney Cove until the early years of the twentieth century. The intensity and duration of conflict varied widely depending on terrain, indigenous population densities, the speed of settlement, the type of introduced economic activity, even the period of first contact. Edward Curr, who had perhaps the widest overview of white-Aboriginal relations in nineteenth-century Australia, wrote the classical account of frontier conflict:

> In the first place the meeting of the Aboriginal tribes of Australia and the White pioneer, results as a rule in war, which lasts from six months to ten years, according to the nature of the country, the amount of settlement which takes place in a neighbourhood,

and the proclivities of the individuals concerned. When several squatters settle in proximity, and the country they occupy is easy of access and without fastnesses to which the Blacks can retreat, the period of warfare is usually short and the bloodshed not excessive. On the other hand, in districts which are not easily traversed on horseback, in which the Whites are few in numbers and food is procurable by the Blacks in fastnesses, the term is usually prolonged and the slaughter more considerable.[3]

While black resistance has gained increasing recognition discussion of Aboriginal motivation is still rudimentary. Nineteenth century writers frequently discussed Aboriginal action but rarely analysed their motives. Compulsions of savagery were often propounded as a satisfactory explanation of black behaviour. 'There are some who affect to believe', observed a humanitarian squatter, 'that it is unnecessary to ask why a black has committed a murder'. 'The cause, say they, is sufficiently accounted for by his savage and blood-thirsty nature'.[4] Modern scholars documenting the resistance have assumed, perhaps understandably, that opposition to invasion is so basic and universal a reaction, that it scarcely warrants discussion, while others have referred to an elemental territoriality. 'All living organisms', wrote Bauer, 'jealously defend to the best of their ability whatever portion of the earth's surface they inhabit'.[5] Regardless of the ultimate value of such generalizations, they offer little to the historian seeking to describe and explain the variety and complexity of Aboriginal behaviour. Yet while biological determinism should be eschewed it is clear that land is central to any discussion of white-Aboriginal relations whether in the nineteenth or twentieth century. Such an investigation must begin with the nature of traditional ownership but that takes the reader into the centre of a major and long running anthropological debate.

LAND OWNERSHIP

There are two basic positions. Radcliffe-Brown argued, and has been supported more recently by Tindale and Birdsell, that Aboriginal Australia was divided into clearly defined, discrete territories with fixed and known boundaries. In an essay of 1913 Radcliffe-Brown referred to a 'very rigid system' of land ownership backed up with strict laws relating to trespass.[6] In his classic 1930 study of the social organization of Aboriginal Australia, he defined the horde as a 'small group of persons owning a certain area of territory, the boundaries of which are known, and possessing in common proprietary rights over the land and its products'.[7] In 1974 Tindale argued that all tribes claim and occupy a 'discrete territory with finite limits beyond which members have a sense of trespass'.[8]

The second view, advocated by Hiatt, Meggitt, Petersen and others, is that boundaries were far less clear and social organization more complex than traditional theories have allowed. The very concept of the self-contained tribe has been called into question with the suggestion that Aborigines identified themselves according to kinship, marriage, territory, totemism, language and ceremony and that these overlapped and intersected in complex ways. Sutton has argued that descent groups owned constellations of sacred sites rather than neat parcels of land. While most of the sites were clustered together a significant number were separated by sites belonging to other groups while some sites were owned by more than one descent group. Estates, he concluded, were not 'whole blocks or tracts of country in the sense of surveyed real estate' but were 'collections of points in a landscape'.[9] Land-use patterns were complex as well. Neighbouring clans intermingled, foraging and hunting on each other's territory; easements were provided for travellers, temporary hospitality for sojourners. While discussing the ritual and economic life of the Yir-Yoront of Cape York Lauriston Sharp carefully defined tribal attitudes to ownership, access and trespass:

> A majority of the Yir-Yoront clans have multiple countries which are not contiguous, and which vary from an acre or two up to a number of square miles in area. The countries of a clan, with their natural resources, are owned by all clan members in common ... The right of exclusion is exercised only in exceptional cases, in which there is an actual or pretended drain on the resources of the land, indicating that one of chief functions of clan ownership of land is the apportionment and

conservation of natural resources. The natives state that a clan
may even forbid a man crossing clan territory to get from one
of his own clan territories to another, but no example of such
extreme clan action could be cited. People gather and hunt, or-
dinarily, in whatever country they will. Thus there is practically a standing permission which opens a clan's countries to
all, but this permission may be withdrawn by the clan for
those who are *persona non grata*.[10]

The second strand of interpretation seems more pertinent for the
assessment of the Aboriginal response to European explorers and
pioneers. As a general rule clans did not react immediately to
European trespass although illusions about returning relatives or
fear of guns may have significantly modified their behaviour. Indeed
the history of inland exploration indicates that local groups toler-
ated the passage of European expeditions provided they behaved
with circumspection. On many occasions Aborigines hospitably allowed squatting parties to establish themselves and even assisted
them during the first few weeks of their occupation. Clearly white
and black perceptions of what was taking place were very wide
apart. Unless forewarned Aborigines probably had no appreciation
of the European's determination to stay indefinitely and 'own' the
soil. After all the first white intruders came and went again in a way
that would have fully accorded with black expectations. Even
Morrell had difficulty in explaining the objectives of the first squatting party to enter his district. He persuaded his clan to go on a
hunting expedition to the hill overlooking the camp of the pioneer
stock-men but his kinsmen were doubtful if they would find the
Europeans in the same spot as earlier reports had placed them.
Thinking that the white men were the 'same as themselves', Morrell
explained, 'they were not sure whether they were there'.[11] Initially
the white intrusion may have seemed an event of merely transient
importance. Cape York Aborigines told the anthropologist Donald
Thomson how the appearance of the Europeans fitted in with their
sense of history and continuity. 'After the Big Men', they explained,
'the Middle People lived, last we come and we find the white
man'.[12] The expectation that the settlers would eventually go away

lingered for many years in some places. In the 1960s old Dyirbal people in north Queensland still had 'a solid hope that one day the white man would be driven out, and the tribe would once more be able to resume peaceful occupation of its traditional lands'.[13] The Europeans had been in the district for ninety years.

DISPOSSESSION

Throughout Aboriginal Australia the appearance of strange blacks carried the threat of revenge killing, abduction of women or the exercise of potent magic. But it did not portend forced dispossession or exile from the homeland. While conflict was ubiquitous in traditional societies territorial conquest was virtually unknown. Alienation of land was not only unthinkable, it was literally impossible. If blacks often did not react to the initial invasion of their country it was because they were not aware that it had taken place. They certainly did not believe that their land had suddenly ceased to belong to them and they to their land. The mere presence of Europeans, no matter how threatening, could not uproot certainties so deeply implanted in Aboriginal custom and consciousness. The black owners may have been pushed aside but many refused to accept that they had been dispossessed; they never conceded the major premise of the invasion. Yet for others ejection from cherished homelands was a shattering experience. The missionary Francis Tuckfield discussed the 'white problem' with Port Phillip blacks who visited his station and complained about being driven from their favourite camping grounds. He concluded that they were acquainted with the 'relative possessions of the Black and White population' and they asked him: 'Will you now select for us also a portion of land? My country all you gone. The White Men have stolen it.'[14]

The white invasion often forced blacks into a more assertive and possessive stance concerning clan territories. E. S. Parker came to the conclusion that it was an 'important and unquestionable fact' that the Port Phillip Aborigines were 'not insensible to their original right to the soil'.[15] He referred to the experience of a settler who was confronted by an old man who told the whites to leave the district because the land and water belonged to the Aborigines. Robinson reported a similar case in the Western District where a party of Europeans were ordered by local blacks to depart because, they said, 'it was their country, and the water belonged to them, if it was taken away they could not go to another country'.[16] A very similar response was reported at much the same time from Ipswich in southern Queensland. A large party of blacks marched up to a recently established station and ordered the Europeans to be off 'as it was their ground'.[17]

But Aborigines reacted less to the original trespass than to the ruthless assertion by Europeans of exclusive proprietorial rights often from the very first day of occupation. It was behaviour probably unheard of in traditional society. Increasingly the newcomers impinged on accustomed patterns of life, occupying the flat, open land and monopolizing surface water. Indigenous animals were driven away, plant life eaten or trampled and Aborigines pushed into the marginal country – mountains, swamps, waterless neighbourhoods. Patterns of seasonal migration broke down, areas remaining free of Europeans were over utilized and eventually depleted of both flora and fauna. Food became scarcer and available in less and less variety and even access to water was often difficult. Attacks on sheep and cattle, made frequently in desperation, provoked violent retaliation: reprisal and revenge spiralled viciously.

The missionary William Ridley described the fate of a group of Balonne River blacks in the 1840s. Their situation was typical of what happened all over the country:

> On this river the effect upon the aborigines of the occupation by Europeans of the country was forcibly presented. Before the occupation of this district by colonists, the aborigines could never have been at a loss for the necessaries of life. Except in the lowest part of the river, there is water in the driest seasons; along the banks game abounded; waterfowl, emus, parrot tribes, kangaroos, and other animals might always, or almost always, be found. But when the country was taken up, and herds of cattle introduced, not only did the cattle drive away the kangaroos, but those who had charge

of the cattle found it necessary to keep the aborigines away from the river ... After some fatal conflicts, in which some colonists and many aborigines have been slain, the blacks have been awed into submission to the orders which forbid their access to the river. And what is the consequence? Black fellows coming in from the west report that last summer very large numbers, afraid to visit the river, were crowded round a few scanty waterholes, within a day's walk of which it was impossible to get sufficient food ... that owing to these combined hardships many died.[18]

Ceremonial and religious life was disrupted by the settler incursion. Important sacred sites were desecrated, albeit unwittingly in many cases, access to them denied and large ceremonial gatherings often dispersed by anxious frontiersmen or officious police detachments. Cave paintings were daubed with graffiti, sacred boards stolen. Members of the Horn Scientific Expedition of 1894 found a cave of great religious significance in central Australia and took sixty wooden sticks and fifteen stone tablets but left axes, knives and other bric-a-brac in return. But dramatic events like desecration or dispossession were not the only sources of conflict; it often rose up out of bitter arguments between settlers and blacks who had lived in proximity and reasonable accord for some time before the outbreak of hostilities. Aboriginal women and European property were major causes of such confrontations. They were deceptively simple. Settlers caught blacks taking their property; angry shouting, blows, spearing and shooting followed. The pioneers usually assumed that Aborigines were compulsive pilferers and few historians have bothered to look any closer at the question although references to black greediness and cupidity abound in the literature. While it is true that European material abundance was a major focus of tension the assumption that Aboriginal envy was the principal cause of conflict is both superficial and ethnocentric.

RECIPROCITY VS PRIVATE PROPERTY

Aborigines could not help being struck by the quantity of possessions owned by even poorer settlers. But it is far from certain that they admired the whites for their abundance which must have appeared to lack any rationale. The jealous possession of large herds of animals would have seemed totally unnecessary especially when so few were killed for food. J. D. Wood, a settler who had shrewdly studied Aboriginal perceptions, commented that: 'greediness in us, is with them a great crime, their ignorance prevents them having a knowledge of the cost of our property.'[19] The anthropologist Donald Thomson made similar observations about traditionally oriented people he studied in the 1920s. 'White men's meanness', he wrote, in hoarding great quantities of tobacco and other things which could not possibly be used in a day or two was 'hard for them to understand'.[20]

Reciprocity and sharing were central to the social organization and ethical standards of traditional society. In her study of the Euahlayi tribe K. L. Parker illustrated how sharing was inculcated from the earliest age. Old women crooned charms over babies to make them generous in later life. She had often heard them singing a song which included the refrain:

> Give to me, Baby
> Give to her, Baby
> Give to him, Baby
> Give to one, Baby
> Give to all, Baby[21]

European observers were struck by the importance of sharing in Aboriginal society. 'They are truly generous among themselves', wrote William Thomas of Port Phillip blacks in the 1840s.[22] 'Meanness is rarely found among these people', noted Donald Thomson while on Cape York a hundred years later. Both men observed that reciprocity was so fundamental to Aboriginal society that the clans they knew had no word meaning 'thank you'. Thomas explained that while food was always distributed among those present it was not considered a gift in the European sense, rather as a right 'and no thanks to the giver'. He was, he thought, the first person 'that taught them the meaning of the word thanks'.[23] European possessiveness was morally obnoxious especially as Aborigines assumed that whites had come by their goods without special effort or obvious virtue. J. D. Wood remarked that the blacks thought whites: 'had only to ask in order that we may receive anything we require and they think us culpable if we refuse them what they covet.'[24] A pioneer squatter told a Queensland Parliamentary Select Committee in 1861 of a pertinent incident which had occurred some years before on the McIntyre River. Local blacks had killed a bullock and advanced on the hut of the beleaguered squatter with the animal's kidney fat stuck on their spears. They called out to the whites offering them a share of the fat saying 'that they were not like the whites themselves – greedy'.[25]

Anger about European possessiveness was clearly one of the motives behind the taking and destruction of their stock and other property. Aborigines acted to make the whites share their goods; the motivation was as much political as economic. It was not so much the possessions that mattered as affirmation of the principles of reciprocity. The great disparity of property merely exacerbated tensions inherent in the situation. Innumerable small skirmishes over European possessions appearing to be little better than unseemly brawls, were in reality manifestations of a fundamental clash of principle, the outward showing of one of the most significant moral and political struggles in Australian history. The settlers were transplanting a policy of possessive individualism, hierarchy and inequality. Aboriginal society was reciprocal and materially egalitarian although there were important political and religious inequalities based on age and sex. Two such diametrically opposed societies could not merge without conflict. One or the other had to prevail.

SEXUAL COMPETITION

Conflict over women was a constant feature of relations between white and black, an aspect of contact stressed by nineteenth century observers and one much more familiar to Aborigines than the struggle for land and water. Women were a major focus of indigenous politics and control of their bestowal was perhaps the principal source of secular power in traditional society. The arrival of the Europeans saw the conjunction of an almost womanless pioneer population and a society which allowed the ceremonial exchange of women and the offer of sexual favours as a means of hospitality or method of diplomacy. The resulting sexual symbiosis preceded, followed, even punctuated periods of interracial conflict. Some explorers reported the offer of women, others were discreetly silent on the matter, none admitted to temptation. Sturt noted that his camp was overwhelmed with offers of sexual accommodation while in the Centre; Giles found that attractive young women were brought up to his men one after another; while on his Lake Eyre expedition of 1874 Lewis observed that despite the fear his party evoked local clans sent 'as is customary with them six of their lubras as a peace offering'.[26] When Moorhouse visited the tribes on the Lower Murray after intense conflict with the parties travelling from New South Wales to South Australia they told him that all the white people they had ever seen before asked for women to be brought up so they could have sexual intercourse with them.

Physical understanding, perhaps even mutual gratification, appears to have quickly bridged the gulf between the cultures but an understanding of the social and political ramifications of sexuality took much longer. For most frontiersmen an encounter ended abruptly with ejaculation and withdrawal; for Aboriginal women and their kin that was often just the beginning. The randy womanless white man was not only encircled in warm flesh: he was also enmeshed in an intricate web of kinship. The acceptance by the settler of what seemed to be quick, casual copulation frequently involved him in expectations of reciprocity, and what was more, continuing reciprocity. Many apparently excessive demands for food, tobacco and the like came from blacks expecting European men to behave henceforth as classificatory brothers, sons and nephews. 'After that familiar intercourse', Moorhouse wrote, 'the Natives seem to claim a liberal and constant supply of food, and in case it is not given, they do not hesitate to use violence in obtaining it'.[27] A similar situation was reported on the Gwydir River in northern New South Wales in the 1830s. Shepherds and stockmen had sexual relations with local Aboriginal women but when they subsequently 'refused the Blacks anything they wanted' attempts were made to kill them.[28]

But beyond bad behaviour stemming from ignorance of Aboriginal custom European men deliberately cheated, raped and abducted black women. The emergent frontier custom of 'gin-busting' trampled over sexual customs and incest taboos. Moorhouse set out to unravel the reasons for black hostility on the overland route from New South Wales to South Australia and sought the help of a Sydney black who had made the trip several times. The riverine clans indicated that they were becoming enraged with the whites because they had:

> used the women ... and much abused them. The abuse (they explained), consisted in the Europeans promising the Aborigines food, clothing and tomahawks for the use of their females, but the Europeans did not fulfil their promises, after gratifying their passions, the women were turned out late in the evening or in the night, and instead of the men having their promised rewards, they were laughed at and ridiculed.[29]

Sexual relations between white men and black women were, then, a major source of misunderstanding, bitterness and conflict. But many Aboriginal attacks on Europeans were motivated by revenge for previous injury or insult whether there had been any sexual contact or not.

REVENGE

Revenge was the mainspring of violence in traditional society, source of ever present anxiety about dangerous magic and surreptitious attack. Death was universally attributed to malevolent sorcery, necessitating an inquest to determine guilt and retribution which characteristically took the form of counter-magic or a revenge expedition aimed at the putative killer or a close relative. But while pay-back killing was endemic in traditional society it was usually contained within the resilient bonds of kinship for if clans were near enough neighbours to fight they were liable to be linked by at least classificatory, if not actual, blood relationships. Customary institutions and practices can be seen, therefore, to have promoted intermittent personal violence while at the same time inhibiting the development of widespread conflict. They fostered the feud but prevented escalation into warfare. Revenge killing was also related very closely to the dominant ethic of reciprocity. It was the means of restoring a status quo upset by prior death or injury; of reasserting the balance of rights and obligations. While discussing conflict in Murngin society the American anthropologist Lloyd-Warner observed that:

> the fundamental principle underlying all the causes of Murngin warfare is that of reciprocity: if harm had been done to an individual or a group, it is felt by the injured people that they must repay the ones who have harmed them by an injury that at least equals the one they have suffered.[30]

How did Europeans fit into this presumably age-old pattern of revenge and reprisal? Deaths resulting from frontier skirmishing could be directly attributed to Europeans and we do not know if inquests were considered necessary in such cases. It is distinctly possible that in the early period of contact Aboriginal enemies were thought to be implicated in marking down the particular victims to be killed by musket balls and bullets. White men may have been seen as unwitting agents of powerful black magic. Did blacks credit Europeans with the powers of sorcery attributed to their own 'clever men'? They initially assumed that guns were magic and may have associated death by European poison with sorcery. In several places in South-Eastern Australia the English word poison was borrowed to describe the powers of local 'clever men'.

Despite the impact of the European invasion the whites may have appeared less formidable than they supposed. Western Australian blacks told the early settlers that they initially considered whites as inferior to themselves, that they saw the Europeans going about unarmed and open to attack, and felt sure of success.

While guns were weapons to be reckoned with the Europeans were
not necessarily perceived as being more dangerous than distant
blacks whose potent magic was blamed for death by accident, disease, deprivation and exposure. At the very time that whites were
shooting down blacks along the frontier more were also dying from
other causes which were typically attributed to the malevolent sorcery of hostile Aborigines. Howitt related the story of a group of
twenty-five Braidwood blacks – men, women and children – who
died after drinking what was apparently poisoned alcohol. Blame
for their deaths was attributed not to the whites, or even to misad-
venture, but to clans from Tumut or Goulburn who had put
Gubburra or evil magic in their drink. Inter-clan fighting and revenge killing continued throughout the period of open conflict with
the Europeans and indeed long after in some places. The pressure
of the settlers on both Aboriginal society and the environment may
have actually increased the amount of fighting between rival clans.
In 1897 the German missionary Poland asked an Aboriginal informant how it was that so many local blacks had been killed in
the previous twenty years. He was told that: 'Blacks have killed
them, who are hostile towards us, or policemen or white men have
shot them or the evil spirit got them.'[31] However a pioneer New
South Wales missionary argued that the growing tendency to at-
tribute death to the whites had led to a decline of inter-clan feuding. It was, he wrote:

> formerly a custom, when any of their number died, to receive
> a challenge from another tribe to go to war, to vindicate them-
> selves, from the imputation of having been the cause of his
> death – but now, they usually attribute their visitations from
> death to the influence of white men. However unjust this may
> be to their white neighbours, it is certainly a blessing to them-
> selves, as it saves them from many a desperate and bloody
> conflict.[32]

But when Europeans were clearly responsible for the death of
Aborigines the desire to exact due revenge remained strong although fear of guns and massive reprisals may have promoted caution and helped determine that sorcery rather than physical attack

would be the preferred method of operation. A Western Australian pioneer wrote to the *Perth Gazette* in 1833 observing:

> the doctrine of taking life for life seems perfectly established, and they avow their determination to act upon it, for though I expressed strong dissent they seemed thoroughly satisfied of its propriety.[33]

A generation later a Queensland squatter remarked that in his experience blacks took 'life for life in some shape or other'[34] though it might take years to consummate and there is no doubt that Aborigines carried out carefully planned executions of specific Europeans for known crimes against kinsmen. Pioneer literature recorded many instances of the kind. In his reminiscences of early pastoral life in Queensland James Nesbit referred to the fate of one McLaren who was expertly tracked for a whole day and was eventually speared when incautiously putting down his gun. G. S. Lang recorded the death of a shepherd on Mt Abundance Station who, during twelve months, never relaxed for an instant while out on the run as he was aware of the determination of the local clans to kill him. A moment's inattention just before his contract expired was long enough to allow a spear to rip through his body. Then there was the case of Anthony Cox who was executed in the Maronoa in 1851. He had been under threat from local clans for three months; eventually an Aborigine walked boldly up to the shepherd's hut and drove a spear into him before the two other Europeans present could intervene although they subsequently shot the executioner.

What happened when the guilty European was unknown or beyond reach? When dealing with other Aborigines the more experienced clan members could draw on their knowledge of kinship networks to determine who could appropriately be punished in particular cases. But with white men the situation was entirely different. The basic problem was that of accountability which was in turn dependent on Aboriginal perception of European social organization. Were whites to be considered as one people and thereby mutually responsible? They did speak the one language but on the other hand those in the bush were divided into small residential

groups. This was one of those white problems probably widely discussed among Aborigines in contact with the settlers. Davis, the
convict escapee, noted Aboriginal uncertainty when they were seeking to determine who to attack in revenge for the 1842 Kilcoy poisoning. They were considering an onslaught on the exploring party
led by Thomas Petrie which ventured inland after landing in Wide
Bay and asked Davis 'whether they belonged to the Whites who had
poisoned their friends'.[35] Davis deflected his kin from their projected attack by arguing that the explorers were totally different
people because they had come from the sea and were therefore not
accountable for the Kilcoy massacre which was perpetrated by shepherds who had arrived overland from the south.

The evidence provided by European pioneers underlines the variety of Aboriginal solutions to this problem. An experienced frontier
squatter was asked by the 1861 Select Committee on the Queensland
Native Police if he knew of any instance when blacks had taken revenge on members of one station for violence dealt out at another. He
answered that his experience suggested that they confined their retribution to the family who had injured them. 'They do not make
reprisals', he said, 'except to revenge themselves upon particular individuals'.[36] Twenty years earlier Swan River Aborigines 'seemed to intimate' that their revenge was limited either to place or person. They
explained to a European confidant that they were 'very bad foes with
respect to some districts' but very good or friendly 'with respect to
others'. 'This shows', the settler concluded, 'they consider us devided
[sic] into distinct tribes' although he endeavoured to show the blacks
that Europeans were all the same; that 'to touch one offended all'.[37]

As well as seeking to punish particular individuals Aborigines
sought to keep revenge proportionate with the original offence as
dictated by the principles of reciprocity. In at least some of their
dealings with Europeans blacks sought to use violence to restore an
equilibrium upset by previous conflict in a manner common in traditional society. This explains the often sporadic nature of
Aboriginal attacks on Europeans, the way in which weeks or
months of concord were succeeded by periods of antagonism. At

Moreton Bay in 1843 the Commissioner for Crown Lands reported that local blacks boldly asserted 'their intention of having a certain number of lives of white men by way of compensation' for kin killed in conflict with the squatters.[38] Blacks around Perth explained that after retaliation had been effected they considered that friendship had been restored. 'White man shoot black man, very bad', they said, 'black men spear white man, very good, very good, plenty shake hands'. Armstrong, the Aboriginal Interpreter, wrote to the West Australian Colonial Secretary explaining that local blacks said that because the settlers had shot one of them they had speared one of the white people and that consequently they were 'all friends now'.[39] J. D. Wood, whose perceptions of Aboriginal behaviour were clearer than his prose, explained in a memo to the Queensland government in 1862 that:

> If you (the Reader or Hearer) kill any Aboriginal his relatives catch me or any other White man supposed to be of the same nation, they will kill us, after which you, (the reader or hearer) may walk about amongst them in perfect safety.[40]

While discussing the consequences of the so called Battle of Pinjarra the Western Australian Advocate-General remarked that up until that event the local blacks had believed that, like themselves, Europeans balanced life against life and were 'content if we took a corresponding number of lives to those taken by them'. But the massive onslaught at Pinjarra had caused the 'complete annihilation of this idea'.[41] These remarks are particularly pertinent because they relate to the impact of European violence on Aboriginal behaviour.

Traditional society we can assume had been able to sustain the level of violence created by pay-back killing over long periods of time and inter-clan feuding continued undiminished until well after the Europeans arrived. Occasional fighting with whites may not have appeared a radical departure from these long accepted patterns of violence. But the settlers had no intention of allowing the continuance of a situation which challenged their monopoly of power and the absolute supremacy of the introduced legal code even though they frequently ignored it themselves when dealing with the

Aborigines. Pioneer communities appeared to be unable to cope with the psychological tensions produced by even small amounts of inter-racial violence. The punitive expedition – official and unofficial – was the almost universal riposte. The objective was simple: the use of overwhelming force to crush resistance once and for all and drown in blood the Aboriginal determination to take an eye for an eye and a tooth for a tooth. Terror succeeded in many places. Massive force did achieve peace for the pioneer, subjection for the blacks. But elsewhere an ascending spiral of violence forced Aborigines to shift decisively into new patterns of behaviour, to concentrate more and more on the struggle with the settlers.

Aborigines were often stunned by the numbers killed in encounters with settlers determined to bring an end to conflict 'once and for all'. The violence must have appeared both totally disproportionate and indiscriminate, sweeping away individuals and sometimes whole local groups who had not necessarily been involved in attacks on the settlers. The desire for revenge, to measure life for life, became increasingly difficult to consummate. The problem of accountability was compounded by the length of the casualty list. At this point some shunned further violence turning to sorcery or sinking into quiescence. But amongst other groups two crucial decisions were made – that white people were mutually accountable and responsible for each other's actions and therefore fit subjects of Aboriginal attack. Colour alone was now enough to identify the enemy. When those conclusions had been reached a shift of decisive importance had been made. For the groups in question the constraints of custom had been circumvented, they had moved from feud to warfare.

Initially, then, the blacks had dealt with Europeans as though they too were Aborigines. Their violence was judicial rather than martial, seeking revenge rather than military victory. But the settlers were determined upon radical changes. They had no interest in peace and equilibrium until the invasion was fully effected and all resistance crushed. Till then violence was bound to escalate. Many contingent factors turned events in the same direction.

Misunderstanding, fear and anxiety merged and simmered in the volatile frontier environment. Violent death and succeeding violent revenge built up brutal momentum as the settlers pushed further into Aboriginal Australia.

THREE CELEBRATED ATTACKS

Three celebrated Aboriginal attacks on Europeans can be examined to illustrate these themes – the *Maria* 'massacre' in South Australia in 1840, and the successful Aboriginal attacks on *Hornet Bank* and *Cullinlaringoe* in Queensland in 1857 and 1861 respectively. Each case was seen at the time as evidence of Aboriginal savagery and treachery and although well reported in contemporary newspapers there have been few satisfactory historical accounts of them.

The events leading up to the *Maria* 'massacre' were deceptively simple. The ship travelling from Hobart to Adelaide was wrecked off the Coorong. Twelve survivors were eventually killed by Aborigines who had initially helped them travel along the beach towards the mouth of the Murray. Six months after the event the Aboriginal side of the story was presented by Dr Richard Penny who as surgeon to the whale fishery at Encounter Bay had learnt the local language and arrived at a sophisticated understanding of traditional society. The blacks explained that they had helped the whites travel by carrying their children and providing them with fish and water. When they came to the end of their own country they tried to explain that they could go no further and demanded clothes and blankets in recognition of the trouble taken up to that point. The Europeans refused to give them anything, saying that when they reached Adelaide the blacks would be fully rewarded. They probably did not understand what the Aborigines were trying to tell them. The blacks attempted to help themselves. The whites resisted. Scuffles ensued, tempers flared, and the weaponless Europeans were killed. Their deaths were not inevitable. With a little luck the survivors might have reached Adelaide full of praise for the friendly blacks of the Coorong.

In October 1861 nineteen Europeans were killed by Aborigines at Cullinlaringoe Station on the Nagoa River in central Queensland. The district had only recently been settled and initially relations between blacks and squatters were amicable. Daniel Cameron, the pioneer of the area, reported that local clans had constantly assisted him during twenty months of occupation and in June 1861 the Commissioner for Crown Lands remarked that the blacks were quiet and friendly on both the Comet and Nagoa. But Native Police patrols were already changing the situation. The Commandant explained to the Colonial Secretary why he had decided to send a large detachment into the district. Blacks were reported to be gathering on the Comet and while they had been peaceably disposed they could not be trusted when able to muster in large numbers. In March the police attacked blacks in the area. Frederick Walker, managing a local property, complained to the Government, warning that Native Police action would inevitably lead to serious conflict. The whole tribe he said was 'dreadfully excited and accused me and all the Europeans, with complicity in what they rightly termed treachery'.[42] C. B. Dutton, a neighbouring squatter, took the matter up with the leader of the detachment, Lieutenant Patrick, speaking of it as an 'unfortunate and untoward event'. According to Dutton's testimony Patrick justified himself by saying that:

> other Police Officers before they had been in the force a fortnight had sent in dispatches (I use his own words) 'of lots of blacks shot. And here had he been in the force six months before he had shot a single black'.

Like Walker, Dutton impressed on the Government that the blacks were moved by feelings of:

> deep implacable revenge for unprovoked injuries. They ask me why they are shot. They say 'bail no me kill white fellow ... bail take ration, what for shoot him?' How are they to be answered, how appeased?

And he answered with venom, 'there is but one answer, you are black and must be shot'.[43]

But not all the squatters opposed the actions of the Native Police. In his memoirs Jesse Gregson recorded his part in the events of 1861. He established himself at Mt Rainworth Station in May. The local clans persistently endeavoured to establish friendly relations but were rebuffed each time. Gregson believed firmly in the policy of 'keeping the blacks out'. One of his shepherds lost a flock of 500 sheep. It was found by the blacks who began to drive it away. Gregson arrived with Patrick and his detachment and, as he termed it, a brush took place. The Aborigines determined on revenge. They gathered men from the scattered clans and attacked the recently established *Cullinlaringoe*. The Wills family, who were not expecting trouble, may have died totally unaware of what had gone wrong with the peaceful pattern of contact established during their few weeks in the district. They may have been attacked because they were the closest Europeans to the gathering point of the clans or perhaps they were regarded as the least prepared to repel an attack.

The events at Hornet Bank are fairly well known. The Frasers were managing the property and had close, if not always amicable, relations with the neighbouring Aboriginal clans camped on or near the station. An apparently well planned and unexpected attack was made late at night and all but one member of the household were killed. It appears that the women were raped before death – an unusual accompaniment of Aboriginal attack Various attempts were made at the time to explain Aboriginal motivation but none could compete with the insistent references to the savagery and treachery. However there are scattered pieces of evidence which enable us to advance beyond the folk-wisdom of the frontier. The Honourable M. C. O'Connell told the 1861 Select Committee on the Native Police that the killings were a consequence of the young men 'having been in the habit of allowing their black boys to rush the gins' in neighbouring camps. Archibald Meston, the Queensland 'expert' on Aborigines, heard from a friend of the surviving Fraser son that the white employees of the family had whipped and raped two local Aboriginal girls. This story was confirmed by W. Robertson who claimed to have discussed the events of 1857 with old Aborigines who as youths had been present at the time. They reported that after the women were raped the local clans attempted to use sorcery against the offending Europeans. When that appeared to have no effect they sent an old woman to the Frasers to explain the circumstances and seek redress. When no action was taken by the whites the clans determined on revenge. So the evidence concurs on the importance of sexual attacks on Aboriginal girls but attributes blame variously to black and white employees of the family. But one account directly implicates the young Fraser men. J. D. Wood explained in a memo to the Colonial Secretary that when arriving in Queensland he made enquiries about Hornet Bank. He was told by a Mr Nicol who had been in the Native Police in 1857 that Mrs Fraser had repeatedly asked him to reprove her sons 'for forcibly taking the young maidens' and that in consequence she 'expected harm would come of it, that they were in the habit of doing so, notwithstanding her entreaties to the contrary'. Several other informants told Wood that the Frasers were 'famous for the young Gins' and all agreed 'that those acts were the cause of the atrocity'.[44]

Of the three cases discussed above the *Maria* 'massacre' was clearly the most unpremeditated, even accidental event, arising out of the tension and misunderstanding inherent in the situation following the shipwreck. At *Hornet Bank* and *Cullinlarin-goe* Aboriginal action was carefully planned and thoroughly considered and followed months of provocation – harassment by the Native Police on the one hand, sexual molestation by some, if not all, the young men on the station on the other. Even the raping of the Fraser women appears in retrospect to have been a deliberate, political act. But there were other aspects of the attack on *Hornet Bank* which call for comment. It appears to have been part of what Wiseman, the local Commissioner for Crown Lands, called an 'extensive conspiracy'. Writing at a time of extreme anger and anxiety he may have mistakenly seen connections between unrelated events. Yet he noted that many circumstances supported his interpretation. Two or three days before the attack the black women and children left the stations on the Dawson and went away in one direction while the men went in the other. News of the successful onslaught was, he believed, known to blacks a hundred and more miles away well before local Europeans had heard of it. On receipt of the intelligence in the camps 'rejoicing immediately commenced'. Several other attacks were launched in the district at much the same time but they were unsuccessful. Wiseman referred to many other circumstances 'too tedious to relate' which illustrated the Aborigine's 'feeling of hatred' towards the settlers.[45]

OVERVIEW

We may never know enough to accurately chart the regional variations of frontier conflict and Aboriginal resistance in every area of Australia. But in a few places the documentary evidence is plentiful. This is true of Tasmania where voluminous official reports, newspapers and other records can be balanced up with the detailed diaries of G. A. Robinson written while travelling extensively in what was still Aboriginal Tasmania. Robinson understood the Tasmanian dialects and spent many hours talking with the blacks at a time when conflict with the whites had reached a bitter crescendo. He provided by far the most important European account of Aboriginal motivation and the cumulative effect of settler brutality. Robinson realized that the Tasmanians had experienced 'a multitude of wrongs from a variety of sources'.[46] The accumulation of private injury and personal tragedy fused to produce the bitter racial hatred and desperate resistance of the Black War of 1827–1830. 'They have' wrote Robinson:

> a tradition amongst them that white men have usurped their territory, have driven them into the forests, have killed their game ... have ravished their wives and daughters, have murdered and butchered their fellow countrymen; and are wont whilst brooding over these complicated ills in the dense part of the forest, to goad each other on to acts of bloodshed and revenge for the injuries done to their ancestors and the persecutions offered to themselves through their white enemies.[47]

The more observant settlers noted the change in Aboriginal attitudes which took place during the second half of the 1820s. One
told an official committee that although he had been aware of black
hostility in the past it had previously been 'excited by some temporary aggression of the Whites the Remembrance of which gradually
gave way to better feelings'. The desire for revenge had not originally extended beyond the 'Tribe; or family, in which it originated'.
But the situation had changed and he now detected a 'determined
spirit of hostility' among the whole black population. He concluded
with the observation:

> I think the Blacks look on the whole of the white population as
> Enemies and are not sensible of any benefit they might derive
> from living with us on friendly terms.[48]

The escalation of conflict which occurred in Tasmania in the
1820s was mirrored in other parts of the continent. The occupation
of the northern pastoral frontier of New South Wales and
Queensland witnessed a similar burgeoning of racial violence as the
pastoralists moved deeper into Aboriginal territory. Bloodshed in
one district built up expectations about its probability in the next.
Squatters came over the horizon with their guns loaded ready to
keep the blacks out until they were willing to submit. Expectation
of conflict was diffused on the other side of the frontier as well. The
pastoralists followed the river valleys and open savannah, riding
along those channels of Aboriginal communication where information was most rapidly disseminated. Conflict of the late 1830s and
early 1840s took place in north-eastern New South Wales and
south-eastern Queensland where inter-tribal contact was strengthened by the large gatherings to harvest the bunya trees in the ranges
north of the Brisbane Valley. Refugees from conflict with the whites
almost certainly found succour among clans still beyond the settlers'
reach 'relating to each other the history of their wrongs'.[49]

There was no G. A. Robinson on the northern pastoral frontier
but it is possible to gather a little evidence from a variety of
sources. Davis provided important material about the Aboriginal
reaction to the poisoning of a large number of blacks – probably

fifty or so – on Kilcoy Station in the upper Brisbane Valley in 1842. News of the terrible deaths spread widely in Aboriginal society over a significant area of southern Queensland and northern New South Wales. There was a large gathering in the mountains where, according to Davis, representatives of fourteen or fifteen different tribes were present. The suffering and terrible deaths of those poisoned were graphically mimed for the benefit of the visitors, a performance which Davis was later to repeat for his white rescuers. The anger of the assembled blacks was unmistakable. They were, said Davis 'much infuriated' by the news and swore to have vengeance.[50] This decision was apparently widely and rapidly communicated. Schmidt, the German missionary at Moreton Bay was warned by friendly blacks that the tribes to the north had determined 'to attack and kill whites whenever they met any'.[51]

Similar sentiments, relayed through intermediaries or expressed in frontier pidgin, were reported at various points from northern New South Wales to central Queensland. On the Mooney River in 1843 a group of blacks told beleagured shepherds holed up in their hut that they intended to 'kill or drive all the white fellows off the Mooney, McIntyre and Barwon Rivers'.[52] At Wide Bay in 1851 a squatter reported that the blacks had sent messages through intermediaries to the effect that as soon as the bunya nut was ripe they intended to 'take all the sheep in the district and kill all the white men'.[53] In 1856 when Charles Archer was about to cross the Fitzroy River the local blacks assembled in great numbers on the opposite bank and openly stated their determination to 'attack and destroy all the whites who might attempt the location of the country in that direction'.[54] Two years later four shepherds were besieged in their hut on Camboon station. They offered their attackers all their possessions. But the blacks retorted that they wanted nothing but the lives of the white men and that they would also 'take the lives of all the b - y [sic] white men in the country'.[55] In 1858 Wiseman wrote to his superior in Sydney about Aborigines who openly proclaimed that they would gradually murder all the whites and rid their land of the invader. He was an intelligent and

experienced official and after fifteen years on the pastoral frontier
had concluded that:

> no tribes will allow of the peaceable occupation of their country
> but, following the counsel of the boldest and strongest men
> amongst them, will endeavour to check the progress of the white
> men by spearing their sheep and murdering the shepherds. This
> I have known to be invariably the case ... some solitary murder
> may occasionally occur owing to the wicked and foolish conduct
> of the white labouring man in his relations to the Blacks ... but
> the greater number of murders which I know of in these districts
> I should attribute to the determination of the natives to pillage
> and murder till they can drive out the white men.[56]

The evidence, then, suggests that Aborigines attacked and killed
Europeans for a variety of reasons. At the time of earliest contact
they struck down threatening beings who it was thought had come
from the spirit world. Subsequently whites were killed in unpremeditated melees arising from the anxiety and tension inherent in
frontier encounters. In many cases Aboriginal action was penal in
objective, punishing Europeans as though they were fellow blacks in
an attempt to impose on the newcomers the moral standards and social obligations of traditional society. The spear was used to assist the
assimilation of the European into the Australian way of life. In many
parts of the country, for at least some of the time, absorption of the
small numbers of Europeans seemed the most practical solution to
the white problem. It should not be seen as less realistic or less worthy than open confrontation which many must have realized from
the start was bound to be both futile and suicidal. Assimilation was
after all a policy premised on a self-confident belief in the value of
Aboriginal society and culture. It was one method of defending them
from the unprecedented challenge presented by European invasion.
When this policy failed two alternatives remained – acceptance of
whatever corner could be found in the new order imposed by the settlers or an attempt to drive the invaders away. In many parts of the
country the blacks fought a war against the Europeans. But it did not
always begin when the whites first arrived. It was more common at
the end of a considerable period of inter-action. In Tasmania, for

instance, conflict did not climax for a generation after the first settlement. Elsewhere the shift from feud to warfare was more rapid but
on the other hand there were districts where accommodation was
achieved before the final stage of conflict was reached and others
where massive retaliation crushed the black resistance almost before
it began.

SORCERY

The role of sorcery is an important aspect of Aboriginal resistance
hitherto overlooked by historians. Magic was, after all, widely used
against enemies in traditional society, supplementing or supplanting
physical attack. That it was similarly used against white foes is
beyond doubt especially when open conflict carried such disproportionate danger for the Aborigines. Sorcery was probably employed
in order to enhance the chances of success for attacks with spear
and club during the earliest period of contact and continued to be
used long after overt resistance had come to an end. In the
Aboriginal mind this hidden side of the resistance may have been at
least as significant as physical confrontation. Unfortunately for the
historian magic was likely to have been performed in secret and
kept hidden from intended white victims. Yet there is enough evidence to illustrate its importance. It comes from a variety of sources
but the most valuable material was provided by officials of the
Aboriginal Protectorate in Victoria and South Australia in the
1840s.

In October 1840 there was a crisis in white-Aboriginal relations
at Port Phillip. Following widespread settler concern about black
assertiveness in the districts around Melbourne a party of soldiers
and border police under the command of Major Lettsom surrounded a large ceremonial gathering a few miles north of the
town and captured the whole assembly. They were marched into
town and imprisoned overnight. One man was shot at the time of
capture and another while escaping from incarceration. The blacks
were frightened and infuriated. G. A. Robinson reported that the

most influential men amongst the tribes in Melbourne warned him
that they intended 'returning to the mountains and forest ranges
and killing every white man they could find unprotected'.[57] E. S.
Parker told a similar story. The blacks had said they would take to
the mountains and try and 'drive the white fellows from the country'.[58] The Protectorate officials – Robinson, Parker and Thomas –
worked hard to restrain the blacks and, given the lack of immediate
physical retaliation, felt they had been successful in defusing the situation. But their accounts make it clear that the Aborigines chan-
nelled their anger into magic in order to unleash the horrifying
power of Mindye the rainbow serpent on the whites and those
blacks who were friendly with them, especially the Port Phillip
clans. Thomas reported that the blacks from his station at Narre
Narre Warren had fled because a celebrated Goulburn River 'clever
man' had said the Mindye was about to come. Parker was even
more specific. Several of the senior and influential blacks were, he
observed, fully sensible of the injustices they had suffered. They
warned that the dreaded Mindye would appear with the threat of a
pestilence which was 'to sweep off the Port Phillip blacks and all the
whites'.[59] Reminiscing later he recalled that at the time of the
Lettsom raid several old men told him confidentially that:

> destruction was coming upon the white population not even ex-
> cepting those whom they knew to be their friends. It was known
> that they were practising secret incantations with this object.[60]

Months after the imprisonment Parker found that the Goulburn
River clans were still furious about their treatment and were prac-
tising magic to call up the Mindye to destroy the Europeans and
those Aborigines who had befriended them.

The reaction of Victorian Aborigines to capture and temporary
imprisonment at the hands of Major Lettsom is of great interest.
Their anger was intense and sustained. Direct physical retaliation
was considered but rejected, whether owing to the advice of
Robinson, Parker and Thomas, as they supposed, or to fear of
retaliation is impossible to determine. The resort to magic illustrated a profound belief in their continuing power to counter the

technological supremacy of the Europeans. It is ironic that they hoped to visit on the whites a pestilence similar to the great epidemic which had struck the Victorian Aborigines a generation earlier and which must have remained vivid in the memories of the older people. The hoped-for pestilence was described to Parker 'graphically enough as producing dreadful sores, dysentry, blindness and death' and he was later able to identify 'the threatened agent of destruction as smallpox'.[61] Yet the action of Major Lettsom and his force was far less violent than the behaviour of whites in many other parts of the country. It is reasonable to assume that the only unique feature of the events in Victoria in 1841–42 was that there were three Europeans in close enough contact with the blacks to be able to report on their objectives and motivation.

Thomas noted a further but apparently unrelated case of anti-European sorcery at Port Phillip. An old and very celebrated 'clever man' was captured and imprisoned for sheep stealing. His incarceration caused great distress among blacks around Melbourne and news of it was carried to the corners of the Colony. Signal fires were lit and could be seen in all directions; messengers from seven different districts came in for urgent consultation; the Melbourne blacks pleaded with Thomas to let the 'clever man' go. When he explained that he was unable to secure the release the several hundred town blacks fled into the bush warning Thomas that the whites should leave for Sydney or Van Diemens Land because the sorcerer would unleash the Mindye. In 1849 there was a similar occurrence in Adelaide. The local Protector of Aborigines reported that four blacks had arrived from the north with the alarming news that 'clever men' were about to create havoc in the town. Many Aborigines fled to escape the threatened catastrophe.[62] Edward Eyre referred to a similar situation a few years earlier when the appearance of a comet convinced South Australian blacks that powerful northern sorcerers were about to destroy Adelaide because a senior man of their tribe had been imprisoned in the local gaol. The comet, Eyre was told, was: 'the harbinger of all kinds of calamities, and more especially for white people. It was to overthrow Adelaide, destroy all Europeans and their houses'.[63] Similar events were reported from New South Wales. During the 1830's there was a:

> solemn ceremony of the Natives in the Country to the west of Bathurst in which all the tribes around seemed deeply interested, they had all met together to call upon the Great Spirit, they perceived how their ranks were thinning and no children born, they perceived the havoc civilization were [sic] making on their hunting grounds and they met together to implore the aid of the Great Spirit.[64]

Anti-European sorcery often merged with ceremony, dance and song and it was in this form that it was occasionally witnessed by white observers. Tasmanian Aborigines sang every night around their camp fires, their favourite songs those in which they recounted their assaults on, and fights with the whites. Widowson referred to a sort of dance and rejoicing, jumping and singing performed by island blacks when celebrating a successful attack on the Europeans. A Queensland pioneer who had wide experience of Aboriginal society in the post-contact period referred to what he called the death to the white man song which was sung frequently at corroborees with intense bitterness. On a North Queensland station in 1874 a large gathering of blacks was seen to make two effigies of white men and then all those present 'after exciting each other with war songs and dances, attacked the effigies with their tomahawks and cut them to pieces'.[65]

There are four reports, widely separated in time and space, of a Queensland corroboree depicting a pitched battle between Aborigines and white stockmen. It is not clear if the dance was created in one place and then widely disseminated or if similar corroborees evolved separately although there is a close resemblance in the descriptions provided by the four European observers. The performance began with a group of dancers representing a herd of cattle. Bovine behaviour was minutely and exactly mimed, then a second group dressed as hunters carefully and slowly stalked the 'herd' and eventually attacked them with spear and club. Some 'cattle' fell to the ground, others stampeded into the darkness. The hunters began to prepare the fallen 'beasts' for cooking when a third troupe of dancers appeared from out of the trees. They were made up to look like Europeans with imitation cabbage tree hats, faces whitened with pipe-clay, bodies painted blue or red to represent shirts and legs done up to simulate moleskins and leggings. European behaviour was carefully depicted; the pseudo white men: 'bit the cartridges, put on the caps, and went through all the forms of loading, firing, wheeling their horses, assisting each other, etc, which proved personal observation.'[66] After a protracted struggle with casualties on both sides the whites were ignominiously defeated and depending on the particular dance either all killed or driven away to the intense delight of the spectators.

The four reports in question all relate to the generation between 1860 and 1890 and to the eastern half of Queensland. It seems probable that such anti-white corroborees were frequently performed. They were obviously entertaining, embodied a good deal of accurate observation of frontier life and allowed the vanquished to experience in art the triumph and revenge no longer attainable in the real world. Whether the Queensland 'battle' dance was associated with anti-European magic is impossible to say. But sorcery was related to a sequence of corroborees danced in far-western Queensland in the 1890s. Roth described a series of dances performed over five successive nights which he called the Molonga corroboree. He determined that it had entered Queensland from the Northern Territory in the early 1890s and travelled from the headwaters of the Georgina River down through western Queensland in the space of two or three years. The German missionary Otto Siebert recorded it as performed by the Dieri in the northwest of South Australia and noted that by the early years of the twentieth century it had passed on as far as Port Augusta at the head of Spencer Gulf. Baldwin Spencer saw the cycle danced by the Arunta at Alice Springs while A. P. Elkin reported performances at Penong on the Great Australian Bight in 1915 and at Horseshoe Bend in 1930.

Roth provided the earliest and most detailed description of the Molonga but he did not understand the meaning or the purpose of the sequence. Fortunately, Siebert provided a brief but fascinating account of the central theme and symbolism of the five nights of dancing. The corroboree had its origin in the desire for revenge against Europeans after the shooting of blacks presumably somewhere in the north-east corner of the Northern Territory. Prominent in the performance were dancers made up to look like Europeans who carried long forked sticks to represent their rifles. At the climax of the sequence a figure – Siebert said a female water spirit – suddenly appeared to devour all the 'European' dancers while the destructive magic was directed out in all directions to kill the settlers and the Aborigines who were friendly with them. Thus it is clear from Siebert's account that the Molonga corroboree was an intensely emotional performance directed specifically at mobilizing the most potent magic available in order to destroy the whites and their black allies.

There may have been other dance sequences created like the Molonga to turn back the tide of European invasion. Magic must have seemed the most realistic method to adopt given the weapons of the Europeans and their propensity to exact violent and disproportionate revenge. But did Aborigines continue to believe in the efficiency of their sorcery? Twentieth century studies make it clear that faith in magic and in the powers of the 'clever men' has been one of the most enduring features of traditional culture surviving longer than almost anything else, even language itself. There were in-built barriers to scepticism – time-honoured methods of rationalizing failure and claiming authorship of the contingent. The obvious inability of 'clever men' to drive the Europeans away could be readily explained in ways well tried in traditional society. The failure of magic to immediately achieve stated objectives could be seen as being due to faults in the ritual or to the influence of counter-magic performed by other and often distant 'clever men'. As Europeans on the frontier were normally accompanied by strange blacks it was probably often assumed that their magic threw a protective ring around the white men. Violent hostility to such 'tame station blacks' may have stemmed in part from this perception of their role in the advance of the European settlers.

But we should not assume that Aborigines believed their magic was without effect. Pioneer settlers were often very vulnerable and must have appeared so to the blacks who may have often concluded that sorcery was responsible for the bad seasons, bad luck, and accidents which befell Europeans in every part of the continent. Many were, after all, financially ruined and abandoned farms and stations. Alluvial miners took up and deserted finds with frenetic speed while ships were wrecked all around the Australian coasts. The immediate cause of the white retreat or misfortune would not have been apparent giving scope to those who attributed European misfortune to the magic of the clever men of near or distant tribes. Aiston and Horne referred to a noted kurdaitcha man from central Australia who claimed to be able to make lightning strike where he liked and to have killed a white man with his power. Mrs K. L. Parker recalled that local Aborigines were convinced that a black from the north-west, beyond Euahalayi territory, had called up a storm which wrecked the stable and store on her station. She made an even more interesting observation about the famous rain maker who it was said was so angry with the white people:

> who were driving away all emu, kangaroo, and opossums, the black-fellow's food, and yet made a fuss if their dogs killed a sheep for them sometimes, that he put his rain stone in a fire, and while he did that no rain would fall. He said that if all the sheep died the white fellows would go away again, and then, as long ago, the blackfellows country would have plenty of emu and kangaroo.[67]

Simpson Newland made a similar assessment of Aboriginal motivation observing that they made no attempt to make rain during long periods of drought. Their intention, he believed, was to drive the Europeans out of their country and given the devastating effect of drought on sheep and cattle stations it is reasonable to assume that blacks believed that their magic was often an effective weapon against the white invaders.

R. M. Berndt collected a number of traditional stories at
Menindee in western New South Wales in 1943 which illustrated
the presumed ability of 'clever men' to unleash their powers on the
settlers. One related to an old 'clever man' called Mulgadown
Tommy who lived on the fringes of Cobar. His dogs were poisoned
by the townspeople and in revenge he brought up the poison which
sorcerers were thought to possess and spurted it out so that the
fumes covered the nearby mine. The result was that he 'cleaned out
a great number of people' until his own friends stopped him. Berndt
did not suggest any source for the story but it may have related to
a fatal mine accident which in the blacks' camp was thought to be
a consequence of powerful magic unleashed to punish the
Europeans. A second story referred to another old sorcerer called
Billy who was working as a shepherd on a sheep station. One morning Billy woke up too late to take some rams out of their pen, a job
which he was expected to do before breakfast. But as the meal was
being served he went and got his food and took it into the yard to
eat. When the white boss saw the rams still in their pen he abused
the old man, grabbed his breakfast and threw it onto the ground.
Old Billy got up and walked slowly towards his camp. On the way
he let out his magic cord which, unknown to the Europeans, attached itself to the doors and windows of the bosses' house. Before
he reached his camp he turned around and looked back at the
house:

> he could see all the string, although these were invisible to the or-
> dinary person. Then he released his assistant totem, the light-
> ning, at the same time pulling sharply on the strings, as he did so
> they went off like a loud report of thunder and an immediate
> flash of lightning igniting the house. The cook ran around
> throwing buckets of water upon the flames, but instead of ex-
> tinguishing the fire it acted like kerosene and the flames flared up
> more fiercely.[68]

It seems probable that there were many stories like these ones.
They were obviously important because they allowed the seemingly
powerless and abject blacks to go on believing in the potency of
their culture and in the ability of the 'men of high degree' to harm

and humble even the domineering white boss. Magic was then a crucial factor in the psychological resistance to the Europeans.

Frontier conflict was then widespread in colonial Australia. Most districts saw fighting between resident clans and encroaching settlers although it varied greatly in duration and intensity. Conflict was triggered by tension and misunderstanding, by the possessiveness of Europeans towards the land and water, by competition over women and by diametrically opposed concepts of personal property. Once blacks had been injured or killed their relations were impelled to seek vengeance. Reciprocal violence quickly spiralled. Sorcery played an important part in the conflict although it was usually hidden from the Europeans. The problems arising from fighting with the white men demanded adjustments to customary ways as well as the development of new concepts and techniques.

Chapter 4

RESISTANCE: TACTICS AND TRADITIONS

The development of appropriate tactics was another aspect of the Aborigines' white problem which we can assume was widely discussed on the other side of the frontier. A critical issue was the degree to which known methods of fighting could be employed against the Europeans and the extent to which innovation was necessary. In his famous study of the Murngin, entitled *A Black Civilization,* Lloyd-Warner distinguished six varieties of conflict. How relevant these definitions are to traditional society elsewhere has never been determined but it is reasonable to examine the two major forms of fighting which the ethnographic record suggests were practically universal – the large pitched battle and the small, secret revenge expedition.

MASSED WARRIORS

Pioneer literature contains many references to battles between large Aboriginal parties and they were still being waged years after the arrival of the Europeans. Typically the two sides met at a pre-arranged site and assembled in loose formations. After much shouting of abuse, spears and boomerangs were thrown back and forth between the wavering lines of warriors. After several hours, considerable minor injury and an occasional mortal wound, peace was restored and a corroboree held to mark the cessation of hostilities. Such large formations, with their obvious similarity to the animal drive, were often used against Europeans. But they presented problems, both tactical and logistic. Under normal conditions Aborigines could only gather in significant numbers on those occasions when there was some local and transient abundance of food. It is not clear if Europeans were confronted at times when large groups were already assembled for initiation and other ceremonies in which case clashes with whites were merely a by-product of the normal functioning of traditional society. Another possibility is that fear of Europeans led to the prolonging of customary meetings beyond their appointed time or to the calling together of unseasonal gatherings to deal specifically with the white problem. This seems to have been the case after the Kilcoy poisoning in 1842.

Special meetings would present the problem of ensuring an adequate food supply which could be met by increased culling of fauna by way of large and co-ordinated drives or, more portentously, by turning to the flocks and herds of the European or even their supplies stored in buildings or in transit on drays. Frontier settlers were convinced that large gatherings of Aborigines inevitably led to increased attacks on animals and stations. The crucial step of commandeering European food led to escalation of conflict which in turn encouraged large groups to remain together even longer to seek the protection of numbers. Frederick Walker, the first commandant of the native police on the northern frontier of New South Wales, understood the situation well. It was, he wrote:

> the hostile bearing of the settlers that causes the Blacks to keep in large numbers, for they cannot continue the assemblies customary to them for more than a few days at a time, on account of the want of food ... They supply this want from the herds of the settlers, and are compelled so to do.[1]

The many reports of large Aboriginal gatherings – though no doubt often exaggerated by anxious pioneers – emphasise the changes brought about on the other side of the frontier as a result of European pressure. Aboriginal clans coalesced to increase their power and to seek security and there is no doubt that large gatherings did over-awe white communities. Parties of armed settlers avoided conflict with Aborigines on many more occasions than is commonly supposed while the official determination of the New South Wales and later the Queensland government to use the Native Police to disperse any large tribal gathering was eloquent of official concern. But like people confronting armed whites in many parts of the non-European world Aborigines found that concentration merely increased the ability of their opponents to bring their superior fire-power into play.

GUNS

European accounts allow us to examine, at least in outline, the development of Aboriginal tactics to cope with guns. News of them spread widely but unevenly through traditional society ahead of the white invaders but the amount and sophistication of that knowledge varied considerably. Some clans greatly underestimated the power of firearms and were shot down as a result of their fatal miscalculation. In central Victoria in the 1840s a group of blacks confronted a party of 16 armed and mounted men. They held up shields to keep off the musket balls only to die with the bark, useless and shattered, in their hands. Christie Palmerston wrote of a similar incident in the northern rainforest forty years later. He was challenged by a small hostile party and reached immediately for his gun. 'Their shields may answer very well for the purposes of their wars', he wrote with brutal satisfaction:

> but my rifle drilled them as if they were sheets of paper. Four of the old generals' [sic] comrades ran to his assistance when they saw him wrestling with death. I ceased firing for they seemed so helpless at my mercy on seeing a seam of blood oozing from the ghastly wound ...[2]

Elsewhere Aboriginal caution betokened prior warning of the danger and capacity of European weapons. G. A. Robinson reported that he had watched blacks cautiously approach overland parties when the least movement of the well armed Europeans would cause them to take shelter behind trees or throw themselves on the ground. Moorhouse, who witnessed some of the pitched battles along the lower Murray, remarked that although the blacks faced the whites in large formations they chose their ground so they could rapidly escape behind trees and into thick vegetation. Perhaps the single most important lesson to learn was the effective range of guns and often this may have been transmitted back beyond the frontier. Pioneers reported that blacks behaved as though they had a rough idea of the distance at which they were safe from ball or bullet. Eventually the Aborigines came to appreciate the limitations of the muskets used in the first half of the nineteenth century which were inaccurate at any appreciable distance, frequently misfired and took some minutes to reload in any but experienced hands. There are numerous reports of confrontations between Aboriginal clans and lone shepherds during which the blacks taunted the European to try and incite him to fire his single charge; the shepherd for his part stood for hours with his loaded musket knowing that his only safety lay in preserving it. Aborigines laughed, made faces and rude gestures when muskets misfired as often happened particularly in wet or misty conditions. When they did attack they chose the moment of total vulnerability when their European foes feverishly sought to reload discharged muskets. However there was far less scope for Aboriginal initiative when they faced settlers armed, as they were later in the century, with revolvers and repeating rifles although a writer in the *Cooktown Herald* in 1875 noted how Aboriginal tactics had changed in the face of European fire power. Initially their attacks had been 'daringly open' but as the 'knowledge dawned on their minds that the white race had a fatal superiority of weapons' their forays became stealthy, cautious and only made at 'great advantages of numbers and situation'.[3] Thus the blacks in the Cooktown hinterland quickly learnt the lesson that European firepower and mobility made the massing of scattered clans a dangerous and self-defeating policy.

REVENGE PARTIES

But there were other traditions to fall back on and especially the revenge expedition or execution party, an institution widely reported in both pioneer and ethnographic literature. The 'stealthy sacrifices' of the Pinya, the Kadaitcha or the Maringo were typically carried out by small groups of men, usually at night and in operations which were well planned, based on good intelligence and timed to allow for the strike and return before dawn. Despite a degree of variation it was a traditional method of punishment, execution and revenge well adapted for use against the Europeans. The opprobrious comments elicited from the settlers were evidence of their unease. 'Their whole art of war', wrote a Tasmanian pioneer, was 'a concealed, silent and treacherous attack'.[4] A contemporary in Perth argued that it was not the 'martial courage of a declared foe' that was to be feared but the 'dastardly duplicity of the secret assassin'.[5] Fifty years later a Cooktown journalist remarked that there was not 'a particle of manhood or even brute bravery about the Aboriginals [sic] ... their weapons being treachery patiently nursed'.[6] Their mode of attack, wrote G. A. Robinson, 'is by surreption ... they lay in ambush for some time before they make their attack, a sudden and unperceived invasion ...'[7] The hunter's skills – expert tracking, stealth, self-control and patience – could be turned to effect when attempting to execute individual Europeans. On returning from the bush Davis acted out an Aboriginal dance which mimed the successful spearing of a shepherd – the creeping through the grass, 'the cat-like watching, the drawing nearer and nearer to the unconscious wretch; the spring, the rush, the fierce blow'.[8]

SURVEILLANCE

The gathering of intelligence was one of the most successful aspects of Aboriginal campaigns. They carefully watched the movements of exploring parties, as indicated above, and continued to monitor the actions of pioneer settlers. Women, children and old people were often sent to observe and report on the Europeans. A traditional story from the Herbert River relates how young boys were regularly sent down to the edge of the rainforest to watch the whites and their Kanaka servants. Aborigines employed on stations and around other European settlements almost certainly provided information about the newcomers for kin still in the bush. Attacks on stations often gave indication of accurate information about household lay-out and domestic routines, raids being frequently mounted when the men had left home and were too far away to intervene. Houses, wrote a concerned Tasmanian settler:

> became an easy prey to these insidious depredators, who will, for days and weeks, watch a house that they have marked out for plunder, till they find the whole of the males absent, they then pounce upon the dwelling, and with a celerity incredible plunder it of every article they consider valuable.[9]

It seems that as a general rule Aboriginal intelligence about Europeans was better than the settlers' knowledge of neighbouring clans. Even the Queensland Native Police had difficulty in tracking down blacks who kept a close watch on their movements at all times.

BUSHCRAFT

Apart from effective surveillance the other advantage possessed by the Aborigines was their knowledge of their own country which was intimate and detailed to an extent that no European could hope to match. It was often of great tactical importance. Knowledge of fords, passes, tracks and caves facilitated escape from pursuit, rapidity of march and speed of communication. Settlers were often unable to find the blacks they were pursuing or did not even prosecute the search through a sense of inadequacy in the bush. They were very reluctant to ride into forest, mountain or swamp where their horses were hampered and their mobility restricted. A South Australian settler explained that the blacks he was pursuing had disappeared into thick scrubs 'to which they invariably retreat, and whence they cannot be followed up'.[10] In 1846 a party of police surprised an Aboriginal camp at the head of Spencer Gulf but it was decided that 'to follow them was out of the question from the rocky surface of the whole country'.[11] In Tasmania where European parties usually travelled on foot the Aboriginal advantage was even more marked. 'They are seldom pursued by the settlers', lamented an island colonist, 'from a despair of finding them in the almost inaccessible fastnesses'.[12] Almost despite themselves the Tasmanian settlers came to admire the bush skills of their black adversaries who had proved themselves 'a sagacious and wily race of people'.[13] They were a most 'intricate set of people to capture';[14] no-one could conjecture how 'crafty and subtle they act in the bush'.[15] Similar observations were made by a squatter on the Gwydir in 1839. He believed that the whole British army would be unable to apprehend one tribe in his district:

> so well acquainted are they with every thicket, reedy creek, morass, cave and hollow tree, in which they can secrete themselves, and so inaccessible to a horse of any white man.[16]

There are several reports of Aboriginal groups expressing their self-confidence by turning and making faces at pursuing whites and shouting abuse at them in pidgin English. In Northern New South Wales a party of settlers confronted a group of blacks who:

> took shelter behind the trees, and kept hooting and telling us they were not frightened, calling us white b ... s [sic] and telling us to come on; we left them as we found them, our force being unable to engage them in the scrubs.[17]

There are a number of accounts of Aboriginal parties, confident of their superiority in the bush, turning their backs on pursuing Europeans and slapping their buttocks in derision. Reports of this sort came from Port Essington in the 1830s, the Darling Downs in the 1840s, the Maranoa in the 1860s and Central Australia in the 1890s. Writing from the Tempe Downs station in the Alice Springs district in 1891 the local police officer referred to a group of blacks who continued to elude him:

> they kept a constant watch for me and when I passed, they came down on the flats below, and killed cattle, they were hard to get

> on account of so many ranges, therefore they got cheeky and
> slapped their behinds at my party.[18]

Aboriginal action fell naturally into the archetypal pattern of
guerilla warfare which was ideally suited to their loosely articulated
clan organization and dispersed population, their hunting and foraging economy and highly developed bush skills. The *Hobart Town
Courier* noted in 1830 that nature had instructed the Aborigine in
her 'original language'; that the black man had adopted the 'natural
weapons of his condition'. The writer concluded that while settlers
might denounce the 'craft, the cunning and the murderous habits'
they were but 'natural tactics of war with which providence has provided them'.[19] Governor Arthur well expressed the anguish of the
frustrated opponent of the guerilla, which is as fresh today as it was
a hundred and fifty years ago: 'They suddenly appear; commit some
act of outrage and then as suddenly vanish: if pursued it seems impossible to surround and capture them'.[20]

For a while on the Australian frontier bushcraft and local
knowledge almost equalled the range and power of guns, the speed
and endurance of horses. But the balance tipped dramatically in
favour of the Europeans as a result of the rapid improvement of
their weapons, their growing confidence in the bush and, above
all, their using the blacks themselves as guides, trackers and more
formally in the para-military native police forces of Victoria, New
South Wales and Queensland. The co-option of black bushcraft
began with the earliest expeditions inland from the infant settlement
at Sydney Cove, George Caley informing Sir Joseph Banks in 1801
that he intended to keep a 'native constant soon, as they can trace
anything so well in the bush'.[21] The use of 'friendly blacks' to
counter the superior bushcraft of clans in conflict with the
Europeans was formally proposed in the 1820s. George Frankland
wrote to Governor Arthur arguing that it would be impossible to
capture Tasmanian Aborigines 'without the agency of one or more
Individuals of that Race'. If the 'peculiar tact' of the blacks could be
employed by the Europeans it would at once 'remove the obstacles
which exist to the capture of the Tribes'.[22] Jorgenson was another

perplexed by the 'superiority of the Blacks' in the bush which would never be overcome 'unless we are taught by them'.[23]

The argument was accepted and mainland Aborigines were brought to Tasmania to assist in tracking down the hostile clans. The later history of the use of Aboriginal troopers in Port Phillip from 1842 and the northern frontier of New South Wales from 1848 is well known. They appear to have had an immediate and decisive effect in crushing concerted Aboriginal resistance in the Western District of Victoria in 1843 and in south-east Queensland in 1849. The Queensland Native Mounted Police continued to patrol the fringes of European settlement until the beginning of the twentieth century. Black fear of the native police is well documented. At one blow Aboriginal superiority in bushcraft was undermined leading to a serious loss of morale. The Aboriginal trooper combined the tactical advantages pertaining to both sides of the frontier; traditional bush skills were wedded to horsemanship and facility with rifle and revolver. Unwittingly the Europeans may have coopted another, unseen weapon: by hostile clans out in the bush the police troopers were thought to possess the potent magic of strange and distant Aboriginal tribes. The greatest dangers of the new white world fused in the figure of the black trooper with the most serious threat which traditional society could produce.

NEW TACTICS

But while traditional skills could be used to considerable effect against the Europeans there was also a need for innovation. The widespread use of European food increased the flexibility of Aboriginal organization allowing large gatherings to stay together for longer than usual or giving greater mobility to small groups released from the need for daily hunting and foraging. Clans in conflict with Europeans could hide away during daylight and concentrate their whole attention on the struggle with the settlers. Jorgenson noted how European food had enabled the Tasmanians 'in a great degree to subsist without hunting' which by compelling them to run over large tracts of ground had exposed them to 'capture and very great danger'. He was also aware of the link between altered patterns of food consumption and modification of methods of resistance. The island blacks, had, he wrote:

> in great measure changed the system of warfare and depredations ... instead of resorting to their usual mode of obtaining subsistence, they have closed in upon the settlement, robbing the huts of flour and other provisions in very large quantities.[24]

Tactics were developed to cope with European firearms and indeed some groups endeavoured to acquire them for their own use. Knowledge of their working was gradually gained particularly from individuals who had worked on pastoral stations or in maritime industries like sealing and pearling. There were frequent reports of blacks using guns to attack Europeans in Tasmania in the 1820s, Victoria in the 1840s and around Cape York in the 1880s and 1890s. The *Port Phillip Herald* reported in 1840 that several hundred Aborigines had assembled at a station to the north of Melbourne and had threatened to burn down the huts saying that they 'did not care for white men, as they had more muskets than them, showing at the same time nearly thirty guns of different kinds'.[25] Robinson met numerous Aboriginal parties armed with guns during his expeditions around Tasmania. He was told they 'intended using them against the whites as soon as they could get ammunition, and that they often practiced with them'.[26] But while guns were used by Aboriginal groups in various parts of the country they were never adopted on a large enough scale seriously to alter the balance of power between white and black and in fact did not compensate for European co-option of Aboriginal bushcraft.

ECONOMIC WARFARE

Beyond the influence of European food and guns there was a clear change of objective from the pursuit of revenge or women which inspired traditional fighting to the development of a form of economic warfare. It began with the straightforward destruction of European property over and above animals taken for food. Sheep were run into swamps and over cliffs or killed and injured with spear and club; cattle were stampeded into rough country or caught and hamstrung. On the troubled McIntyre frontier the squatter Jacob Lowe lost seventy-five cattle in a single night raid. The local clans had clubbed and speared the herd but none had been taken for food. In fact only two carcases had been cut open. The hearts had been taken out and were placed on two poles stuck into the turf facing one another. The message was unmistakable. Lowe subsequently told a parliamentary committee that the Aboriginal objective was clearly not food but the desire 'to drive us away out of the district – to frighten us'.[27] Attacks on stations were often highly organized and devastating in effect leaving animals dead, everything moveable carried away and all else put to the torch.

In various parts of the country tactics were developed to attack and pillage loaded drays at the most vulnerable point of their journey. When a group of drays reached a steep gradient it was common practice for several teams to be combined to pull the drays over the rise one at a time leaving the others vulnerable to sudden attack. If done quickly the raiding party could be out of sight before the bullock drivers were able to intervene. But perhaps the most sophisticated attack on European communications was made on the dray road from Ipswich to the Darling Downs in 1843. The road was barricaded with logs and the stalled drays were attacked by blacks hiding in surrounding vegetation. Two separate sources suggest that the Aboriginal objective was to prevent all supplies reaching the properties on the Darling Downs thereby starving them out. The local Commissioner for Crown Lands was told by 'an intelligent Aborigine named Toby' that the mountain clans had 'formed a plan of intercepting all communications by the high road to the Darling Downs'.[28] The Government Resident at Moreton Bay took the threat seriously and a military detachment was stationed in the area for three years. A pioneer Darling Downs squatter visiting Brisbane at the time was told by a friendly black not to return to his property because the Aborigines intended to fence up the road, cut off all communications and attack the stations.

In other places Aborigines came to appreciate the crucial importance of horses to the European economy. At the simplest level this meant choosing to carry out raids on sheep and cattle during heavy rain when boggy conditions kept horsemen at home and allowed operations to proceed without fear of attack. In one or two districts there appear to have been systematic attempts to kill all the horses in order to immobilize the Europeans. This seems to have been the case on the Palmer River where several massive raids were made on miners' horses. The *Brisbane Courier* estimated in 1883 that in the previous ten years over 200 horses had been speared though not all fatally. A recent study has determined that 133 horses were killed on the road from Cooktown to the Palmer in six years during the 1870s. But the evidence is even more specific in relation to the McIntyre River district in the 1840s. Not only were many horses killed – one writer suggested 100 head between 1843 and 1846 – but local Aborigines specifically stated their intention. A northern squatter wrote to the *Maitland Mercury* in 1843 arguing that the blacks were well aware of the crucial role of horses and from what they had told him he had 'every reason to believe that they will destroy all our horses, and thus disable the men from attending to the cattle'.[29] Five months later another writer referred to the continued attacks on European animals which were 'part of the plan of these fellows' which showed the 'premeditated and systematic manner in which they set about the work of plunder'.[30] A further incident was reported at much the same time. A group of shepherds besieged in their hut were dared by their attackers to venture outside. The blacks said they had already 'killed all the horses'[31] and would now kill the settlers. Five years later another McIntyre settler reported that the Aborigines had driven off all the horses and made massive attacks on the cattle:

> The threats they used of killing all our horses first, and then the men, accompanied by the most dreadful yells and shouts, had the effect of striking terror into some of our party.[32]

Attacks on livestock in general and horses in particular were among the most effective tactics employed by the Aborigines in their struggle with the settlers. Fire was potentially an even more potent weapon. The blacks were, after all, experts in the use of fire in the Australian environment; traditionally they understood its value in regeneration of vegetation, its role in the control of undergrowth, the relative fire resistance of various plant species, the importance of such variables as wind, time of day, temperature and fuel build up. Given the expertise readily available the surprising thing is not that fire was used as a weapon but that it was not used more often. The settlers were particularly vulnerable given the general dryness of the climate and in fact they realized the destructive power latent in the simple fire stick. Fear of Aboriginal-induced conflagration was apparent from the early years of the first settlement on the Cumberland Plain. George Caley told Sir Joseph Banks that had the blacks 'been bent for to do us as much injury as we had done them' then the settlement would have been endangered 'for it was in their power for have done us almost an irreparable injury by fire'.[33] Governor Hunter shared the unease about the possibility of Aboriginal attack by fire. In 1800 he wrote:

> the mischiefs which these people can with ease to themselves do to us renders it highly essential to our own comfort and security that we should live on amicable terms with them. Fire in the hands of a body of irritated and hostile natives may with little trouble to them ruin our prospects of an abundant harvest, for that is the very season in which they might spread desolation over our cultivated lands, and reduce us to extreme distress; and they are not ignorant of having that power in their hands, for after the destruction of the above two boys they threatened to burn our crops as soon as it could be effected. I caution'd the settlers in consequence that they might be upon their guard. They did not, however, attempt it.[34]

As a rule Aboriginal use of fire cohered with the level of conflict as a whole – it was sporadic and used more against individuals and their property than the whole of the white community. But where, as in Tasmania in the 1820s, the struggle had escalated into racial warfare, fire was used more systematically and with much greater effect. After witnessing the burning of houses, fences, crops and haystacks throughout the district the settlers of the Clyde Valley met at Bothwell in 1830 and moved an address to the Governor warning that Aboriginal action was 'affecting not only the lives of the Colonists' but also 'threatening the extinction of the Colony itself by firing our Crops and Dwellings'.[35]

DIMINUTION

Frontier conflict was ragged, sporadic and uneven. It was uncommon for hostilities to embrace everybody even in relatively small districts. There were usually a few Aboriginal clans that avoided confrontation with the settlers and on the other hand a minority of Europeans who refused to be forced into open antagonism with their black neighbours. Complete racial polarization only occurred at times of very high tension. On the other hand hostilities rarely came to a sudden or complete conclusion. Instead conflict inched away uncertainly. Aborigines eventually decided that the cost of open attacks on Europeans was prohibitively high and only took life when the chances of discovery were low as in the case of lone travellers or solitary prospectors. They learnt to adjust the level of resistance to keep it below the assumed threshold of violent retaliation although European behaviour must have seemed dangerously unpredictable. Forecasting their probable reaction became one of the crucial skills of the emerging interracial politics.

Attacks on property became more selective, secretive, surreptitious. The adjustment of objectives was noted by European observers. The Queensland squatter William Forster argued that after a period of open war the blacks reached a different stage altogether:

> when they understand our superior power, and at the same time their predatory habits are still in existence – they will carry on small depredations and will no doubt take life at times, but their object is not to take life – it is not war.[36]

The Commissioner for Crown Lands on the Darling Downs noted a similar diminution of resistance. The local blacks, he wrote in

1845, were no longer at open war with the squatters driving off whole herds of cattle and flocks of sheep but had adopted instead 'a system of pilfering that no foresight can prevent'.[37] Thirty years later and over a thousand miles away the *Cooktown Courier* distinguished between districts where 'a state of warfare' still existed and those where the Aborigines had given up all avowed hostility 'their depredations if they commit any, taking the nature of larceny'.[38]

THE IMPACT OF RESISTANCE

Considering the advantages possessed by the European the resistance was often surprisingly effective and unexpectedly prolonged. A high price was exacted from many pioneer communities in tension and insecurity as much as in property loss, injury or death. Aboriginal attacks on property had devastating effects on the fortunes of individual settlers and at times appeared to threaten the economic viability of pioneer industries – squatting, farming, mining and pearling. There were occasions – as in Tasmania in the late 1820s, New South Wales in the late 1830s and early 1840s and Queensland in the early 1860s – when Aboriginal resistance emerged as one of the major problems of colonial society. An editorial in Queensland's leading newspaper in 1879 summed up the impact of Aboriginal resistance in the colony:

> During the last four or five years the human life and property destroyed by the Aboriginals in the North totals up to a serious amount ... settlement on the land, and the development of the mineral and other resources of the country, have been in a great degree prohibited by the hostility of the blacks, which still continues with undiminished spirit.[39]

Yet Europeans were only rarely willing to recognize the intelligence and courage which informed the resistance. When they did their comments were particularly interesting. In 1830 a writer in the Hobart paper *The Colonial Times* referred to 'a cunning and superiority of tactics which would not disgrace some of the greatest military characters'.[40] Another island settler remarked that the blacks had 'oftentimes evinced superior tact and clearness of head'.[41] The official Tasmanian Aborigines Committee thought the blacks a 'subtle and daring enemy', a 'sagacious and wily race of people'.[42] A report of 1831 observed that the island blacks:

> now conduct their attacks with a surprising organization, and with unexampled cunning, such indeed is their local information and quickness of perception, that all endeavours on the part of the whites to cope with them are unavailing.[43]

In 1834 Governor Stirling informed his superiors in England that West Australian settlers had found the blacks 'very formidable enemies, and if they could avail themselves of the advantages of combination it would be useless to attempt a settlement in this quarter with our present numbers'.[44] A pioneer colonist concurred, remarking in 1833 that if in addition to their knowledge of the country the local Aborigines had 'firearms and a little discipline' they would 'put an end to the settlement in less than a month'.[45] The Commandant at Port Essington wrote in 1834 that local blacks had shown 'excessive cunning, dexterity, arrangement, enterprise and courage' in their attacks on Europeans.[46] A generation later in north Queensland a writer in the *Cooktown Herald* remarked that the miners had difficulties enough to contend with:

> without having to enter into guerilla warfare, and risk their lives fighting their sable foes, who are immeasurably their superiors in tactics and bush fighting.[47]

But perhaps the most generous tribute was paid by Edward Eyre who wrote:

> It has been said, and is generally believed, that the natives are not courageous. There could not be a greater mistake ... nor do I hold it to be any proof that they are cowards, because they dread or give way before Europeans and their firearms. So unequal a match is no criterion of bravery, and yet even thus, among natives, who were labouring under the feelings, naturally produced by seeing a race they were unacquainted with, and weapons that dealt death as if by magic, I have seen many instances of an open manly intrepidity of manner and bearing, and a proud unquailing glance of eye, which instinctively

stamped upon my mind the conviction that the individuals before me were very brave men.[48]

The long running debate endemic in pioneer communities between those who wanted to 'let the blacks in' and others equally determined to 'keep them out' was undoubtedly reflected on the other
side of the frontier. 'Staying out' or 'going in' to white society was
a major question for Aboriginal clans all over the continent. Either
choice presented hazards. The unpredictability of European behaviour made any approach to station, farm, mining camp or township
a dangerous and uncertain exercise. Yet life in the bush became increasingly hazardous and eventually 'staying out' became the
greater of the two evils. Dwindling indigenous food supplies put
enormous pressure on clans seeking to live in isolation from the
Europeans. Malnutrition stalked many camps and children and old
people may have often died of hunger in the bush. A western
Queensland pioneer was told by local blacks after they had come in
that during the era of frontier conflict the Europeans:

> used to starve numbers of the old men, women and children to
> death; for, being hunted into the desert, they had neither the
> means of carrying water nor of catching game ... and of course
> the weaker members of the tribe felt it most.[49]

Many clans were faced with a simple, stark choice. They could take
European animals and supplies to meet their immediate and press-
ing needs with the certainty of ensuing retaliation or they could
move in to the fringes of the nearest European settlement to escape
the tightening vice of hunger and violence.

DESTITUTION

Evidence of destitution can be adduced from many parts of the
country. The officials of the Port Phillip Protectorate wrote of the
plight of Victorian blacks within a few years of the European invasion. After a journey through the Western District in 1841 G. A.
Robinson reported that the condition of the blacks was deplorable,
their poverty the 'extreme of wretchedness'.[50] The missionary

Francis Tuckfield was told by Aboriginal informants that there was scarcely anything left to eat in the bush while E. S. Parker observed that the earliest settlers acknowledged that:

> the Natives are now in a much worse condition and present a far less robust appearance than when they arrived – and that it is their decided conviction, that they must occasionally suffer great privations, from their altered and often emaciated appearance.[51]

The picture was similar in other parts of the continent. In 1856 Wiseman saw a group of blacks on the banks of the Fitzroy River who appeared to be desperately hungry. They kept striking their bellies and crying out in broken English 'Plower, Plower'. He concluded that they were 'very probably starved' as fear had pinched them into an isolated and barren corner of their territory.[52] In 1877 a correspondent of the *Queenslander* wrote of the fate of the blacks on the Palmer River. The country, he explained, was infertile and poorly stocked with game and the Europeans had occupied all the watercourses with the result that the local clans were half starved. In 1882 a journalist from the *Sydney Morning Herald* spent a day with a small group of blacks in the coastal rainforest near Cairns. They complained that they found it 'very difficult to get food' and because the whites had taken all the good country 'they had to go to the mountains or rocky places on the coast, where the fish was not plentiful'.[53] Near the Gulf of Carpentaria the blacks were driven away from the cattle stations and 'sent to starve along the coast or in the ranges'. 'The few I saw', wrote a correspondent to the *Queenslander* in 1886, 'are really being starved to death'.[54]

'GOING IN'

Many of those who went into white settlement were refugees from the danger, deprivation and insecurity of life in the bush: they were pushed reluctantly towards European society. Yet in other cases blacks were attracted, or pulled, in the same direction giving rise to Stanner's aphorism that for every Aborigine who had Europeans thrust upon him, at least one other sought them out. Many aspirations combined to attract Aborigines to white settlement. Intellectual curiosity was obviously important – an expedition from the homeland in to the nearest European outpost was an adventure to be equated with foreign and overseas travel in white society. The desire to experience new food, clothes, weapons, sights, sounds, textures, tastes had been apparent even before the arrival of the pioneer settlers. Writing of central Australia in the late nineteenth and early twentieth century Chewings noted that many blacks living far from European settlements had: 'at some time or other journeyed in through some friendly tribes' country to some cattle, telegraph, or railway station, just to see what the white man really is like.'[55] Like travellers anywhere Aboriginal sojourners did not necessarily intend to stay within the European orbit although return became progressively difficult as months and then years passed. Those who willingly but tentatively approached white settlements were not in a position to foresee the degradation which came to dwell in every fringe camp on the continent and the disease, malnutrition, alcoholism and social disintegration which followed inexorably and almost universally from the move into European society.

During the twentieth century there have been many well-documented examples of voluntary migration from tribal homelands in towards European settlements. This has been particularly important around the fringes of the central and western deserts although outstation movements of the last few years have partially reversed the trend. But twentieth century developments do not necessarily throw interpretive light back onto events of a hundred and more years ago. When applied to the nineteenth century, Stanner's aphorism is not so much wrong as anachronistic. However, it is true that voluntary migration was prevalent in the vicinity of the major towns. Sydney, Melbourne, Adelaide and Perth all attracted Aborigines in from their hinterlands and authorities in Melbourne and Adelaide vainly endeavoured to keep distant clans away from the urban fringe. But outside the compass of major towns the situation was usually quite different. From the start of settlement the Aborigines were comparatively safe in the urban areas – at least from powder and shot if not from fist and phallus. In the bush life was much more dangerous. Violence was so common that it must have seemed an ever present possibility. Aborigines were far less likely to move in towards white settlement because they feared for their lives. Curiosity and the attraction of a new world of experience could not counter the danger which encircled the Europeans like an evil penumbra. For their part the settlers were usually so insecure that they were highly suspicious of Aboriginal attempts to approach station, camp or farm. Tentative initial contact had so often been followed by bloodshed that frontiersmen decided that the only safe procedure was to keep the blacks beyond the range of their ever ready rifles.

ATTEMPTED NEGOTIATION

There were aboriginal groups which sought a political solution to their white problem, a middle way between the stark alternatives of staying out or going in. The desire for a negotiated settlement may have been far more widespread than the available evidence will ever suggest yet there are four relevant examples widely separated in time and place. At the height of conflict on the Hawkesbury River in 1804 Governor King met three local blacks who said they objected to the ever increasing spread of settlement along the valley. They were determined to hang on to the few places left on the river bank and told King that 'if they could retain some places on the lower part of the river they would be satisfied and would not trouble the white man'. King thought the request so 'just and equitable' that he assured the blacks that no further settlements would be made lower down the river.[56] Forty years later in northern New South Wales the pioneer settler E.O. Ogilvie came across a group of local blacks living in hostile seclusion in the mountains following a period of conflict with the whites. A limited knowledge of the local dialect helped him exchange views on the existing state of relations between indigenes and settlers. The blacks told Ogilvie to return to his station in the valley. 'You have the river', they said, 'and the open country, and you ought to be content, and leave the mountains to the black people. Go back – keep the plains and leave us the hills'.[57] Ogilvie claimed that he wished to live in peace and wanted nothing in their territory except the grass. An understanding was reached which continued to exert a beneficial effect on race relations in the district. Howitt related an even more interesting story. He was returning from an expedition in central Australia and travelling towards the settled districts of South Australia. While at Lake Hope near Coopers Creek he met a celebrated Dieri called Jelinapiramurana who asked him if he would:

> tell the white men who were coming up to his country, according to the information sent him by tribes further down, that they should 'sit down on the one side (Lake Hope) and the (local clans) would sit down on the other, so that they would not be likely to quarrel'.[58]

James Morrell, the Queensland castaway, was able to fully discuss the white problem with his clansmen. When the first few settlers arrived in the neighbourhood he explained that they were merely the harbingers of a much larger white population. He warned his black kin that 'there were a great many people, many more than themselves' and they had plenty of guns, and that if the blacks went near 'they would be killed'. Morrell told them quite bluntly that the white men had come to take their land away. 'They always understand', he explained 'that might not right, is the law of the world'. But the blacks told Morrell:

> to ask the white men to let them have all the ground to the north of the Burdekin, and to let them fish in the rivers; also the low grounds, they live on to get the roots.[59]

Once restored to European society Morrell appears to have made little attempt to shield his companions of seventeen years from the onslaught of the frontier settlers. Their attempt at negotiation was swept aside as being unworthy of consideration.

There was no neat or decisive end to conflict between Aborigines and settlers; neither armistice nor treaty; no medals, no speeches, no peace conference. Black resistance did not conclude when the last stockman was speared although methods were modified and objectives altered. Sorcery was probably increasingly favoured over physical confrontation as a means of challenging white domination. Killing ceased but raids on European property continued. The most immediate motive was economic; blacks stole to survive. But there was always a political element in Aboriginal behaviour. They continued to believe that Europeans were under a moral obligation to share their abundance, both because sharing was so central to Aboriginal values, and to provide compensation for the loss of land, water and game. The settlers for their part often regarded Aboriginal depredation as a continuation of resistance in a new guise. They said so on many occasions. A typical remark was that of a writer in the *Queenslander* in 1871 who said that Aboriginal crime had assumed:

> a different aspect from the old time spearing of cattle, or the massacre of station hands. The criminal black fellow of the present day frequents the town, gets drunk, robs houses, insults women and otherwise conducts himself like a civilized blackguard.[60]

BANDITS

Aboriginal and part-Aboriginal bandits or bushrangers were common in the generation after settlement. Typically they were young men who had grown up in fringe camps and had worked in varying capacities for the Europeans. They were often competent horsemen and handy with guns while still proficient in the ancient bush skills. Though rarely a serious challenge to European society the black bandits created anxiety in small frontier communities and problems for colonial police forces. 'All settlers will agree with me', wrote a correspondent to the *Port Denison Times*, that the 'half-civilized blackfellow is a more dangerous and troublesome customer to deal with than the myall'.[61] Queensland seems to have had the largest contingent of such men. The provincial papers of the 1870s and

1880s abound in reports of their careers, crimes and capture. In 1878 a Gladstone correspondent wrote of *Billy Burmoondoo* who had been 'a terror to the district for years'.[62] Ten years later the *Port Denison Times* reported the capture of the notorious *jimmy*, an object of terror and alarm and in 1882 referred to the shooting of *Murdering Harry*. At Tambo in 1876 the notorious *Saturday* was taken after 'many depredations' as was *Sambo* at Wide Bay a few years later. The latter had defied the police for years and during 1875 the terror of 'club law' had become so great that the women accompanied their husbands into the fields 'rather than remain unprotected in their homes'.[63] *Sambo's* career called forth a comment from the Maryborough correspondent of the *Queenslander*:

> It is difficult to catch these blacks, who are very cunning, and some of them are noted for the number of successful robberies they have committed. One outlaw by the name of Sambo, is a regular Rob Roy, his stealings have been on such an heroic scale. He has been wanted for years past, and all they know is that he is in the district still. The other blacks shield him as sedulously as in some parts of Ireland they shield a gentleman who has had the misfortune to shoot his landlord.[64]

Whether other bandits received as much protection as Sambo is impossible to say. Some seem to have been outcasts from both black and white communities and there is as much evidence of Aboriginal betrayal as of support and sustenance.

Between 1878 and 1880 the part-Aborigine Johnny Campbell defied the police in a wide area of south-east Queensland during which time he was the 'sable terror of the whole Wide Bay District'. It is hard to find any detail about Campbell's life before he took to the bush. But it seems that he rejected his Aboriginal heritage taking pride in his command of English and his skill with horse and rifle. Campbell rode the watershed between the tribal resistance of his Aboriginal grandparents and the world of the white bushranger. He was, a writer in the *Maryborough Chronicle* argued the 'local representative of the Ned Kelly fraternity'.[65]

With Jimmy and Joe Governor the watershed was crossed. The brothers were part-Aborigines and the white community reacted to their rampage by reference to deeply embedded racial stereotypes. They were dubbed the 'Breelong blacks', newspapers referred to the 'black horror' while the *Mudgee Guardian* argued that violence was to be expected from Aborigines 'when the inbred passions of the savage nature assert themselves'.[66] There probably was some element of racial antagonism in the Governor's behaviour. A police sergeant at Wollar reported to his superiors that their mother Annie Governor was a woman 'with a grievance' who had 'encouraged her sons to do acts of violence, as she states that the Government took the poor blacks' country, giving them nothing in return'.[67] But Jimmy Governor was, according to his wife Ethel, 'particularly touchy about his colour' and did 'not like to be called a blackfellow'.[68]

The Governors wanted to be bushrangers. Their model was Ned Kelly not the tribal warrior. Ethel reported that Jimmy was an avid reader of stories about bushrangers. Several months after their marriage he said he would 'be a bushranger before long' and in the period before the murders of the Mawbey family the brothers were frequently 'talking about bushranging at night'.[69] The desire to go out bushranging was a characteristic the Governors shared with many of the poor, rural working class youth of the time. Contemporaries greatly overemphasised the Aboriginal element in their behaviour. Those observers who remained free from racial hysteria realized this. A journalist who travelled with Jimmy Governor on the ship from the northern rivers to his trial in Sydney reported that:

> The outlaw has no trace in his speech of the usual dialect of the Aboriginal. His language is just the same as that of any white Australian ... and most of the 'black fellow talk' which has been interwoven with remarks attributed to him has either been introduced with an intention of lending supposedly needed colouring or has been insensibly conveyed from the mind to the lips or the pen of the narrator by reason of the fact that Jimmy Governor is usually spoken of as an aboriginal and is so dark skinned. His grammar is not, of course, of the most elegant description, but his only dialect is the dialect of the average bush labourer. Of the latest slang he is a master, and he freely uses 'flash' talk and slang in his conversation.[70]

With Jimmy Governor the bushranger had supplanted the tribal warrior; class had superseded race.

DEATH TOLL

How many people died as a direct result of frontier conflict? It is a question which white Australians have rarely posed and never satisfactorily answered. The few official estimates made in the nineteenth century are of limited value and normally underestimate the numbers of Aborigines shot down by the settlers. However, recent research work in various parts of Australia provides a more satisfactory basis for assessment. It is much easier to determine the number of Europeans who died violently than to make comparable estimates for the blacks. Loos and Reynolds estimated that 850 Europeans and their allies – Pacific Islanders, Chinese, acculturated Aborigines – died by spear and club in Queensland between 1840 and 1897. Though the count was careful, precision was impossible and the figure may have been as high as 1000. Similar estimates were subsequently made in other parts of Australia. In Tasmania the official figure for European mortality was 160 but Ryan has recently argued that 200 is more realistic. Christie has suggested 200 as a reasonable estimate for Victoria; Green has accounted for 25 deaths in the south-west corner of Western Australia between 1826 and 1852 and Prentis 20 for the northeast corner of New South Wales. There is now enough regional accounting to make an intelligent guess about the country as a whole. It seems reasonable to suggest that Aborigines killed somewhere between 2000 and 2500 Europeans in the course of the invasion and settlement of the continent. There were many hundreds of others who were injured and carried both physical and psychological scars for the rest of their lives.

Calculating the Aboriginal death toll is much more difficult. Conflict is better documented in Tasmania than anywhere else in the country and Ryan's estimate of 800 is possibly more accurate than any other we can make. Green has accounted for 102 Aboriginal deaths in his segment of Western Australia and Prentis for 100 in the northern rivers district of New South Wales. Christie has recently argued that the whites killed 2000 blacks during their occupation of Victoria while Reynolds suggested that as many as 8000–10000 Aborigines died violently in Queensland. For the continent as a whole it is reasonable to suppose that at least 20000 Aborigines were killed as a direct result of conflict with the settlers. Secondary effects of the invasion – disease, deprivation, disruption – were responsible for the premature deaths of many more although it is almost impossible to arrive at a realistic figure. Many blacks were wounded but recovered. After an expedition to survey the Aboriginal population in central Victoria in 1846 G. A. Robinson reported that many of the adult men had gun shot wounds and 'other marks of violence on their person'.[71] In 1969 an old Northern Territory black recalled that when he was a child a lot of his people had bullet marks on their arms, legs and backs and one had survived although half his mouth had been shot away.

The ratio between black and white deaths varied considerably from four to one in Tasmania up to ten to one in Queensland. Such a discrepancy demands explanation. The rugged island terrain undoubtedly assisted Aborigines in both defence and attack. Horses were less common on Tasmanian properties than on sprawling mainland stations and convict servants usually travelled on foot. They were often unarmed as well. The free settlers were unwilling to give guns to their workers because the 'black war' followed a period of serious conflict with gangs of bushrangers. The struggle in Tasmania was over before European weapons underwent their rapid mid nineteenth century improvement with the introduction of breech-loading, repeating rifles and six shot revolvers. Conditions in Queensland were much more favourable to the settlers. The introduction of responsible government in 1859 removed many of the political constraints that had previously held back the full force of white violence. The frontier was vast and in most places favoured the European on horseback while the Native Mounted Police developed into an efficient weapon to 'disperse' Aboriginal tribes.

There is then a marked discrepancy between the ratios of white deaths to black in Tasmania, the south-west of Western Australia and north-east New South Wales on the one hand and those in Queensland on the other. This may reflect a wider difference between settlement in the south and east of the continent in the first half of the nineteenth century and that of the second half in northern Australia. Christie's ratio of ten to one in Victoria may be anomalous. It is possible that his figure of 2000 Aboriginal death is too high although E. S. Parker kept a careful account of conflict in his area of north-central Victoria and estimated that Europeans killed seven Aborigines for every white man speared. Elsewhere he spoke of a fearful preponderance in the settlers' favour.

The figure of 20 000 Aboriginal deaths in frontier conflict will be thought too high by some, too low by others. However, the evidence concerning the ubiquity of conflict is overwhelming. It can be found in almost every type of document – official reports both public and confidential, newspapers, letters, reminiscences. Settlers often counted black bodies either in anger or in anguish; members of punitive expeditions confessed to their participation in a spirit of bravado or contrition. Later observers came across bones and skulls; buried, burnt or hidden and occasionally collected and put proudly on display. In a few districts officials and settlers assessed the role of violence in the decline of local populations; others noted the disproportionate number of adult women following frontier conflict and the widespread and prolonged mourning for butchered men-folk. The evidence for a great loss of life is voluminous, various and incontrovertible.

Some will think a figure of 20 000 dead too low considering the alarming decline of the Aboriginal population from about 300 000 in 1788 to not much more than 50 000 in a little over a century. Given ample evidence of massacres should we not significantly extend the death list? To answer this question several points should be made. They relate to both sides of the frontier. An overemphasis on the significance of massacres tends to throw support behind the idea that the blacks were helpless victims of white attack; passive

recipients of promiscuous brutality. Such an argument runs easily
along well worn channels of historical interpretation. Paternalism
and sympathy have often merged in support of the view that the
Aboriginal experience was a story 'infinitely pathetic – children as
they were, stretching out frail hands to stay the flood tide'.[72]

But such an assessment parodies the Aboriginal role in frontier
conflict. Blacks did not sit around their camp fires waiting to be
massacred. They usually knew of the dangers accompanying white
settlement even before the Europeans arrived and took action to
minimize those perils. While the settlers normally had the advantage of guns and horses the blacks were far more competent in the
bush and undoubtedly had a superior intelligence network.
Aboriginal clans usually knew in advance what European parties
were doing and simply avoided contact. White numbers were too
small to scour the country thoroughly while settlers could not afford the luxury of long patrols which took workers away from productive work. Even the Queensland Native Police seems to have
spent much of its time in fruitless patrolling without seeing any
Aborigines. Clans were most vulnerable when they were in camp
and punitive parties often endeavoured to advance on them in the
darkness and attack at first light. White tactics succeeded sometimes but the failure rate was certainly very high. Aborigines were
inured to fear of night attack from their tribal enemies. It was in
consequence hard to take a camp by surprise especially for clumsy
and heavy booted Europeans. Many measures were adopted to
counter nocturnal danger. Fires were either not lit, kept so small
they could not be seen in the distance or shielded by screens of
saplings. Without the distant glow of camp fires sleeping blacks
were almost impossible to find. Camp sites were chosen on the
edges of rivers and swamps and forests or among broken and boul-
der strewn country to expedite flight and there are numerous accounts of European parties galloping into camps that had already
been vacated. Aborigines were acutely observant and their camps
were usually surrounded by dogs keen from hunger who provided
an effective early warning system.

There were important constraints on European action – legal, political and moral – which operated even in Queensland where control of Aboriginal policy passed to the settlers while there were still large indigenous populations beyond the reach of the whites. But equally important in determining what happened along the frontier was the action of the Aborigines themselves. Their skills, intelligence and tactics were always a significant element in the equation of contact. The settlers may have wanted to kill more blacks than they did, may have dreamed of easy assassination, but counter-action by the blacks frequently frustrated them. The ratio of four or five deaths to one in favour of the Europeans may have been the best that they could achieve during the first half of the nineteenth century with their inefficient guns and fumbling bushcraft.

DEMOGRAPHIC DECLINE

Another fact of considerable importance when assessing the frontier death rate is that while the demographic evidence is far from complete it seems that there were still large Aboriginal populations in most areas when open conflict came to an end. The demographic decline did not cease when the shooting stopped and was equally significant in those few relatively peaceful districts where it scarcely began. Disease decimated Aboriginal communities – colds, influenza, T.B., measles, whooping cough, dysentery, malnutrition – all took their grim toll. Epidemic diseases were probably more lethal than punitive expeditions. While traditional culture provided skills to deal with guns there were no effective answers to introduced illness. Even a people like the Kalkatunga (or Kalkadoons) who stood up to the Queensland Native Police proved more vulnerable to measles than Martini-Henry rifles.

The catastrophic fall in the birth rate was another factor of demographic significance. Aborigines not only died at unprecedented rates; they were not born, or did not survive childhood, in anything like sufficient numbers to replace the loss by premature death. 'A child is now but rarely to be met with', wrote a white official in melancholy mood, 'a birth but seldom known'.[73] The missionary Benjamin Hurst commented in 1841 that he knew of only two children under twelve within a forty mile radius of his station on the western side of Port Phillip Bay. A settler at Lake Colac noted that amongst one hundred or so local women there had not been more than six or eight children born in the previous three years. A contemporary could recall only two births in five years in his district and both children later died. William Thomas kept detailed records of the Port Phillip and Western Port clans. Between 1848 and 1858 the population fell from 92 to 56 and only one child survived. The story was similar all over the continent. In district after district children were found to be 'few beyond all proportion'.[74] Many of the factors – malnutrition, exposure, disease and especially V. D. in a variety of forms – were only too apparent. But beyond even their lethal reach there was the loss of land, the dislocation of the known universe, a previously unthinkable disruption of the cosmic cycle of birth and death and reincarnation. Some groups exhibited an unquenchable determination to survive; for others the onslaught of invasion had destroyed everything. The future itself had been extinguished. Death from disease and chronic infant mortality merely proved that the times were irrecoverably out of joint. The Port Phillip Protectors reported Aboriginal comments eloquent with despair, leached of all hope. Thomas referred to 'this indifference to prolong their race, on the ground as they state of having no country they can call their own'.[75] 'No country, no good have it pickaninnys', one Aborigine explained, while another lamented 'no country now for them ... and no more come up pickaniny'.[76] A contemporary of Thomas reported that he was asked: 'Why me have lubra? Why me have piccaninny? You have all this place, no good have children no good have lubra, me tumble down and die very soon now.'[77] During the nineteenth century, European observers frequently argued that given the importance of disease and the plummeting birth rate that frontier violence was only a minor factor in the decline of the Aboriginal population. The argument was a perfect anodyne for the tender colonial conscience but nevertheless did contain an element of truth, certainly sufficient to convince those eager to be persuaded. But it ignored the European input into almost every source of Aboriginal misery and cloaked the full significance of frontier violence which was political just as much as demographic. Violence was used to force submission; the impact spread far beyond the actual casualties. Fear and insecurity ran like fire throughout Aboriginal Australia and the scars of that great conflagration have still not healed. The horror of the punitive expedition was graphically captured by a Victorian black who told James Dredge in 1840: 'Blackfellow by and by all gone, plenty shoot em, whitefellow – long time, plenty, plenty.'[78]

The memory of the dead, all 20 000 and more, lived on, stamped deeply and indelibly into the consciousness of the survivors, their children, and their children's children. It is probably the most politically potent folk memory in Australian society. Oral history has tapped a number of stories of massacre; sagas of sudden death, of unforgettable horror. Despite the lapse of time the terror is still alive coiled snake – like in the awful narratives. The following story was told by an old black north Queenslander just before he died in the 1970s:

Big mob come up from Atherton
all the native police come up
all got the rifle, all got handcuffs
fire for bullock, roast im, altogether
bullock is for tucker
shoot im altogether, shoot im altogether
chuck im in the fire
all the revolvers going on
talk about smell
nobody gonna be alive
chuck im in the fire, half alive,
sing out
you all finished no more
Native police shot im all
Widow come back cryin
she lose im husband
all finished, they shot em live
all cryin come home
to this valley here[79]

Chapter 5

THE POLITICS OF CONTACT

ATTRACTION

Aborigines reacted in complex ways to the European invasion; there was a variety of situation and diversity of motivation which will continually confound the over-confident or over-simple generalization. Yet patterns did recur. One was the interplay of attraction and resistance which ran through the politics of post-contact Aboriginal society. While Europeans were far more likely to notice the resister there were blacks who endeavoured to find a place in the new society. The missionaries and officials at Port Phillip noted several such cases. E. S. Parker claimed that many young blacks were willing to accept European ways and that they openly avowed 'their dislike for the wandering and comfortless habits of their own people'. He instanced the case of youths who established themselves on his station and built themselves 'permanent habitations of saplings and reeds in imitation of one built by Government men'.[1] The Commissioner for Crown Lands in the Monaro in the 1840s reported the case of a local man and woman who separated themselves from their clan, cleared a block of land, built a hut and began farming. When the first Aborigines were recruited for the Port Phillip Native Police Force they 'broke unsolicited their spears and other native weapons' and throwing them into the river said 'they would no longer be black fellows'.[2] The missionary Francis Tuckfield noted in his journal that young blacks had expressed themselves in the 'most decided and encouraging manner about becoming settled and adopting the European mode of living'. Some had made strenuous efforts to do so but had been compelled by their kin to return to the bush. He referred to the case of Kam-kam who built himself a house and when urged to join his clan hunting and skirmishing brought his 'instruments of war to the Missionaries that he might urge this as an excuse for not going'.[3]

To explain the attraction of white society we must consider how it must have appeared to Aborigines coming in from the bush. We can assume that those young blacks who went willingly towards the Europeans fully expected to be able to participate in their obvious material abundance. Reciprocity and sharing were so fundamental to their own society that they probably expected to meet similar behaviour when they crossed the racial frontier. They presumably thought that residence alone would win them equality, that kinship and sharing would flow naturally from contiguity. Though Aborigines were accustomed to differences in power and status based on age and sex they had no experience of the extremes of wealth and poverty which existed in European society. Material equality was one of the central characteristics of traditional life throughout Australia. Those blacks who wished to live like Europeans can hardly have imagined that the desperate poverty of the fringe camp could sit so near the plenty of town or farm or station.

YOUNG VS. OLD

But misconceptions about white society and expectations of reciprocity were only one side of the story. Aspects of traditional life must also be considered. Aboriginal society was loosely articulated; during a typical year groups waxed and waned, clans coalesced and dispersed. Visits to European camps or stations could be easily encompassed within the normal pattern of movement about tribal territory. What is more the attraction of the white settlements worked on latent divisions within traditional society. Discipline was maintained by the older men who managed both the pace at which the young were initiated and the bestowal of women and girls as they became available for marriage. While the fully initiated men controlled the only possible, or conceivable, passes on to the plateau of full adulthood their authority over the young remained unshaken. The Europeans, often unwittingly, challenged that dominance. This was particularly true in the case of young men and women who had not been fully incorporated into traditional society. Still awaiting final initiation they were the group least firmly attached to customary mores. At the same time it was the young who were most useful to the Europeans. They learnt new skills and mastered rudimentary English before the old people and in the case of girls were more sought after as sexual partners by white frontiersmen. So beneath the over-arching clash between black and white there were subsidiary tensions between those who were attracted to and those who resisted the Europeans. This secondary conflict often coincided with lines of stress latent in traditional society and especially those between young and old.

One of the most interesting accounts of intra-tribal conflict was written by A. C. Grant in his unpublished account of life on a pastoral property in the Burnett district of southern Queensland. The old men, he observed, did not like the changes which gradually deprived them of their authority. The arrival of the Europeans had the effect of making the active young men 'of more importance than the old fellows, who were beyond learning English' and found it difficult to acquire the new skills. They never learnt to ride while the 'youthful generation became adepts'. The young men began to openly challenge traditional food taboos and scoffed at tribal custom although their new assurance rapidly fell away when they were sick. The tribal elders battled to retain their authority by means of 'sacred cor-roborees, incantations, magic bones and stones, etc'. Grant described how the Aboriginal camp was swept by a mania for marble playing and little circular rings of cleared ground could be found everywhere. Even in such a minor aspect of European culture the old were disadvantaged:

> Old men, grey headed warriors, Grand fathers, sage in council, valiant in war, played with little demons of grandchildren satanic in their nimbleness of finger, and sureness of aim, and superior in the jargon and tricks of the game ... The amusing and saddening feature to me was the airs of equality which an English speaking, useful brat of nine or ten years, would assume towards his grey headed and battle scarred old grandfather.[4]

Yet in many tribal groupings the old men managed to minimize the defection of the young. They were often helped by European violence which united the clans in hatred and temporarily closed off the option of going in to white settlement. Among the Walbri, for instance, the Coniston massacre reinforced the authority of the older men who had previously tried with only limited success to 'dissuade their juniors from becoming entangled with white men'.[5] Many nineteenth century sources provide evidence of the effective assertion of tribal authority. The Commissioner for Crown Lands on the McLeay River observed in 1846 that many of the young people who worked casually for the Europeans would be happy to remain permanently about the settlements 'were it not that they were absolutely prevented by the old members of their tribe'.[6] A Victorian settler noted similar developments in the Western District where the old men invariably took away any boys who manifested 'an inclination to leave their wandering habits'.[7] On the far side of the continent Governor Hutt concluded that the older natives, both men and women, were opposed to innovations and expressed 'decided hostility against the youths ... who indicate any inclination for civilized habits'.[8]

Tribal leaders used an array of methods to preserve their authority – threats, sorcery, ritual spearing, even execution. Howitt referred to the fate of a young Dieri man who accompanied his expedition north into central Australia. He deserted when the Europeans ventured into what to him would have been hostile territory and returned to his own country. However, Howitt learnt that he had been pursued by an armed party of kinsmen and executed because he had become 'too familiar with white men'.[9] The Commissioner for Crown Lands in the Maranoa described the great animosity felt by blacks still in the bush for those working on the stations. 'Every effort and trick is resorted to', he wrote, 'to seduce them away, to destroy their fidelity and attachment'.[10] He instanced the case of his guide Jemmy who had been indispensable to him. Jemmy returned to his tribe for a week only to reappear emaciated almost beyond recognition. He told the Commissioner that he had to immediately leave the white man's service because he had a stone in his stomach and the old men had told him he would die if he stayed with them. Taplin told a similar story of conflict among the Narrinyeri of South Australia. The old men began to complain to him because the young people would not conform to their customs. A youth called Tungeriol eloped with a girl he had no right to and went to live under the protection of Europeans on a nearby cattle station. Some months later he was decoyed into the bush, grabbed by five men and smothered. Taplin tried every means to discover the executioners but was never able to do so. But the fate of the defiant Narrinyeri youth illustrated an issue of much wider significance.

CONTROL OF WOMEN

The control and bestowal of women was a major focus for inter-clan conflict both before and after the arrival of the Europeans. Three aspects of traditional society fostered sexual competition and conflict – a marked masculinity in Aboriginal populations, the widespread practice of polygamy and the control by old men over the bestowal of women. Elopement, adultery and abduction were, as a result, common occurrences. The sudden intrusion of an almost womanless white population added considerably to existing tensions. Frontiersmen abducted women and often took them away for considerable periods of time. On the other hand Aboriginal women may have gone to European men willingly and actually sought them out either to escape undesired marriage or tribal punishment or to gain access to the many attractive possessions of the Europeans. The disruption caused by the settlers provided the opportunity for young men to grab control of women from the elders and seek sanctuary among the white men in order to escape retribution. Such a situation was described by the West Australian Inspector of Aborigines on the north-west coast at the turn of the century:

> The tribal laws and customs have been annulled through the natives coming into constant contact with Asiatics; where in former days old men had the young women, who supported them through hunting, to-day most women are in the hands of young men and boys (who by tribal law are not entitled to them), having stolen them from their rightful owners by brute force, leaving the old to fossick for themselves, whilst the young men, with their so-procured women, follow up the pearling boats or go into Broome.[11]

Where the old men continued to exert their authority they were able to use their control over the bestowal of women to discipline the young men. F. J. Gillen reported the case of a young central Australian man who had lived with Europeans since childhood and so had missed out on initiation and the related operations of circumcision and subincision. Though he spoke good English and had practically forgotten his own language he eventually decided to accept initiation. Gillen explained the circumstances:

> One day he came to me and said 'I think I will go and get cut'... and I said 'look here, Jim, you are a fool to submit to that'. He said in reply 'Well, I can't put up with the cheek of the women and children. They will not let me have a lubra, and the old men will not let me know anything about my countrymen.[12]

In some cases the old men seemed to have welcomed the chance to send the young away to work for Europeans for the difficult and often prolonged period between puberty and marriage. They appear to have used the pastoral stations or pearling luggers as safety valves to relieve some of the pent up pressures of traditional society intensified by rapid change. Several perceptive observers of Aboriginal society noted this practice. Writing of South Australia in the 1840s Moorhouse noted that young men were persuaded to live with the Europeans in order to keep them away from the old men's wives. At the end of the century W. E. Roth, Queensland's Northern Protector of Aborigines, claimed that old men encouraged youths to ship with pearlers so as to retain their control over the young women. Europeans frequently tried to protect blacks threatened with tribal punishment and their power was often sufficient to provide effective sanctuary from physical violence if not necessarily from sorcery. When faced with interfering white men the blacks turned to secret and surreptitious methods to punish or execute those who continued to defy tribal authority. Governor Hutt endeavoured to uncover the hidden influence of the old men which 'paralysed and menaced' the attempt to assimilate the young, but he was continually frustrated because the 'threats were so vague, the influence so carefully concealed'.[13]

WHITE PRESSURE

But the pressure of an assertive white legal system and the physical scattering of tribal populations progressively sapped the power of the old men. They looked on with impotent fury as European influence penetrated deeper into Aboriginal life. E. S. Parker wrote of a clash he had with two influential Loddon River blacks. They objected to Parker's assertive promotion of European culture and the continuous subversion of their children. Parker explained that one of them:

> complained in his anger that the white fellows had stolen their country, and that I was stealing their children, by taking them away to live in huts, and work, and 'read in book' like white fellows.[14]

Simpson Newland wrote of an old man from the upper Darling who remained intransigent in face of the pervasive influence of European culture. Although he recognized that further resistance was futile and acquiesced in the submission of his kin he refused to have any contact with the white man 'much less work for him, wear his clothes, or even eat his food'.[15] At times the gap between the old people and the young grew so wide that the elders refused to pass on the traditions and beliefs of their tribes. F. J. Gillen saw it happen in Central Australia. No sooner, he wrote, do the blacks come into contact with the white man than the younger men:

> break away from the control of the older men, who, in normal conditions of the tribe are all powerful. It is only the older men who are really acquainted with the ancient customs and traditions, and these they will not reveal to the younger ones who have broken away from the tribal rules, and refuse to be governed by what to the old men are laws rendered sacred, because they have been handed down from the far past.[16]

The decision of elderly Aborigines to reject the youth of their own clans was by no means a universal one. Yet in many camps across the continent old men and women drifted towards death, lonely, bitter and disregarded.

Clearly the European invasion put great pressure on indigenous political organization and undermined traditional authority. But did new patterns of leadership emerge as a response to the white challenge? It is by any reckoning a complex question and will take some time to answer. The problem is compounded because Europeans who provided most of the evidence often believed that either Aboriginal society had a system of chiefs or should acquire one. In the early period of contact settlers were frequently convinced that renegade Europeans – escaped convicts and the like – had taken control of the Aborigines out in the bush and were stirring up trouble. Thus an official notice of 1796 suggested that two escaped convicts 'direct and assist' attacks on the settlers.[17] Five years later another Government report stated that there was reason to believe that 'some vagabonds' were living with the blacks and 'instigating them to commit many acts of violence on the settlers'.[18] Similar suggestions were made in Tasmania and at Moreton Bay where the blockading of the road to the Darling Downs was attributed to the fact that 'pale faces were at work amongst them'.[19]

From what we know of traditional social organization and of the experiences on the other side of the frontier of people like Davis, Morrell, Thompson and Buckley there is little reason to suppose that stray Europeans had any significant influence on Aboriginal behaviour. G. A. Robinson thought the idea of renegade white leaders 'one of the most puerile inventions that was ever conceived'.[20] Far from being thought worthy of emulation Buckley and Thompson were considered as rather simple souls whose minds had been affected by their journey back from the dead. We also know something of a European who lived for years on the islands of the Western Torres Strait. He was neither a powerful chief nor 'the Wild White Man of Badu' and was only able to survive by being both useful and circumspect. Barbara Thompson met him and reported that he was called Weinie by the islanders:

> and had no particular authority, being the joint property of two brothers, and was very useful to them in repairing their canoes. She had often heard her own people remark that they would be glad to catch a white man like Weinie to work at their canoes for them.[21]

The idea that rogue Europeans were responsible for tribal resistance served two functions – like any conspiracy theory it could be used to explain away black hostility while at the same time confirming white belief in Aboriginal incompetence.

LEADERSHIP

Settlers' accounts abound also in references to powerful Aboriginal chiefs who it was thought directed the attacks of warrior bands on the lives and property of the Europeans. Names like Eaglehawk, Jupiter, Belba and Oromonde were coined for these largely fictitious figures. Much of the evidence concerning Aboriginal leadership was provided by people with little understanding of, or interest in, traditional society and must for that reason be regarded with great suspicion. Moorhouse, the South Australian Protector, carefully observed black methods during one of the large scale attacks on overlanding parties on the lower Murray in the early 1840s. These were possibly the biggest groups ever to confront the settlers but even then Moorhouse could detect no indication of military leadership in the European sense. He wrote that:

> the natives had no chief or leader. They appeared to be arranging their intervals of distance with each other on their approach towards us. I have nothing to lead me to infer that they have chiefs.[22]

There is more evidence to hand relating to a number of young men who became prominent by their resistance to the Europeans in and near the major colonial towns – Pemulwy in Sydney, Yagan in Perth, Dundalli in Brisbane. They were certainly well enough known to be recognized by the settlers and they were clearly at the forefront of skirmishes with the Europeans although their motives may have been those of personal revenge rather than racial retribution. Each of the three created considerable anxiety among the Europeans who saw them as symbols of black resistance. Pemulwy was, according to Collins, 'said to be at the head of every party that attacked the maize grounds'[23] and to others 'a riotous and troublesome savage', a 'most active enemy to the settlers'.[24] Yagan was thought to be 'at the head and front of any mischief'.[25] In the eyes of another he was 'the Wallace of the Age'.[26] The evidence concerning such people as Yagan and Pemulwy is very much more substantial than what we have about any individuals on the pastoral frontier. But we are still no closer to the question of leadership. Clearly they were courageous and resolute in their reaction to Europeans but that does not mean that they were leaders of their own people especially as they seem to have been relatively young men. In traditional society the old men were paramount in matters of ritual and belief but in more secular areas the fundamental egalitarianism of Aboriginal society militated against the emergence of permanent leadership. Europeans who knew the Aborigines best were aware of this. Symmons, the West Australian Protector, remarked in 1841 that the blacks were a people 'owning no chief – literally a pure democracy'.[27] Writing of South Australian Aborigines Taplin noted that 'all members of the clan are held to be equal'.[28] The early New South Wales missionary William Walker

thought Aboriginal society would be better if there was more subordination. But if a man:

> whom Englishmen have called chief, should in the least degree,
> offend one of those over whom he is placed in authority, he will
> raise his waddy and knock him down.[29]

Despite the cultural barriers to the emergence of strong secular
leadership it is possible that Aborigines were influenced by what they
saw of European society with its officers and overseers, governors and
superintendents. Evidence for such cultural influence is very difficult
to find although there are one or two suggestive scraps of information. The West Australian pioneer G. F. Moore was handing out
Government rations to a group of blacks at York when one man came
forward saying: 'Give it to me, I, Darrama am the Governor among
the Yoongar, as your Governor is among the white men.'[30] Many
years later when Logan Jack was on his expedition across Cape York
he met a young man who had worked on the pearling boats. Speaking
in English he told the white explorer that he was captain of many canoes. Both these cases are interesting but it is impossible to know if
the two men in question had merely borrowed English words or if
they had also adopted the concepts which they expressed as well.

There is still another aspect of leadership to consider. It seems
that in some places groups of mainly young Aborigines who had
broken away from tribal authority coalesced into gangs, or as they
might be termed, reconstituted clans, under powerful authoritarian
leaders who based their power on personal charisma. Mosquito, the
leader of Hobart's 'tame mob' is perhaps the best documented example. He was doubly an outsider – a mainland rather than a
Tasmanian Aborigine and considerably acculturated as well. Yet he
seems to have exercised great authority over his companions although we will never be certain about the inner dynamics of these
groups. A contemporary observed that the 'tame mob' consisted of
twenty to thirty blacks who 'had absconded from their proper tribes
in the interior' many of them having 'transgressed tribal laws in
their own districts, and were obliged to live abroad for a season'.
Mosquito, he explained, had power over them: 'in a sense superior

to any known among the equality-loving Tasmanians, and governed them after the approved European model.'[31]

The case of the Tasmanian woman Walyer is even more interesting although the evidence is more fragmentary. Like Mosquito she was considerably acculturated having lived with the Bass Strait sealers. She spoke English, could use guns and had presumably adopted other aspects of European culture. Robinson is the main source of our knowledge about her and he attributed his information to several other Aborigines. She was, he wrote, 'at the head of an Aboriginal banditti' and was known to issue her orders 'in a most determined manner'. As with Mosquito's tame mob her companions were 'the disaffected of several nations'. It was said of her that she:

> boasted to the other women how she had taught the blackfellows
> to load and fire a musket, and instructed them how to kill plenty
> of white people, and that she was wont to recount her exploits
> how she used to tell the blackfellows how to act when they used
> to rob a hut.[32]

There may have been other 'banditti' like those of Mosquito and Walyer in other parts of the country and indeed the case of Pidgeon in the north-west of Western Australia in the 1890s springs immediately to mind. The members of these gangs seem to have shared many characteristics with Aborigines who rode on the other side of the white man's law, the trackers and troopers of the native police forces. Both outlaws and 'police boys' were typically young, having grown to adulthood after the arrival of the settlers, were considerably acculturated and often rebels against tribal authority. The parallels were underlined by the fact that many outlaws crossed from one side of the white man's law to the other. Mosquito, Pidgeon, the Dora-Dora brothers and many others began their careers riding with the European police and ended up trying to evade them.

THE DISCIPLINE OF LABOUR

The move from the bush into white society was not merely a spatial journey. Among other things it was a transfer from one economic

system to another, from the domestic mode of production to the
burgeoning capitalist economy of colonial Australia. When groups
of blacks walked into camps and stations and townships they carried few material possessions. But their cultural luggage was very
much richer and more important in determining their reaction to
the new world. They came from a society where economic activity
was geared to immediate use not to the creation of a surplus for exchange. Once the current needs had been met each day could be de-
voted to leisure – to sleeping, gossiping, sexual intrigue, to politics,
ritual or ceremony. Like hunters and gatherers elsewhere the
Aborigines do not seem to have spent more than three or four hours
in the field seeking food. Each family unit had direct access to the
means of subsistence and each embodied all the various skills
needed for survival, if not for sociability. This was the irreducible
foundation on which the equality of traditional society rested. Thus
Sahlins argued:

> Primitive peoples have invented many ways to elevate a man
> above his fellows. But the producers' hold on their own eco-
> nomic means rules out the most compelling history has known:
> exclusive control of such means by some few, rendering depend-
> ent the many others.[33]

Europeans were quite clear as to the economic and social role
appropriate to Aborigines who came in from the bush. Governor
Macquarie argued that when they had given up their 'Wild wandering and Unsettled Habits' they would become progressively useful to the country either as 'labourers in Agricultural Employ or
among the lower Class of Mechanics'.[34] A generation later
Governor Gipps gave his attention to the means by which the
Aborigines 'could be induced to become voluntary labourers for
wages'. Though 'by nature wild' he believed that proof existed that
they could be 'induced to submit to the restraints which are imposed
on ordinary labourers'.[35] Numerous plans were devised to impose
the required discipline on Aboriginal workers. In Perth in the 1840s
the Government issued a directive that blacks would only be admitted to the town if they were wearing a woollen shirt which had

to be earned by labour, thus practically conveying the lesson 'of the value of acquiring property'.[36] Education of the children was held out to be the great hope especially if they could be separated from their parents and brought up in institutions. A West Australian official put forward a scheme for the socialization of black children in 1840. He argued that an institution be set up to which the children be induced 'and even compelled' to go and enter upon a 'field of action which would gradually wean them from their present erratic habits'. This scheme was quite elaborate. He suggested the children should be taught to walk to and fro for a limited distance in *'Gangs* merely to form a *habit'*. The next step would be to make each boy bring back any loose wood that might by lying about to be used for cooking. Subsequently they would be made to carry an axe to cut wood 'thus gradually bringing them on *by steps* to a *habit of labour'*.[37] Other gangs would meanwhile collect ballast stones, grow vegetables, break up ground or make roads.

Several attempts were made to encourage Aborigines to become gardeners or small farmers and thereby 'feel the sweets of property'.[38] In 1815 Macquarie endeavoured to settle a group of Sydney blacks on the shores of the harbour and provided them with huts, small patches of garden, rations, clothes and a European assistant in order that they would learn to prefer 'the productive Effects of their own Labour and Industry to the Wild and precarious Pursuits of the Woods'.[39] The failure of this and similar schemes has usually been attributed to the Aborigines' total lack of understanding of agriculture. Yet traditionally they did harvest root crops and wild grasses and often from the very same patches of soil appropriated by the settlers for agriculture. The big difference lay in the fact that they did not see the need to sit around and wait for the crops to grow. Confident in their knowledge of the environment and their ability to ensure, by appropriate ritual, its continued flowering they arranged their timetable to return to an area when a new crop had matured and ripened. Clearly there was a big gap between the productivity of Aboriginal foraging and European horticulture even in the crude colonial environment. But the crucial difference was not in the use of the land but in the institution of private property. Small European farmers and gardeners remained in one place not just to nurture their crops but because they owned the land and all it produced and residence was required to effect and affirm that ownership.

During the first half of the nineteenth century there were numerous settlers who appreciated that the difficulty of 'bringing in' the blacks 'to a habit of labour' was due to lack of motivation rather than incapacity, to the 'difficulty of finding some inducement sufficiently powerful to excite them to continuous labour'.[40] Samuel Marsden remarked in 1825 that he was pessimistic about the future of the Aborigines. 'The time', he wrote:

> may come when they may feel more wants than they do at present – they seem to have all they wish for Idleness and Independence. They have no wants to stimulate their exertions and until they have, I fear they will remain the same.[41]

Perhaps the clearest analysis of the problems of attempting to impose the discipline, punctuality and regularity of wage labour on Aboriginal society was provided by Jack McLaren in his account of his life at the tip of Cape York at the turn of the century. He set out to establish a coconut plantation using the local blacks for labour. Being a solitary European the option of force was not available to him and he was required to use patience and diplomacy to extract the amount of work he required. The blacks sought access to his trade goods but otherwise they could continue to survive independently. He provided an interesting catalogue of his problems. It was, he wrote, no easy matter to persuade the natives to work on succeeding days:

> We worked yesterday and are tired and would rest, they would say adding pointedly that in their habitual mode of life they worked not at all, and hunted only when the need for food was on them. Whereupon I would point out that in their wild life they had no tobacco, or flour, or coloured cloth, or tinned meats or tinned fish, or any other of the luxuries they coveted, and that the only way to obtain them was by working all day every day.[42]

To his annoyance the blacks took a long time over their meals. Even their method of eating appeared unnecessarily time-consuming. After the midday meal the whole camp would sleep and if McLaren did not wake them they would doze the afternoon through. Even while they were working there were constant distractions. When they came across food they would immediately down tools to dig the yams, cut out the sugar bag, pursue the wallaby, causing disruption which might last several hours. Unless he supervised their work all the time they would sit down, smoke or go to sleep the minute his back was turned. 'Often in those early days', he reminisced:

> did I return from a brief absence to find the whole of the labourers stretched like black shadows on the ground, I tried upbraiding them. It was no use. I tried ridiculing – saying scornfully that they worked like women or children, that they had neither strength nor endurance. That was no use either ... There were, in fact, no means by which I could persuade them into sudden acceptance of a daily routine of toil.[43]

UNWILLING WAGE LABOURERS

The historical record bristles with colonists' complaints about their problems in trying to get Aborigines to behave as 'voluntary labourers for wages'. Governor Hutt concluded that black attitudes to labour were the 'chief and serious difficulty'[44] which had hampered assimilation. They would not work regularly; would not settle; they were unpunctual. 'Every species of labour seems to be irksome to them',[45] wrote the Commissioner for Crown Lands at Moreton Bay. 'Nothing', commented a woman settler from New England, 'can really repay them for performing any labour beyond that necessary to procure them enough game to enable them to exist from day to day'. Occasionally local blacks worked on her property but 'they all looked on working for us as a personal favour, and gave us to understand as much'.[46] 'If they do service for others', wrote J. B. Walker of the Tasmanians, 'they do it through courtesy'.[47]

But it was not just the habit of labour that had to be induced but also those concomitants the subordination of servant to master and the separation of the worker from the means of subsistence and production. The second was the most difficult because it was hard to convince the Aborigines that they were working for their own benefit and not for white employers. G. A. Robinson explained to the Superintendent at Port Phillip that on the stations of the Protectorate the blacks were 'taught to feel that their occupation is for their own advantage'.[48] E. S. Parker was even more acutely aware of the problems of convincing the Aborigines of the advantages of wage labour and imbuing them with the ideology of capitalism. In a report from his station on the Loddon he explained how it was essential to bring the blacks 'under the influence of Christian principles' which would provide the fundamental underpinning for the socially desired behaviour. Even then it was essential:

> that in all cases where they are employed they should be made to feel that their occupation is for their own benefit rather than for the advantage of the employer. They appear generally to feel that they owe us nothing and that they are under no obligation to work. If the suspicion therefore be aroused in their minds that they are working more for the benefit of the whites than their own advantage they will speedily recede from their employment.[49]

It has often been assumed that the blacks were unable to acquire enough skills to compete successfully in colonial society. The evidence suggests otherwise. Aborigines displayed their adaptability within a few years of the settlement at Sydney Cove. Collins believed that if well treated they 'certainly might be made very serviceable people'; in a number of occupations they proved themselves 'as handy and as useful as any other persons could have been'.[50] By the 1840s the catalogue of Aboriginal occupations had grown much larger. G. A. Robinson noted that:

> as far as they have been employed, they have been found faithful guides, able Bullock drivers, Efficient Shepherds, Stockkeepers and Whalers, good Boatmen, Horsemen and Houseservants, Husbandmen, Policemen, Handicrafts and other useful employments [sic].[51]

When they had only recently arrived on the fringe of white society Aborigines must have found many European occupations incomprehensible. As they lacked any immediate rationale they may have been thought to have ritual significance. Yet many jobs in the colonial economy required only limited formal skills and in some the blacks had distinct advantages. In much of rural industry they may well have been more immediately useful than new-chums from urban Britain. But while they were able to pick up the actual mechanical tasks associated with various jobs they were not willing to accept the social relations and cultural milieu in which they were set. While they might handle the tools of the labourer they were reluctant to accept the discipline that went with them.

TRADE, PROSTITUTION, BEGGING

Aborigines living in and around colonial towns did develop small scale trade in products gained by hunting, fishing or collecting. Fish, shell-fish, crustaceans, bark, sandalwood, skins, birds, feathers were at various times bartered with or sold to Europeans. But markets were uncertain and the blacks were regularly cheated. E. S. Parker noted in 1839 that Victorian Aborigines were the mainstays of a profitable trade in marsupial furs and lyre bird feathers yet the whites acquired them for almost nothing. He endeavoured to secure conditions which would obtain 'for them the just value of the produce of their hunting excursions' and drew up a scale of 'prices' for Aboriginal commodities which he vainly hoped the Protectorate could enforce. The basic unit was the pound of flour:

    1 Kangaroo skin – 2 lbs flour, 3 lbs if large
    2 Oppossum skins – 1 lb flour
    1 Basket, large – 6 lbs flour
    1 Basket, middle – 4 lbs flour
    1 Basket, small – 2 lbs flour[52]

One pound of flour was to be equivalent to 1 lb of rice and 1 lb of meat, $1/_4$ lb of sugar and $1/_4$ of rice and one knife. A tomahawk had the value of 2 lbs of flour.

Many Aboriginal groups discovered that prostitution provided a more certain return than vestigial hunting and gathering. In some places a large and lucrative trade developed and especially around the northern coasts where prostitution became one of the essential service industries supporting the pearling fleets. From the critical comments of white authorities it is obvious that substantial sums of money were earned by black communities in towns like Broome and Thursday Island. 'The trading with young girls is very profitable to the natives', wrote the Inspector of Aborigines at Broome, 'as for one nights debauchery from ten shillings to two pounds ten is paid in rations and clothing'.[53] The situation at La Grange Bay would, he said rather coyly, 'speak for itself'. For eight months of the year 'an average of 150 coloured men came into contact fortnightly with the natives'. Money and food earned by the women was shared in the fringe camps allowing most of the men to avoid the need to labour for the Europeans, to 'make a living in ease and idleness'.[54] At Cape York at much the same time officials reported that the ex-trackers Waimara and James were the 'bosses' who organized labour for the luggers and women for the crews. Whether such indigenous entrepreneurs emerged elsewhere is impossible to say.

Officials in both West Australia and Queensland were determined to stamp out the trade. Waimara and James were deported to a Reserve; police in Broome drove the blacks out of town. Their motives were mixed. There was genuine official concern at the massive health problems accompanying a widespread epidemic of V.D. but it was equally clear that the colonial governments were determined to prevent the blacks from becoming economically independent. When the Western Australian Inspector of Aborigines visited a Broome purged by the local constables his first remarks were instructive. He noted that very few blacks could be seen about the town and residents told him 'they could now get hold of a native willing to work'.[55]

Begging was another means by which blacks could avoid the need for regular wage labour. The morality of the practice looked very different to blacks than to censorious whites. Moorhouse wrote in 1842 that he found it a difficult task to make Adelaide Aborigines believe that 'begging lessens them in the estimation of Europeans and that their supplies would be more certain and more creditable, if gained by cultivation of their own ground'.[56] Begging was a natural response from people who shared without question and who believed that reciprocity was the greatest social good. The conviction that the white man owed a great debt for appropriated land merely strengthened their determination to continue a practice which helped to augment meagre diets and maintain a precarious existence on the rim of European society.

THE CASTE BARRIER

Many Europeans believed that they genuinely offered their culture and religion to the blacks. Yet white society was less able than Aboriginal society to assimilate outsiders on terms of equality. The only entry point available was at the very bottom of the social hierarchy where resistance to assimilation was at its strongest. For all their fine words colonial elites were not offering equality to the blacks but merely space on the lowest rungs of society. Unskilled Europeans could not afford a similar generosity. They feared the economic competition of cheap labour and were never willing to concede equality to the black outsider who was 'a good deal bullied by the white labourer, who lost no opportunity of asserting his superiority over him'.[57] Unfortunately, wrote E. S. Parker, 'there exists an aversion on the part of most European labourers to see the natives taught to work, avowedly for the reason that a successful result might interfere with the price of labour'.[58] Similar arguments were presented in the Adelaide Examiner in 1842 by Dr. Richard Penny, one of the most perceptive European observers of Aboriginal society in nineteenth-century Australia. His comments are worth quoting at length:

> All the efforts for civilizing the native, have been with the object
> of his becoming a portion of our labouring, civilized, population,
> and forming an integral part of it, and it has been this, that has

caused all such attempts, to end in failure. The two races can never amalgamate – the white labourer, and the native, (be he ever so useful), can not be brought to work together on equal terms. We could never succeed in incorporating the native with the mass of the labouring population, for there is always enough of that antipathy of races existing, to induce the settler to place the native, however deserving, in an inferior position to his white servants, and to give him the more menial offices to perform; but if the settler being a friend of the Aboriginal cause, were not disposed to make any distinction, but that of merit, the servants themselves would not perform those offices, whilst they could shift it on that of the blacks.[59]

When it came to sexual relations the caste barrier was raised even higher preventing almost all contact between black men and white women. 'No European Woman', wrote William Shelley in 1814, 'would marry a *Native*, unless some abandoned profligate'.[60] Over sixty years later John Green told a Victorian Royal Commission that he had known of several cases where Aboriginal and part-Aboriginal children had been brought up with European families. All would go well, he remarked:

> until they came to an age that they would like to make love. As soon as this was known by mamma or papa, there must be something done to stop it, so the white daughter or son is told they must not make so free with the darky; they must remember that, although he or she has been educated in the family, it would be degrading to make love with them. So the cold shoulder is soon turned on the darky; they soon feel it, and a change is seen in the darky; instead of one of the most cheerful they will mope about until they can find a chance to join their friends the aborigines.[61]

With neither property nor marketable skills the Aborigines were stranded, poverty-stricken and powerless, on the fringes of colonial society. A few individuals temporarily escaped the inexorable dictate of the market by being kept in social and even geographical isolation allowing them to achieve an elevated status which could not be sustained once the special circumstances were brought to an end. Guides on exploring expeditions often attained an importance unmatched by blacks elsewhere in the society as a consequence of their special skills, the paramilitary nature of the exploring party and the social limbo of the inland journey. Children and youths taken into the homes of the colonial elite were afforded a status dependent on their hosts' class position rather than their own. Native police troopers were deliberately kept in isolation from the wider community and encouraged to feel superior to the white working class. The original regulations for the force at Port Phillip specified that the troopers were to be prevented from 'associating with those who may instruct them in vicious and disorderly habits'. They must be made to 'discriminate between the differing classes of white people', avoiding the working class while showing 'respect to the upper and well conducted'.[62] Settlers seem to have often adopted similar policies with their Aboriginal servants. The Tasmanian pioneer J. H. Wedge did not allow 'his blackboy' May-day to 'live with or associate with servants'.[63] But once troopers left the native police, expeditions came back from the bush, upper-bourgeois protectors returned to England, the artificial platform was removed. The assertion of social reality, the sudden descent, was a harsh and often shattering experience. This may well explain why so many ex-trackers and ex-troopers ended up as renegades alienated from both white and Aboriginal society. These themes can best be illustrated by reference to the careers of a few blacks who suffered these experiences.

Bungaree was a New South Wales Aborigine who was well educated, could speak Latin and behaved 'as a gentleman in elegant society'. He entered the native police but found his position in society anomalous in the extreme and remarked to his superior officer in a 'melancholy tone':

> I wish I had never been taken out of the bush, and educated as I have been, for I *cannot be a white man*, they will never look on me as one of themselves; and I *cannot be a blackfellow*, I am disgusted with their way of living.[64]

Mathinna was a young Tasmanian girl who was temporarily adopted by Governor and Lady Franklin. 'She had dwelt in the Colonial palace', wrote Bonwick, 'had been taught, petted, and trained to high hopes'.[65] When the Franklins returned to England it was thought that Mathinna's health would not stand the journey. She was placed in an orphanage and virtually abandoned to eventually drown while drunk at the Oyster Cove settlement for the remnants of the Tasmanian tribes. At much the same time in South Australia a young Aboriginal girl called Maria was taken into Government House in Adelaide. Seduced by a prominent merchant she was sent away when her pregnancy became apparent and fell 'into disreputable habits of life'[66] and was not even acceptable at the Poonindie mission. George Grey discussed the career of the West Australian youth Miago who sailed for several months on the *Beagle* and proved a 'temperate, attentive, cheerful' servant. But on his return to Perth he found European society uncongenial and went back to the bush. Grey considered the reasons why:

> Miago when he was landed, had amongst the white people none who would be truly friends of his – they would give him scraps from their table, but the very outcasts of the whites would not have treated him as an equal – they have no sympathy with him – he could not have married – he had no certain means of subsistence open to him ... He had two courses left open to him – he could either have renounced all natural ties, and have led a hopeless, joyless life amongst the whites – ever a servant – ever an inferior being – or he could renounce civilization, and return to the friends of his childhood, and to the habits of his youth.[67]

RESISTANCE TO ASSIMILATION

But most Aborigines were not frustrated guests waiting patiently to be admitted to an unwelcoming white society. Generally speaking blacks were not impressed by what was offered. 'They do not court a life of labour', wrote a Victorian Justice of the Peace in 1849:

> that of our shepherds and hut-keepers – our splitters or bullock drivers – appears to them one of unmeaning toil, and they would by no means consent to exchange their free unhoused condition for the monotonous drudgery of such a dreary existence.[68]

It was difficult to persuade Aborigines to accept the inequalities of white society. Taplin noted that Aboriginal men had 'quite a dignified bearing with an air of freedom altogether different from low class Europeans'.[69] They do not 'understand exalted rank', wrote a Victorian clergyman, 'and, in fact, it is difficult to get into a blackfellow's head that one man is higher than another'.[70] James Gunther, the pioneer New South Wales missionary, commented on the consequences of the blacks' 'peculiar form of government' which:

> admitting of no distinction of rank, but allowing each man to share in their consultations and decisions as to any questions arising among them stamps a feeling of independence and even haughtiness with an appearance of dignity on the character of the men rarely to be met among differently governed natives. As they have no titles for distinction nor a proper name for a chief so they have neither a word in their language to signify a servant ... no man has an idea of serving another, this idea of their own dignity and importance is carried so far that they hesitate long before they apply the term Mr. to any European even when they know full well the distinction we make (between master and servant).[71]

The value of economic incentives was undermined by the egalitarianism and reciprocity of Aboriginal society. Increased wages awarded for improved efficiency were immediately shared with kin whether they were employed or not. It was difficult, a north Queensland missionary wrote, for Aborigines to 'understand individualism'.[72] Their system of socialism', commented another, was a barrier to progress because it hindered 'any improvement or rightful ownership'.[73] Taplin observed that South Australian Aborigines 'always resent the payment of superior wages to one man because he is a better workman than another and never will allow he is more worthy of it than themselves.' This aversion, he wrote:

> to acknowledge superiority is a great evil when the Aborigines come in contact with the colonists. They will never permit one of their own people to be placed over them as a ganger or overseer.[74]

Thomas Mitchell pondered on the problem of the Aboriginal response to white society when he returned to the settled districts after his Queensland expedition and was required to consider what should happen to the guides who had accompanied him into the interior. He appreciated the importance of equality in traditional society – 'all there participate in, and have a share of, Nature's gifts. These, scanty though they be, are open to all'. But among Europeans the 'half clad native finds himself in a degraded position ... a mere outcast'. Experience in Australia and elsewhere, he argued, had shown the 'absurdity of expecting that any men' would leave their woods purely from choice 'unless they do so on terms of the most perfect equality'.[75] Drawing on his experiences of white-Aboriginal relations in South Australia Richard Penny concluded that if the black was:

> to accept the terms of civilization that we offer him, everything would conduce to keep him in the lowest scale of society, he would be constantly subject to all sorts of oppression, and would make but a bad exchange for his native independence.[76]

Penny argued that not only was this the objective situation facing the Aborigines but that they were fully cognizant of it. 'These are things', he wrote, 'which the friends of the Aborigines overlook: but the natives themselves ... are well aware of this, and it is a reason assigned by them for not remaining at the stations of the settlers.'[77] Bonwick argued that young Aborigines were not content with their position when living with white families. 'However English lads may reconcile themselves with a life of subordinate servitude' the same could not be expected of the blacks as it was 'too opposite' to their instincts.[78] Backhouse and Walker believed that many experiments with the Aborigines, had failed because they had been 'placed in situations where they felt themselves looked down upon by the whites'.[79]

AFFIRMATION

By the middle of the nineteenth century many settlers had concluded that the Aborigines would never adopt European civilization, that they were incapable of 'improvement' and were indeed a doomed race. Yet a minority of whites appreciated that black behaviour manifested faith in their own culture, that it betokened strength not weakness, affirmation not failure. The problem they realized was not the incapacity of tribesmen but their 'intractableness', their 'martial spirit'.[80] The present generation, wrote a Victorian settler, 'cling to confirmed habits and old associations with a tenacity which nothing can overcome'.[81] From the Darling Downs the Commissioner for Crown Lands wrote in 1850 that the 'roving life' still had charms for the blacks 'far too powerful ... to overcome'.[82] The Protector of Aborigines in Western Australia observed that:

> the bush has so many attractions, that they prefer the precarious subsistence it affords to the food of the white man which must be earned by labour. Their ... roving life still has charms for them far too powerful for any inducement that the habits and customs of civilization can offer to overcome.[83]

A majority of Aborigines endeavoured to maintain direct access to their land both for its spiritual significance and the means of subsistence that it provided. They sought to preserve their independence from the labour market and the abject position that it assigned to them. This increasingly meant that hunting and foraging had to be supplemented by returns from casual labour, prostitution, begging and pilfering. 'Why should they vex themselves with the drudgery of labour' asked a New South Wales settler in the 1830s:

> they are not labourers at all, and for the same reason that any other gentleman is not viz. that he can live without labour. So also can they, and as comfortably as they wish to live.[84]

Clearly fringe-dwelling blacks did not live as comfortably as they would have liked but it is essential to stress the element of choice in their predicament. They chose to maintain the maximum degree of independence possible in the circumstances at the cost of their standard of living, even of their well being. They opted for Aboriginal values, settlement patterns, family life, rhythms of work even when that choice meant a miserable level of material comfort. Although Europeans increasingly imposed restraints, and on reserves and missions they were almost overwhelming, the blacks continued to exercise choice and thereby shape their own history. There were great penalties – malnutrition, ill-health, despair, population loss – but by retaining even a small area of autonomy nineteenth-century fringe dwellers ensured the survival of at least elements of Aboriginal culture in those parts of the continent where the impact of the invasion had been most devastating. It was a course of action fraught with risk yet the Aboriginal renaissance of the last decade suggests that ultimately the sacrifices were justified.

Chapter 6

THE PASTORAL FRONTIER

INITIAL ENCOUNTERS

For a majority of Aborigines their first experience of permanent settlers came when pastoralists arrived in their clan territories bringing with them horses and drays, cattle and sheep and the varied equipment of the pioneer station. The fear evoked by the white man, already discussed above, was soon matched by concern for local ecologies which quickly showed the impact of the exotic animals. The castaway James Morrell witnessed this process in north Queensland in the 1860s. His clansmen brought him news of a large herd of cattle which had suddenly appeared, surrounded a favourite waterhole and emptied it, leaving fish stranded in the mud. Though tempted to rush in and pick up the dying fish they were too intimidated to venture out of their hiding places. The explorer Thomas Mitchell was another who witnessed the impact of cattle herds travelling out beyond the fringes of European settlement in northern New South Wales and southern Queensland in 1846. An Aboriginal guide was taking Mitchell's party to a shallow creek where he expected to find water but on arriving on the bank he was disappointed to find that cattle had already been there and had drunk it all. The black showed Mitchell the 'recent prints of numerous cloven feet' and the explorer was made to feel 'in common with the Aborigines, those privations to which they are exposed by the white

man's access to their country'. The experience was repeated the following day. The party approached a pond well known to local clans
only to find once again that cattle had drunk the water and trodden
the ground 'as dry as a market place'. Elsewhere Mitchell came
across springs and ponds which local clans had tried to protect by
cutting down nearby trees and placing the logs over the water. Thus
it was, he mused, that the Aborigines 'first became sensible of the
approach of the white man'. He wrote of the fate of the small man-
made waterholes in dry stretches of bush which were like oases surrounded by lush green grass. Cattle, he wrote:

> find these places and come from stations often many miles dis-
> tant, attracted by the rich verdure usually growing about them,
> and by thus treading the water into mud, or by drinking it up,
> they literally destroy the whole country for the Aborigines.[1]

WATER

Mitchell's experience illustrated the widespread conflict over water
which arose in arid areas all over the continent and in well watered
areas as well during dry seasons. It often began as soon as the
Europeans appeared. This was certainly the case in the desert
where thirsty camel trains and horse teams consumed huge
amounts of precious water in Aboriginal wells and springs and
soaks. The pioneer Queensland squatter George Sutherland related
a similar experience which illustrated the competition for water in
a parched environment. He was driving a flock of thirsty sheep
through waterless country towards the Georgina River in western
Queensland. The local clans, camping around the only available
surface water, scattered in terror when the whole flock stampeded
towards the billabong.

Conflict was sharpened by the widespread belief among frontier
squatters that 'niggers and cattle don't mix'; that the half-wild herds
were unsettled by the mere sight or sound of Aborigines. As a result
the blacks were repeatedly driven away from river frontages and lagoons. They were shot at or ridden down and stock-whipped.

Relevant evidence for this is voluminous, coming from all parts of
the continent. 'All the freshwater is surrounded by cattle', wrote
Burketown's policeman in 1897, and if a black was unfortunate to
be seen by the station hands he was 'hunted, whiped [sic] and se-
verely maltreated'.[2] Inspector Foelsche of the Northern Territory
police noted how local squatters kept the blacks away from the inland lagoons and billabongs which were important both as meeting
places and sources of food. The Protector of Aborigines at
Camooweal remarked in 1901 that the station owners and man-
agers claimed that the sight of the blacks disturbed the cattle with
the result that the blacks were 'dispersed by the station hands'.[3]
Writing of northern New South Wales in the early 1850s the
Commandant of the Native Police noted that with the exception of
a few stations the Aborigines were 'in a manner outlawed in their
own country, being hunted from the river and creek frontages, and
thus deprived of means of lawfully obtaining food'.[4] The impact of
these policies on black communities was graphically described by an
old Roper River black who recalled in old age the hardships suffered by his people when he was a boy during the early years of the
twentieth century:

> Oh terrible days we used to had: We never walk around much
> 'mongst the plain country or groun'. We use to upla hill alla time
> to save our life. Our old people you know used to take us away
> from plain or river or billabong. Only night time they used to
> run down to get the lily, alla young men you know. Can't go day-
> time, frighten for white people.[5]

Cattle and sheep were destructive of the environment in other
ways as well. Their close cropping of the vegetation destroyed native flora while plants growing in or around water-holes or lagoons
were eaten or trampled under hard hoofs. A north Queensland pioneer wrote of the impact of cattle along the Gulf of Carpentaria
coastline:

> they trample out the signs of turtles found in dried up swamps,
> the trail of the crocodile to his nest; they eat the tops of yams,
> and eat and destroy the lillies, all of which make their (the
> Aborigines') natural food scarcer and harder to find.[6]

Other introduced animals – pigs, rabbits, camels – damaged sensitive local ecologies as well. An Aboriginal woman from the north Queensland coast told a European visitor in 1895 that feral pigs had eaten large amounts of traditional food. 'I think altogether we die soon', she lamented, 'pig-pig eat him yams; plum fall down, wild pigs too much eat'.[7]

BLACK SHEPHERDS

Pastoral settlement presented a massive challenge to Aboriginal society, altering ecologies and disrupting traditional economies. But clans responded creatively to that challenge all over the continent. They studied the Europeans and their animals and began to weave new ideas into long established patterns of social and economic life, co-opting sheep and cattle for their own use and learning the skills of the shepherd and herdsman. There was, after all, a considerable overlap between the methods of the hunter and the herdsman. Kangaroos and emus were driven long distances to be trapped in rudimentary stockyards made of logs and bushes. There are numerous references in the pioneer literature to the discovery of long races of sticks, boughs and bushes which had been used to control the movements of the larger marsupials. Thus Giles referred to what he termed dilapidated old yards, where the blacks had formerly yarded emu or wallaby; K. L. Parker observed that the Euahlayi tribe made bush yards and caught emus in them. Buckley recalled that the clans he had lived with pursued kangaroos in order to hunt them into corners like flocks of sheep. Writing of north-western Queensland Roth noted that local Aborigines mustered emus like cattle driving them into nets and palisades. G. F. Moore found that West Australian Aborigines used the word *yekan* meaning to drive or to chase to describe the European's herding of cattle. But while traditional methods overlapped with new we should not overlook the wide ranging adaption apparent in Aboriginal tactics to capture or kill sheep and cattle. There seems to be no doubt that these skills were consciously developed and deliberately improved and that the blacks were proud of their evolving mastery of the new techniques. Davis was told by his Aboriginal hosts in southern Queensland 'with much minuteness how dexterously they had succeeded in carrying off sundry sheep at different times without being even perceived by the shepherds'.[8] How did the blacks so rapidly become efficient sheep stealers and adept shepherds?

Stragglers were driven away when out of sight of the shepherds or grabbed by blacks lying immobile in the grass; dogs were trained to rush in and cut out sections of flocks. An observer in southern Queensland noted that local blacks had well developed techniques which exploited the terrain. They waited until the flock approached the summit of a steep ridge, or the trench of a deep gully and then rushed in with their dogs to cut out twenty or thirty sheep and drive them into rough or broken country. The manoeuvre was executed so quickly that the blacks were beyond reach before the shepherds were aware of the raid. Some techniques seem to have been even more sophisticated. A report from the Western District of Victoria in 1842 described how local blacks enticed ewes out of their pens at night without arousing the suspicion of the shepherds:

> Breaking the leg of a lamb, the natives placed it at about 50 yards from where the sheep were penned. The bleatings of the poor little animal soon drew the attention of the ewes, and several of them leaped the hurdles, and made for the spot where it was lying. From this they were attracted by the cries of another lamb, placed at a little distance onwards. The same expedient was followed by the savages of mutilating lambs and placing them at distances from each other till they had succeeded in decoying the old sheep several hundred yards away from the hurdles. They then rushed between the hurdles and the sheep, and drove the latter from the station. So silently was the robbery accomplished, that the sheep were not missed till the following day.[9]

Skilful cutting-out was only a start. To avoid violent retaliation from the settlers, or at least the loss of the animals in question, it was essential that the flock be driven away as far and as quickly as possible without allowing the sheep to scatter. Consequently pursuing whites often came up with disputed flocks many miles from their station of origin. In the Portland district in 1843 a squatter and his men pursued a flock of 480 sheep across country for 250 miles. A few years later at Wide Bay in Queensland a settler reported that he had followed a group of Aborigines who had successfully taken 500 sheep over two mountains, through a mile and a half of rain forest and on to another mountain. The blacks quickly learnt that success depended on their ability to cover their tracks before the Europeans ventured in pursuit. Many of the methods employed were probably carried over from traditional society for clans were adept at hiding their movements from their enemies. A group of blacks from the Western District of Victoria were found with a flock of sheep twelve miles away from the station where they had been secured but they had been taken on a circuitous route of at least forty miles and through a series of swamps to confuse white pursuers. On the Glenelg River a flock was driven back on its own tracks to blot them out and was then divided into three lots which were driven in separate directions. Elsewhere the blacks burnt grass for a considerable distance around plundered pens to hide the tell-tale tracks.

Rivers presented a considerable problem to black shepherds. Europeans following the tracks of stolen flocks concluded that Aborigines often made repeated attempts to rush their newly acquired sheep down the river banks in order to force them across the water and there are several reports of blacks making log bridges to facilitate the movement of their flocks across stretches of water. In 1850 a party of Wide Bay squatters actually found local blacks in the process of building a bridge[24] while a few years earlier in the Grampians, a native police detachment, pursued a group of Aborigines for eight days through gullies, over ridges and across mountain streams where the blacks had made bridges strong enough for the troop horses to pass over.

But even when blacks had escaped with their commandeered flocks and evaded pursuers there remained the need to prevent the sheep from straying. A common solution to this problem was to break or dislocate the sheeps' hind legs. The pioneer Victorian squatter Hugh Murray reported how the Colac Aborigines took their animals to some secure neighbourhood and feasted upon them, 'breaking the legs of those they did not at once kill, to detain them'. It was, wrote a fellow squatter 'a cruel sort of tethering resorted to in those days.[10] But less drastic means of securing sheep were widely adopted. Naturally enclosed patches of grass were selected for use, squatters in Wide Bay for instance finding sheep high up on a mountain in a small space surrounded by rain forest which was, they realized, a 'natural paddock'.[11]

Of even greater interest was the widespread construction by Aborigines of folds and stockyards to secure captured flocks, a practice obviously adopted from European shepherds though owing something to traditional use of brush fences to control and corral native animals. There are many such reports and they come from widely scattered parts of the continent. Research to date has turned up over thirty separate eye witness reports from districts as far apart as Yorke Peninsula in South Australia, the upper Burdekin Valley in north Queensland and the Champion Bay district in Western Australia. A few examples will suffice for purposes of illustration.

In 1840 a party of Western District squatters followed a group of blacks into almost inaccessible mountains and discovered 'a very ingeniously constructed brush yard where the sheep had been kept during the night'.[12] Six years later at the head of Spencer Gulf local blacks took a flock which they regularly folded 'whilst they were regaling themselves upon divers roasted legs and shoulders'.[13] The South Australian Protector of Aborigines reported finding a yard made of branches and capable of holding from two to three hundred sheep. A party of Maranoa settlers following tracks of stolen sheep found that the blacks had made bough yards for them every night, 'as well as a white man could have done'.[14] In the Burdekin Valley blacks drove 400 sheep into the ranges after a successful raid on a station and built a 'proper yard' and regularly shepherded the flock showing 'how closely and for what a length of time they must have watched the habits of Europeans'.[15] The rapid development of Aboriginal sheep raiding techniques was noted by a writer in the

Adelaide Observer in 1846. Attacks which were originally 'ill considered and accidental' had been superseded by 'well planned forays':

> the flock is steadily driven, and carefully folded – taken with dexterity and retained with determination. The captors feed upon the sheep until all are consumed – then sally forth in quest of a fresh supply.[16]

CATTLE HUNTERS

Cattle presented Aborigines with a different set of problems. The half-wild animals of frontier districts were larger, faster and more aggressive than sheep and much harder to kill. Indeed it was difficult to kill them at all with traditional wooden or stone-tipped spears. Numerous pioneer squatters reported cases of cattle coming in off the range covered with spear wounds or with the weapons still stuck in their bodies. A Western District settler found one of his bullocks still alive with thirty spears sticking into its tortured flesh. There is no doubt that one of the principal motives for the adoption of iron tipped spears was to facilitate the killing of the large European animals including draught bullocks as well as horses and cattle. The *Portland Gazette* reported in 1845 that local blacks were adopting iron spears and were systematically attacking cattle herds with them. Clans living close to the growing networks of telegraph lines adopted spear heads fashioned from porcelain insulators while the Loritja people of central Australia were said to have adopted a cruder and hence more expendable spear for killing cattle.

The greatest problem for the cattle hunters was to immobilize the large beasts long enough to be able to close in for the kill. Many different techniques were tried. The most common appears to have been to rush selected beasts into swampy or muddy ground and then attack them while they were unable to move quickly. 'They now proceed in a most systematic manner', wrote the Commissioner for Crown Lands at Moreton Bay in 1844, 'rushing the cattle into swampy ground during the wet weather and then hamstringing them'.[17] The explorer Thomas Mitchell reported that in northern New South Wales local clans had driven off 800 head of cattle when the country was in flood and the horsemen were unable to travel. In such conditions the cattle stuck fast 'in the soft earth' and were thus 'at the mercy of the natives'.[18] But swampy ground was only available to some clans and for limited periods of time. Elsewhere other techniques had to be developed.

On the Mulgrave River in north Queensland local blacks dug pits on well used cattle tracks and then speared the trapped beasts. Clans in the Western District rushed in and killed cows while they were calving; in the Bowen hinterland animals were driven through a narrow pass into an enclosed valley. A Riverina pioneer reported that he found a large party of blacks on his run and that they had driven his cattle into a tight circle and were 'ringing them around' and 'riddling them with spears all the time'.[19]

Experienced frontiersmen noted the development of Aboriginal techniques. The Commissioner for Crown Lands on the Liverpool Plains remarked in 1842 that local blacks had become 'much more expert and cunning in watching and hunting cattle' and had trained their dogs to be most efficient assistants to them'.[20] A correspondent wrote to the *Moreton Bay Courier* in 1849 explaining that on the Pine Rivers the Aborigines had developed:

> a new system of securing their prey, by wounding the beasts in such a way with their tomahawks that they are easily killed after being driven to the scrubs. This is a considerable improvement on their old system and shows the determined and systematic manner of their outrages. Previously, when the cattle were speared on the river there was a great chance that the savages would be disturbed before they could cut up the carcases and carry them off; and if they drove the herd to the scrubs they would no doubt have considerable difficulty in slaying the infuriated beasts. It was not gratifying ... to find that many of their victims escaped after being speared or died too near to the stations for them to secure the anticipated feast. Their present plan has, therefore, been adopted in order that the maimed cattle may fall easily before their spears, when they reach the scrub, exhausted and faint from their previous wounds.[21]

It appears that some groups killed cattle as near as possible to a river bank in order to use water transport for the large and heavy carcases. A Queensland pioneer reported that the blacks on the Burnett killed cattle on the north side of the river and then conveyed the meat in canoes across to the sanctuary of the rain forest on the south bank. Frederick Curr who settled in the Etheridge district in north Queensland recalled that he had to keep his herds away from the Einasleigh River because local blacks were able to kill the beasts while they were in the water and then tow the carcases downstream where they could be safely cut up and carried away.

Aborigines reacted quickly and creatively to the settlers' flocks and herds. They turned to good effect their traditional skills while accepting the need for innovation in both techniques and social organization. Ready access to large amounts of beef and mutton enabled groups to meet more frequently and stay together longer. Cooking methods were modified and diet changed with a probable decline in the collection and consumption of native plants. Yet reactions to cattle and to sheep were qualitatively different. When they pursued, killed and consumed cattle the Aborigines were still behaving like hunter-gatherers though they had modified traditional methods to cope with the introduced animals. But in their use of sheep many black clans had clearly travelled beyond the confines of customary experience. They had become effective herdsmen in their own right presenting a fundamental challenge to European pastoralists. All over the continent Aboriginal groups learnt to shepherd their sheep for long distances over difficult terrain, to train their dogs to assist rather than hinder their operations and to feed and water and corral their commandeered flocks. There are a few reports which suggest that the women took over the new role of shepherd while the men continued to hunt the larger indigenous animals as well as the introduced ones.

These developments were arguably the most striking examples of creative adaptation in the history of the Aboriginal response to the European invasion. Yet they have been almost completely overlooked by historians and anthropologists, due in part to the fact that the evidence is widely scattered and often in obscure sources. Another reason is that the Aboriginal venture into pastoralism was confined practically everywhere to a very short period of time coinciding with the moment of maximum conflict with the Europeans and coming abruptly to an end when black resistance was crushed and the survivors were let in to pastoral stations and frontier towns.

CO-ORDINATED ATTACKS

But the Aborigines also attacked and destroyed the European animals as part of their resistance to the invader as was indicated briefly above. A long list of such onslaughts could be compiled for each colony but a few examples will suffice for the purposes of illustration. In 1830 Tasmanian blacks beat 100 ewes to death on a Longford property; a few years earlier on the north-west coast a similar number of Van Diemens Land Company sheep were driven over cliffs into the sea. In 1816 in New South Wales 200 sheep of the Malgoa estate were destroyed; fifty were mangled and blinded, the rest thrown down a precipice. On the Liverpool Plains thirty years later four hundred young ewes were left dead in a heap on Cobb's Station. In 1842 McIntyre Aborigines killed a horse, cut off its head and two legs and hung the entrails out from bush to bush while on the New England plateau the local blacks burnt 1200 ewes and lambs. On a McIntyre River station local blacks killed eighty head of cattle in a single night and hamstrung others while some of the heads were cut off the carcases and put up on sticks. In 1848 forty cattle were drowned by Aborigines in the Brisbane River. Writing to his father from Bowen Downs in central Queensland in 1867 B. D. Morehead reported that the local clans had destroyed his sheep 'not to satisfy their hunger, but their spite, as in some of their camps there were more than fifty lying dead ... or wounded lying about brutally murdered'.[22]

Aborigines launched systematic attacks on individual properties which were quite devastating in their impact. Ovens river blacks attacked Dr Mackay's station in 1840 in the absence of the Europeans who returned to a scene of total devastation. Three valuable horses and a working bullock had been destroyed, all but seven of a herd of 1500 cattle driven away; a large barn and four roomed hut burnt to the ground along with forty bushels of wheat, agricultural implements, tools, bedding and clothes. Fifty years later and on the far side of the continent Northern Territory Aborigines burnt and looted Welleroo Station. They killed 30 or 40 fowls and threw them in a heap and carried away almost all moveable property including 20 bags of flour, 4 bags of rice, over 60 pounds of tobacco, all the pipes and matches, two dozen new dungaree suits, two dozen pairs of boots, all the clothes, rugs and blankets, 4 Winchester rifles and 300 cartridges.

Aboriginal attacks were occasionally massive enough to ruin pioneer squatters. Two men so affected petitioned the government for assistance leaving a record of their tribulations. In 1840 Victorian blacks raided David Waugh's Station killing the shepherds, running off most of the sheep and taking everything 'that could be, or supposed to be, of use to them'.[23] Waugh's losses which he computed at £1200 were crippling. A generation later John Yeates, one of the pioneer settlers of the Bowen district, assessed his losses while petitioning the Queensland government. The local clans raided his property on several occasions during a three month period in 1867. They took two flocks of sheep amounting to 1300 animals which he valued at 10s a head, 36 rams worth over £2 each and stores worth £55. His total loss of £800 could not be sustained and he abandoned the station.

But spectacular attacks on individual properties should not obscure the smaller, more typical Aboriginal operations, which were cumulatively important. Occasionally neighbouring squatters met to discuss their losses and petition distant governments for protection leaving a valuable record of frontier conditions. In 1842 Port Fairy settlers petitioned the Superintendent of Port Phillip computing their collective losses over a few months at 3600 sheep, 100 cattle and 10 horses. Seven years later the squatters on the Condamine wrote to the local Commissioner for Crown Lands complaining that during a four-month period the blacks had taken 6000 sheep and killed 8 shepherds while doing so. In 1851 the Magistrates of the Maranoa met at Surat and petitioned the local native police officer detailing the losses sustained by the squatters which amounted to 6000 cattle and 2000 sheep in the previous eighteen months.

But the violent and persistent retaliation by frontier squatters and their men forced the blacks to adjust the level of their assaults on European property and seek means to avoid imputation of responsibility. The *Sydney Gazette* reported in 1824 that the blacks living around the outer settlements had learnt to kill cattle by spearing them carefully in the skull, perforating a hole about the size of a musket ball subsequently claiming that white men were responsible for discovered carcases. In 1847 the *Portland Gazette* observed that local Aborigines were suspected of killing a bullock but that they had buried the head and skin in a pit in order to avoid detection. In the 1890s on the Diamantina local blacks cooked a bullock in a deep pit dug under a well worn cattle track in order to disguise their culinary operations. At Albany in 1842 a group of blacks devised a scheme to steal one or two sheep from their folds each night over a long period of time. So careful was the operation that the loss was not discovered for several months. A few years later on the Darling Downs the Commissioner for Crown Lands commented that 'everywhere' the blacks had adopted the 'same plan'. Visiting the stations in small numbers 'under the guise of friends' they allowed:

> no opportunity to escape of pilfering the huts or destroying any stray cattle they may meet on their way. In several instances they have killed milking cows close to the huts, without so much as being suspected till the Bones of their victims happen to be accidentally met with some days later; in one or two instances they have even buried the Bones...[24]

ACCOMMODATION

Accommodation between Aborigines and pastoralists was reached everywhere sooner or later, although it took place gradually and unevenly. Occasionally a group of neighbouring squatters made a collective decision to let the local clans in but more commonly it

occurred fitfully, station by station, and over a considerable period
of time. Aborigines responded tentatively. Typically a few individuals cautiously approached the Europeans and gradually over a year
or two their kin began to spend a greater proportion of their time
at station camp sites assigned by the squatter. Europeans kidnapped
individual blacks for labour or sex; as hostages, even as tutors in
local dialects. Equally the Aborigines sent women or young men
into the white men's society to act as spies and go-betweens. A settler on the Gascoyne River told a government official in 1882 that
he had 'no doubt the women kept by the whites act as spies for their
friends in the bush'.[25] Aboriginal shepherds and stockmen furtively
fed their kin who had not come in. A government official investi-
gating squatter complaints about sheep loss in the north west of
Western Australia concluded that:

> in the great majority of cases the sheep have been given away by
> the shepherds at night. In the day time they allow them to go
> astray in order that their friends may pick them up.[26]

In some cases it appears that small groups or individuals remained
out in the bush refusing to accept European domination. Simpson
Newland wrote of his experiences on the New South Wales-
Queensland border with an old and recalcitrant black whom he
called Baldy:

> Our new employees never gave us the least trouble, and as
> soon as they understood that neither the Queensland police
> nor our squatting neighbour would bother them while in our
> country we had the whole lot at our service – good, bad, and
> indifferent – all except the redoubtable Baldy. I had messages
> sent to him to come in, that no one should molest him, but all
> in vain. I never saw him in all my rides, drives, or walks, nor
> did the overseer, who was constantly on the run for many
> years. Much of the country was densely covered with thick
> polygonum swamps, and we were well aware Baldy lurked
> there during the day, and late at night often joined the shep-
> herd's camps. Sometimes he went out in back country, away
> from the hateful white man, and lived the old hunter's life, ob-
> taining water from the roots of the Kurrajong-trees growing
> on the dry tableland to the west of the Upper Paroo. On an

excursion out there on one occasion I saw his tracks and the thick roots drained of their contents. Probably the untamable savage was close by, maybe our blackboy even saw him, but Baldy would hold no communication with the white race, though in return for the protection given and kindness shown to his people he kept the tacitly understood truce.[27]

On some stations formal understandings were reached between squatters and neighbouring blacks. A Queensland pioneer explained to a Parliamentary Committee in 1861 that he had met the local clans and reached an understanding, telling them that he was 'master on the open ground and they were masters of the scrub and the mountains'.[28] On Gamboola station on the Mitchell River Edward Palmer came to an agreement with the blacks of the district undertaking 'to protect them and give them a beast once a month or so – and let them have one side of the river to hunt upon'.[29] Blacks on Merivale Station in southern Queensland negotiated with the whites to secure the right to hunt and hold corroborees and similar agreements were reached on Woodstock and Jarvisfield Stations in north Queensland. On Strathdon in the Bowen district an Aboriginal woman who had lived on the station for a year acted as an intermediary between the local clans and Bode the resident squatter. The blacks agreed to stop killing cattle and threatening the stockmen while Bode promised his protection against the Native Police as well as hunting rights, free access to the river and supplies of blankets and steel axes. These examples are all from Queensland but it seems reasonable to assume that similar understandings were reached between pastoralists and blacks in many parts of the continent.

STOCKMEN AND CONCUBINES

Most squatters were only too willing to exploit the labour of the Aboriginal camps. Within a very short time young men were working with the stock and women in and around station homesteads. It is probable that the blacks' eagerness to work for the Europeans varied widely. There are many reports of Europeans using force to recruit and keep their workers and all over Australia young women were forced in concubinage. The evidence for this is overwhelming. Mr Justice Dashwood, the Government Resident of the Northern Territory, told a Select Committee of the South Australian Parliament in 1899 that the 'forcible taking away of lubras' was a commonplace of outback life. Police officers who had spent their whole careers on the frontier had told him 'how men on stations seeing lubras in the bush will pursue them, run them down on their horses, and take them away'.[30] A policeman based at Camooweal said that he felt sure:

> that if half the young lubras now being detained (I won't call it kept, for I know most of them would clear away if they could) were approached on the subject, they would say that they were run down by station blackguards on horseback, and taken to the stations for licentious purposes, and there kept more like slaves than anything else. I have heard it said that these same lubras have been locked up for weeks at a time – anyway whilst their heartless persecutors have been mustering cattle on their respective runs. Some, I have heard take these lubras with them, but take the precaution to tie them up securely for the night to prevent them escaping.[31]

Young men were kidnapped too and taken to be 'trained up' for stockwork. But evidence of a voluntary acceptance of pastoral work can also be found. A squatter settled near Bowen explained in 1869 that he had allowed local clans to camp near water holes close to his head station and that on the following day a few men had come up on their own accord and joined his kanaka servants at their work, although 'they were more in the way than of service'.[32] Cattle stations probably provided more congenial work for Aboriginal men than any other European undertaking with the possible exception of the maritime industries for sea-coast peoples. There was considerable overlap between the old economy and the new. Local knowledge, the ability to track and to live off the land; all of these were carried over into the life of the Aboriginal stockman. Knowledge of sheep and cattle gained before coming in was rapidly augmented in minds trained to closely observe animal behaviour. 'I don't know what we pioneers should have done without the blacks', wrote a

Queensland pioneer cattleman in 1884, 'for they can't be beat at looking after horses and cattle'.[33] Horse-riding was an exhilarating experience for people who had known no means of locomotion other than their own legs. 'Above all', a pioneer squatter wrote of the Burnett blacks in the 1850s, 'horse riding enchanted them'.[34] 'They are ambitious to learn to ride' Chewings observed of young Aborigines in Central Australia, 'and do not mind a few falls in acquiring the art'.[35]

The pastoral industry provided many young Aborigines with a role in the European economy in which they could find satisfaction and scope for both traditional and acquired skills. That it was not conducive to greater Aboriginal advance was due to the pull of traditional society on one side and the power of white prejudice on the other. Aboriginal workers were given little incentive to increase their efficiency. They were typically underpaid, given no formal training, were rarely praised and often bashed and kicked and whipped. Even when consideration replaced brutality the paternalism remained. The Thargomindah correspondent of the *Queenslander* provided an unblinking account of the situation of Aboriginal workers in the south-west of the colony in 1885. There were he wrote:

> On all stations ... in this western portion of Queensland a certain number of black boys and gins all employed, and it is difficult to see how stations could be worked without their assistance. The vast majority receive no remuneration, save tucker and clothes. They are, of course, bound by no agreements, but are talked of as my, or our ... niggers, and are not free to depart when they like. It is not considered etiquette on the part of one station to employ blacks belonging to another. Cases have occurred where blacks belonging to both sexes have been followed, brought back and punished for running away from their nominal employers. For the main part they are fairly well treated, clothed and fed.[36]

The pastoral industry was clearly a major determinant of the pattern of white-Aboriginal relations in many parts of the continent. Yet there were other areas where the first permanent white settlers were not squatters but farmers, miners, missionaries, sealers, pearlers and townsmen.

Chapter 7

OTHER FRONTIERS

SEA COASTS

Relations between coastal clans and sea-faring Europeans provide an interesting contrast to contact on the land frontier. There were some important differences. Europeans who landed from ships were usually in quite small parties – no more than could conveniently fit into a rowing boat. They were necessarily on foot and had little knowledge of the terrain beyond the tree line or the dunes. The journey by dinghy both to and from the shore was often hazardous, doubly so if potentially hostile blacks were standing on the beach. While stretching uncertain sea legs they could not hope to catch up with local blacks seeking to avoid them either by flight or conceal- ment. When Europeans came upon parties of Aborigines we can as- sume that it was because the blacks had made a deliberate decision to meet the white men. Though there were violent skirmishes on every part of the Australian coast peaceful contact may have been more common on the shore than it was inland. Both parties stood to benefit from amicable meetings – the Europeans could obtain water, local intelligence and perhaps sexual release; the Aborigines access to the white man's goods without the disadvantages of per- manent European settlement. The belief that meetings on the coast were potentially peaceful seems to have been established among the Europeans sailing remote shores and may have influenced their behaviour. Searcey, the Northern Territory pioneer, wrote in 1905, that it was a 'well known fact' that whites from the sea were 'better received than those coming from inland'.[1]

Aborigines participated in maritime industries from the early years of European settlement. They were involved in sealing and bay-whaling around the southern coasts during the first half of the nineteenth century and in pearling and bêche de mer gathering around in the northern ones during the second half of the nineteenth century and the early years of the twentieth century. Sea-based industries were probably less disruptive of Aboriginal life than either mining or pastoralism. The Europeans who harvested the sea had no need for land other than small plots for bay-whaling stations and bêche de mer processing depots. Bay whaling fitted easily into accustomed patterns of life along the southern coasts. Coastal clans were used to gathering in large numbers to eat whales cast up on the beaches and may have assumed, as they had done in the past, that Aboriginal magic was responsible for bringing the whales into shore. The Europeans for their part were able to supply local Aborigines with large quantities of unwanted whale flesh. Around the northern coasts from the north-west of Western Australia to the Gulf of Carpentaria the European search for bêche de mer would have been immediately comprehensible to clans who had seen for centuries the seasonal coming and going of the Macassar men.

While sealers, pearlers and whalers had no hunger for land they often relied heavily on Aboriginal labour for the profitability, and even the survival, of their industries. Bass Strait sealers depended on Aboriginal women from northern Tasmanian clans while at some of the bay-whaling stations Aboriginal crews manned rowing boats, receiving the same pay, or share of the profits, as the whites. The Commissioner for Crown Lands in the Monaro wrote in 1842 of three boats crewed by blacks at Twofold Bay. They were:

> stationed on the opposite side of the bay to the other fishermen and they adopted the same habits as the whites. They lived in huts, slept in beds, used utensils in cooking, and made the flour

into bread; but as soon as the fishing season was over, they all
returned to their tribes in the bush.[2]

In northern Australia Aborigines and Torres Strait Islanders were
even more extensively employed. During the last quarter of the
nineteenth century a thousand or more blacks a year worked during
the pearling and bêche de mer seasons.

Traditional expertise was carried over into the maritime trades
much as it was on the pastoral frontier. Local knowledge of the location of beds of shell launched the north-western pearling industry.
Aboriginal skill and endurance in the water ensured its success on
both the east and west coasts until the diving dress was generally
adopted in the 1880s. The expertise of the Tasmanian women on
both sea and land allowed the European sealers to survive on bleak
Bass Strait islands. James Kelly observed their hunting techniques
when on Tasmania's east coast in 1816. The women walked to the
edge of the water and wet themselves all over to prevent the seals
from smelling them. They swam to the rocks where the seals were
lying and, keeping to the wind-ward, they crept up to the reclining
animals and lay perfectly still allowing the seals to inspect them:

> The women went through the same motions as the seal, holding
> up their left elbow and scratching themselves with their left
> hand, taking and keeping the club firm in their right ready for
> the attack. The seals seemed very cautious, now and then lifting
> up their heads and looking round, scratching themselves as be-
> fore and lying down again, the women still imitating every move-
> ment as nearly as possible. After they had lain upon the rocks for
> nearly an hour, the sea occasionally washing over them ... all of
> a sudden the women rose up on their seats, their clubs lifted up
> at arms length, each struck a seal on the nose and killed him.[3]

The predominantly male work force of the northern maritime
industries sought Aboriginal and Torres Strait Island women for
sexual gratification. The degree to which blacks assisted them in
this pursuit varied widely according to time and local circumstances. On some occasions Europeans abducted women and kept
them by force just as their land-based counterparts did on the pastoral frontier. Torres Strait Islanders told a government official in

1882 that the white men had so ill-treated their women in the past that when a boat was sighted the young women were buried in the sand and kept there until the Europeans sailed away. Yet at other times local communities actively participated in the trade extracting the best possible deal for the services of their women. On both the northwest coast and around Cape York the pearling fleets supported a large and lucrative prostitution industry. Aboriginal clans reorganized their pattern of migration to travel down to the sea coast when the pearling luggers were laid up for the monsoon season and remained there until they sailed away again. The demand for the young women was such that all other clan members could live off the proceeds of their copulation for the duration of the lay-up season.

The complexity of Aboriginal motivation was apparent also in the recruitment of labour for the sea-based industries. Force and fraud played a major role in the beginning as it had done in the early years of the labour trade in Melanesia. There is considerable evidence of this from all parts of the continent. In the papers of the Tasmanian settler, J. E. Calder, there is reference to a group of island men who sailed to Port Phillip during the 1820s where they enticed a party of young women on board and then sailed for the Bass Strait Islands where the women were bartered for seal skins. A pioneer of the north-west coast of Western Australia remarked that the method of obtaining labour for the local pearling industry was 'better imagined than described'; it was 'sufficient to say that it was crude'.[4] Having been obtained in diverse ways the blacks were kept for as long as possible. They were 'planted' on off-shore islands on both the north-west and north-east coast during the off-season and picked up when the luggers put to sea again; they were abandoned in coastal towns like Broome, or Thursday Island or Cooktown, far from home, where further recruitment was the only means of survival.

But force and fraud probably became less important with time. The Queensland and Western Australian Governments began to exercise some supervision around the northern coast from the 1880s and the blacks themselves rapidly grew wise to the ways of the white men. Force and fraud after all could only work once or twice. To suppose otherwise is to assume that the Aborigines were unable to learn from experience. The essential weakness of the European position must be re-emphasised, along with a realistic assessment of what had to be done to recruit labour by force. The white men had to come ashore on a little known coast; protect themselves against attack; catch observant and fleet footed blacks on their own intimately known territory; secure captives; and then take them off the coast in small rowing boats. If the trade were to continue in the use of force this operation would have to be repeated many times over.

It is apparent that many blacks chose to work on the pearling luggers and bêche de mer boats – incited by their own curiosity, a desire to gain European goods, or to escape punishment or other trouble at home. After recent research on the North Queensland coast Anderson concluded that the relationship between the Aborigines and the lugger captains was not entirely a matter of one-way exploitation. For the blacks employment on the boats was often 'a way out of strife and tension on the domestic scene'. He concluded that there was evidence 'of men escaping the consequences of an adulterous affair, and of men dissolving an unsuccessful or undesirable marriage by simply going out on a lugger'.[5] The Europeans were, then, often used for Aboriginal ends. They provided a new means to implement an old custom – the traditional device of 'resolution of conflict by fission'.[6]

The experience of labour on the luggers seems to have been woven into traditional patterns of life in other ways as well. The missionary E. R. Gribble noted how at Yarrabah the return of the men from the pearling fleets at the beginning of the wet season was marked by a distinctive ceremony. They were, he wrote:

> given a great welcome by the natives, and a peculiar ceremony was gone through on the arrival, as they came along the beach in a compact body, they were met by John and an old man, who conducted them along until they sighted the camps, they then stopped short, and facing each other gave a shout, then facing about marched on, each man singing and beating time with a

spear on a shield; getting close to the camps a woman met them, bearing in her hands two green boughs, and, dancing along in front of them, led them to a cleared space in front of the little huts ... here they stopped, and standing in a circle continued singing, with the woman dancing round the circle, shaking the boughs over their heads until another woman from a group standing near rushed up, and putting her head over the shoulder of one of the men gave a yell and this concluded the ceremony.[7]

Another important aspect of recruitment was the co-operation of influential older men with the Europeans in order to encourage young men, and young women in some places, to ship with the whites. There is evidence of this from several parts of the continent. In her study of white-Aboriginal relations in Tasmania Ryan has drawn a clear picture of the relations between the Bass Strait sealers and the clans of the north-east coast. The blacks altered their pattern of movement about their territory remaining on the coast throughout the summer in order to keep in contact with the Europeans who bartered hunting dogs and other commodities for the temporary use of young women for their labour and sexual favours. The coastal people abducted women from traditionally hostile clans to meet increasing demands from the Europeans. This picture of relations between the sealers and the Tasmanians was confirmed by such visitors to Bass Strait as James Kelly in 1817 and William Hovell and Dumont Durville during the 1820s. Hovell met sealers and their Aboriginal concubines and discovered that:

> the way these men get those Girls and Women is by purchasing or more properly speaking bartering for them of the different chiefs along the East Coast of Van Diemens Land.[8]

Some girls, he believed, left without regret; others resisted strongly but were forced by the older men to go with the Europeans.

The situation on the north coast later in the century seems to have been very similar. Young men were encouraged to sail with the whites by the old men who received a commission from the lugger captains. When demand was high the elders could extract substantial rewards. During the 1902 season, for instance, officials at Thursday Island issued permits for 990 recruits but only 334 were forthcoming. W. E. Roth, the Northern Protector of Aborigines, noted how the blacks had taken advantage of this situation to demand large bonuses of tobacco and flour in advance. The desire of the old men to gain exclusive possession of the young women was possibly another reason to send the youths away with the Europeans. Roth concluded that about one third of recruits were married and on their return they usually found their wives living with one or other of the old men. Anderson's work on the oral history of Bloomfield River people led him to the belief that the old men had used the pearling luggers:

> to increase their own power and wealth by acting as recruiters of young males for work on the boats – a service for which the old men received tobacco, flour and decreased competition for wives.[9]

Working conditions in the maritime industries were often harsh and there was a high mortality rate from disease, personal violence and work-related accidents. Yet many Europeans quickly appreciated that good conditions and fair treatment resulted in greater productivity and certainly less tension on the cramped and stinking luggers. On the other hand the Aborigines and Torres Strait Islanders were more than passive units of labour. They could use the universal stratagems of forced and unwilling workers – going slow, feigning sickness, losing and breaking equipment or simply refusing to find shell under the water. As Europeans rarely dived they were ultimately at the mercy of the blacks who did. A pioneer of the north-western pearling industry wrote in 1886 that 'a kind of freemasonry exists between the men'. At times they agreed amongst themselves not to bring up shell. He referred to a 'notable instance' when divers of four ships declared for days that they could find no shell. When eventually Malay divers were sent down they found the shell stacked in heaps on the bottom.

Aborigines and Torres Strait Islanders were in many respects the experts about coastal waters. European and Asian skippers often came to depend on their judgement. The blacks made many of the day to day decisions about diving in much the same way that Aboriginal stockmen determined many questions relating to the management of cattle herds. In fact European pearlers and bêche de mer seekers were probably more dependent on their black assistants when out on the coral reefs than were the squatters on their inland pastoral stations. An official report of 1880 on the Torres Strait pearl fishery concluded that the Aborigines and Islanders were 'quite capable of taking care of themselves'. In fact the divers had:

> almost entirely their own way, and will not bear any superintendence from the whites whilst fishing, so that the practical part of the getting of the shell i.e. the management of the boats, the locality of the fishing, the times of fishing, besides the actual gathering of the shell is entirely left to the divers.[11]

But the prevalence of peaceful contact around the coasts should not obscure the significance of Aboriginal resistance to sea-faring Europeans. It took many forms. Ships lying at anchor in estuaries or close inshore were raided in many parts of the continent. This was particularly common along the Queensland coast where the sheltered, island studded, waters inside the Barrier Reef gave Aborigines an offshore mobility unmatched elsewhere. The use of outrigger canoes in Torres Strait and along the north-east coast increased the range of blacks living along shore lines and on nearby islands. Reef waters were hazardous at night and ships frequently anchored till dawn leaving them vulnerable to nocturnal attack. This was particularly so in such waterways as the Whitsunday and Hinchinbrook Passages.

Aborigines and Torres Strait Islanders (and Papuans as well) launched numerous attacks on Europeans living at isolated bêche de mer stations. Many young men recruited for pearling or bêche de mer voyages eventually turned on the white men killing them or throwing them overboard and then sailed the commandeered vessel back to their mainland or island homes. It was often done simply to get home, sometimes long after an agreed contract period had expired. But boats were also taken to run them ashore, strip them of everything useful and then scuttle or burn them. It appears that eventually groups of young Aborigines and Islanders set out systematically to recruit, kill the Europeans or Asians, take the boat and then if possible repeat the process.

Attacks on the Europeans in the bêche de mer and pearling industries around about Torres Strait were serious enough to create
deep concern in coastal communities. A writer in the *Cooktown
Independent* claimed in 1890 that in the previous sixteen years at
least 100 Europeans who had sailed from the port had been killed
by Aborigines, Islanders and Papuans and many others, as a consequence, had been 'driven back upon southern civilization'.[12] The
accuracy of this assertion is difficult to determine. Yet similar anxiety about Aboriginal resistance was voiced in official government
reports. One on the fisheries of North Queensland published in
1890 was eloquent with European disquiet:

> Of late years, and in the Torres Straits district more particularly,
> outrages committed by these labourers; in which the boat-owners
> or their agents have been assaulted and lost their lives, or the
> boats with stores on board have been stolen, have become so fre-
> quent as to paralyse the industry to a very large extent.[13]

FARMING DISTRICTS

Fertile, well watered river valleys notch the east coast of Australia. In
most of them Aboriginal clans had their first prolonged contact with
timber getters cutting cedar and other valuable trees in sub-tropical
and tropical rain forest. They, in turn, were followed by small farmers
who grew potatoes, maize, bananas and other crops in patches of
cleared land. The overall pattern of race relations was similar to that
on the pastoral frontier but there were some significant differences
which require comment. Heavy forest provided food and sanctuary for
resident clans for many years in some places and slowed down the impact of the Europeans although customary patterns of clan migration
and local ecologies were disrupted. Water was normally much easier to
find than in the dry inland and many local groups continued to have
access to estuaries, stretches of coastline, and off-shore islands.

Conflict commonly arose over the question of access to
European crops. Blacks not only refused to concede that white
farmers had suddenly become the 'owners' of small pockets of clan

territory, they also attempted to secure a share of the new vegetable foods which grew there. The increasing pressure on traditional food supplies intensified their determination to harvest the new crops growing on their land. Whenever they could they reaped 'by stealth the product of a tract of land they are themselves too indolent to cultivate'[14] as the *Sydney Gazette* complained in 1805. Inter-racial tension was often seasonal, culminating when grain crops ripened and potatoes matured. 'These enormities', noted the same paper 'are periodical in their commencement'; the blacks were most threatening 'when the fields of ripened maize were open to their pillage'.[15]

Aboriginal raids on the crops often involved many hands. Several acres of maize were taken in one night from a Moreton Bay farm in 1846 and there were similar raids on the corn crop on the Don River in the 1870s, farmers losing 100 bushels or more in a single week. On the Herbert River a few years later a farmer complained that he had lost all his banana crop, one half and one third of successive corn crops, and all of a third one, while from another property the local blacks took all the sweet potatoes, most of the corn and a hundred bunches of bananas. A Barron Valley selector wrote to the *Herberton Advertiser* in 1888 detailing the impact of black raids on his property:

> I deem it my duty to make known to intending settlers the losses, through blacks, I have suffered during the present year. On January 12th they visited my selection; stole corn, and were shot at leaving a dilly bag and bone bodkin, used for husking corn, behind them. On the 13th they again stole corn ... on nine occasions between the 12th of January and April 5th the niggers stole corn. On the 14th April, 23rd and 30th May, and June 4th, they stole corn. Off 4 acres planted in July I gathered 10 bushels; off 4 acres planted in November 6 bushels; and off 2 acres in January I got nothing – the niggers had the rest. They have now started removing English potatoes and pumpkin.[16]

During successful raids on European crops the Aborigines clearly employed many of their traditional hunting skills – stealth, patience and the ability to move without sound. Farmers at Bowen complained in 1873 that the blacks had succeeded in taking crops growing within ten yards of their huts. The *Wild River Times* reported in 1887 that tents were raided while selectors were working only fifteen paces away. The Commissioner for Crown Lands at Maryborough explained in a letter to his superior in Sydney in 1852 that the local clans had taken his sweet potatoes despite a watchdog and a paling fence six and a half feet high. He had, he said, found blacks actually 'lying within five yards' of his sitting room at 8:00 o'clock in the evening. They had been watching him write at his table while their companions 'dug the potatoes at about twenty yards further off down the hill'.[17] When Aborigines gathered potatoes they often carefully replaced the stalk and leaves. There were reports of this from places as widely separated as Albany, Portland and the Tasmanian Midlands. It is not clear if this was done simply to escape detection, as the Europeans assumed, or if it was related to the traditional practice of replacing parts of yam plants after harvest. But in his reminiscences of pioneering in Tasmania and Victoria G. T. Lloyd had no doubt about the deliberation involved in Aboriginal tactics. 'Potatoes were rooted up and carried off by the hundred weight', he wrote:

> whilst the cunning fellows re-arranged the ridges so neatly as to hide all appearances of their having been disturbed, erasing their footmarks also with brushwood as they retired. In this manner many industrious farmers found themselves most unaccountably mistaken in their estimate of their crop.[18]

Both Aboriginal and European population densities were higher in the fertile coastal valleys than on the pastoral frontier. Properties were very much smaller and European neighbours closer together. To be successful Aboriginal raids had to be stealthy and well organized and usually conducted at night. A writer in the *Wild River Times* observed in 1888 that the local blacks evinced 'a knowledge and cleverness in the manner in which they plan and carry out their raids', which, he concluded, 'could scarcely be rivalled by London cracksmen'.[19] Trickery and deception were called into play to secure the crops of vigilant resident selectors. In 1804 the *Sydney Gazette* reported that blacks on the Georges River had made a social call on a farmer's wife and kept her talking while others cleared a whole acre of corn and carried the cobs off in canoes. Eighty years later Atherton Tableland clans found a way to rob a German selector who had up till then foiled every attempt made on his crops. An Aborigine approached his hut making rude and insulting gestures. He took the bait and chased his tormentor into the nearby forest. While he was gone a small party moved quickly into his hut and took everything – food, clothes, tools and other personal possessions. The fate of the impulsive German selector illustrated the fact that in many respects the conflict between white and black in small farming districts was more evenly balanced than in all but the most marginal pastoral country and much more even than on the mineral fields of north Australia.

GOLD RUSHES

In most parts of Australia mineral discoveries were made after the initial phase of settlement. Miners typically entered districts where Aborigines had already undergone considerable acculturation and where overt resistance had been crushed. But in north Queensland and in one or two parts of Western Australia miners leap-frogged ahead of the most remote pastoral stations and came into contact with clans whose members had never experienced permanent white settlement. The Gilbert was probably the first such field to be followed by the Etheridge, Mulgrave, Palmer, Hodgkinson and Croydon Rushes. Of all forms of European economic activity mining was probably the most devastating in its effects on resident Aborigines. Numbers alone were of decisive importance. Hundreds of miners arrived en masse at sites of promising finds. Even on small fields the Europeans rapidly outnumbered local clans and prospecting parties fossicked their way into the remotest corners of Aboriginal territory. Innumerable sacred sites must have been desecrated as the Europeans scrambled across the ancient landscape in their frenetic search for mineral wealth. The impact of alluvial miners on the environment was massive and immediate – they gouged up the soil, polluted the streams, pillaged nearby stands of timber. The average mining camp had relatively few animals which could have compensated local Aborigines for the destruction of vegetable food and the shooting and driving away of indigenous animals.

Mineral rushes put unrelenting pressure on the Aborigines forcing them to seek safety in whatever sanctuary of scrub or mountain left to them. The European impact was exacerbated by the long dry season of north Australia which must have been a lean time for local blacks even before the whites arrived. Of all the European activities mining must have appeared to be the least rational, the most incomprehensible. A correspondent writing from the Etheridge field believed that the local Aborigines were very curious 'as to what the white men were rooting up the sand and soil for'. Their first belief, he remarked:

> was that the object was something to eat, and, as the prospectors proceeded further up the river, down they would come, and commence rooting also in the abandoned holes. This they did perseveringly as the prospectors could see on their way down the river again.[20]

Miners felt little need to accommodate the blacks. Unlike squatters and farmers who were settling on the land the diggers were transients without commitment to the soil they so industriously turned up. They had little use for Aboriginal labour and the preponderance of European numbers obviated the need for the sort of negotiation noted on the pastoral frontier. They often lived in canvas and galvanized iron packed in from the coast rather than in bark huts made from nearby trees; they ate and drank commodities produced in factories in Sydney or Melbourne or even the northern hemisphere and rarely developed the sort of relationship with the environment which elsewhere led Europeans to an appreciation of indigenous knowledge and expertise.

Blacks in the mining areas were often forced into resistance from the earliest period of European intrusion. Violence did not escalate slowly out of personal vendetta as in many districts of older settlement; in many places it was open and indiscriminate from the start.

The local clans developed tactics to deal with the specific problems of the mining frontier. They made frequent attacks on the bullock teams supplying the remote mine fields, choosing night time for raids at known staging points along the dray roads and they speared large numbers of horses both to immobilize the Europeans and to eat their large animals. Sudden, well organized raids were launched against prospecting parties in the remoter parts of the mineral fields. Tents were constantly robbed, silently and skilfully, while miners worked nearby claims. So persistent were these robberies that it became customary on northern fields for one man to remain in camp during working hours to guard the tent. But despite their spirited resistance mining pushed the Aborigines to the edge of starvation more rapidly than any other European activity giving their attacks a desperation not often matched in other parts of the continent. 'The white men occupy their only hunting grounds', wrote a Palmer River resident in 1877, 'and in default of the fish, roots and game of the waterholes and creek bottoms, they are in a manner compelled to eat horses and bullocks'.[21] Aborigines presented, 'a very emaciated appearance, as a rule. They appeared to be in very great distress and were, in many cases, starving.'[22]

MISSION STATIONS

During the last quarter of the nineteenth century Aborigines in a number of localities in northern Australia had their first continuous contact with missionaries rather than with pastoralists, pearlers or miners. This was true at Yarrabah, Bloomfield, and Hopevale on the east coast of Cape York and Mapoon and Weipa on the Gulf of Carpentaria; of Daly River and Beagle Bay in the North West; and of Hermannsburg in the Centre. The relations between Aborigines and pioneer missionaries were exceptional enough to merit a brief mention.

The reaction of local clans to the sudden appearance of missionaries appears to have followed a common pattern. After cautious surveillance from a distance one or two men ventured to meet the white people. Gradually the numbers visiting the missionaries increased and when mutual confidence had been established women and children followed their men folk into the embryonic stations. Individual visits were prolonged till eventually semi-permanent camps developed on the mission reserves and young children and old people were left behind while their kinsfolk faced the rigours and dangers of the bush. The greatest advantage of the missions was that they provided a sanctuary from the depredations of white pastoralists, miners or pearl fishers and from those of traditional Aboriginal enemies as well. Both black and white foes were constrained from attacking clans actually camped within reach of the missionaries.

Blacks who lived for part of the time on mission reserves seem to have carefully chosen the time of their visits to coincide with the leanest and least pleasant period in the bush – the dry season around Hermannsburg, the time of the cool, wet south-easterlies on the east coast of Cape York. Poland, the German missionary from Hopevale, wrote realistically of what motivated local clans to come into the mission:

> April! Australian Autumn. Not much more fruit to be gathered in the bush. The cold wind makes fishing harder and less rewarding. The natives and their dogs are getting thinner. They are beginning to feel cold, their tobacco is almost at an end. So they have to make the bitter decision to give up their free and easy life for a while and go to the mission station and work there.[23]

The missionaries were important as a source of desired European commodities like steel axes, flour and especially tobacco. Work on the mission station and attendance at often incomprehensible prayer meetings was an accepted price to pay for access to them. But the blacks soon learnt how to bargain for more generous supplies. A local clansman told the Trappists at Beagle Bay that it was a case of 'no more tobacco, no more 'allelulia'.[24] The blacks were able to play the missionaries off against the other Europeans, quickly appreciating the political possibilities inherent in the situation where different groups of white men were pursuing irreconcilable objectives. 'They do not like working in the fields', noted a north Queensland missionary, and they consider that 'our issues of food and tobacco are not very generous'. The Aborigines asked him pointedly, 'Does the One up in Heaven tell you to give us so little?'[25] The missionary retorted that the gospel taught that he who did not work would not eat. With that the blacks replied by praising the townspeople of Cooktown for their generosity to the blacks.

Whatever success the missionaries had with Aboriginal children the adults strongly resisted the attempts to proselytise them. 'They hold so firmly to their fables', wrote Kempe of the Hermannsburg blacks, 'that they have already told us straight out that we tell them nothing but lies'.[26] At about much the same time Poland was writing of his difficulties with the Aborigines at Hopevale. He had endeavoured to explain the significance of Christmas but the adults looked at him with an 'air of utter disbelief'. They said mockingly that their ears were blocked to his message because they had to sleep on the ground all the time.[27]

But blacks often developed the ability to appease the missionaries and keep on good terms with them. Poland gave an account of an exchange he had with a group of men just returned from a fishing trip. They had explained how the eldest member of the party had tied up the wind to facilitate their journey and that he could also make rain. The discussion continued with the missionary exclaiming:

> 'Oh, don't talk such rubbish, I am telling you the truth; only God can let the rain come'.
> 'Of course he is right', says the rainmaker and looks mockingly at his friends.
> 'Be quiet and don't mock him', says another one a little anxiously.
> 'Don't make him angry', another one repeats.
> 'He may not give us any tobacco otherwise'.
> 'Now let him talk!', exclaims one man, 'haven't I been telling you all along? He talks well and we ought to stay with him'.[28]

Poland concluded ruefully that the 'bored look' on the face of the last speaker left him in no doubt about the total insincerity of the statement. On other occasions the Aborigines deliberately played down to the low opinions of their ability held by the missionaries. 'We blacks simply can't learn', missionary Hoerlein was told at Bloomfield, 'our heads are too hard. Nothing ever goes in. Learning is only for white people like you.'[29] The missionary's task was all the more difficult because the Aborigines often thought that by letting their children receive instruction they were actually working for the benefit of the white men. The experience of the German missionaries at Moreton Bay in the 1840s was typical of misunderstanding apparent elsewhere. The mission diary for May 1842 contained the passage:

> they consider still their attendance a labour for us, from which they suppose we derive advantage and threaten us sometimes, when they are not quite pleased, no more to work in the school for us.[30]

Aborigines found many advantages in the missionary presence, especially in those areas where they continued to have ready access to their own country and the food it provided. But conflict emerged in regard to the education of the children and the questions of marriage and burial where Christian and Aboriginal traditions met head-on. The missionaries attempted to suppress traditional mortuary ceremonies and endeavoured to prevent the tribal marriages of young girls who had grown up on the stations, although it is quite likely that the girls sometimes used the missionaries in order to avoid the dictates of the old men. E. R. Gribble described the tension resulting from the struggle over who would bury the body of a little girl who died at Yarrabah in 1895:

> After placing it in the coffin I waited some time before putting on the lid; one old woman stepped up and put an old garment and several pieces of bark into the coffin. Then I placed the lid on, and as soon as I did so the old women set up a most fearful din, and acted in a truly disgusting manner, rolling in the sand, throwing it at the coffin and over each other ... They did not want the whites to have anything to do with the dead.[31]

The missions set up in remote localities in the late nineteenth century did shield the Aborigines from some of the worst excesses of frontier contact. It is probable that around the missions the decline of the population was less dramatic, and that demographic recovery occurred sooner, than in many other parts of the continent: health on the missions was normally better than in the typical fringe camp. But the missionaries mounted an intellectual challenge to Aboriginal society and culture far more deliberate, and consistent, than any other group of Europeans in colonial Australia. It was most apparent in the separation of children and parents by the establishment of dormitories which became common on Australian missions established during the late nineteenth century and early twentieth. Developments at Yarrabah during the 1890s illustrated a common trend. Gribble summed up his objectives in a number of reports written in the middle of the decade. In the first one of September 1895 he explained that the dormitory was nearing completion, an event eagerly awaited because the Europeans would 'then have the children more under control'. By having them 'under lock and key at night' the mission staff would be able to 'prevent the camp natives taking them off at all hours for corroborees etc'.[32] The old people objected strongly to the incarceration of the children, complaining that the boys and girls were 'getting too much like white fellow.'[33] News of the missionaries' behaviour spread quickly to clans living in the hinterland. Gribble described an incident which took place a few months after the opening of the dormitory. He was travelling in the bush with two black guides some distance away from Yarrabah. The party approached a camp on a creek bank just before sundown. The local men came up to the visitors and interrogated the two guides. Gribble described the following exchange:

> At first little notice was taken of me, the people being busy questioning the two boys while I stood a little apart. Presently one man asked Harry who I was, and on his saying quietly the one word 'Missionary', the effect was wonderful to behold, the women gave me one look full of fear, then clasping their children tightly, vanished; the men stood their ground, but looked as if they would like the ground to open and swallow either me or themselves.[34]

Gribble subsequently learned the reason for the hostile reception. Aborigines for miles around had heard of the mission, he wrote, and the idea was 'among them that we intend taking their children forcibly from them'.[35]

FRONTIER TOWNS

Colonial towns played an important role in the history of contact and acculturation. Almost every European community on the continent had at least one fringe camp at some time in its history. Many blacks were driven into these camps just as Aborigines elsewhere were forced onto pastoral stations by the violence of the bush and dwindling indigenous food supplies. 'They are driven from many stations in the bush', wrote a government official in Rockhampton in the 1860s, 'and their dogs which they use for hunting are poisoned ... so that the use of their own country is literally taken away from them'.[36] A similar situation was outlined by an Aboriginal woman interviewed in the bush near Cooktown in 1899. She was camped with a small family group which had just returned from town with meat and bread. When asked why she and her kin did not go into the bush and live off the land she replied: 'White fellow along a yarraman, too much break him spear, burn yams, cut him old man with whip, white man too much kill him Kangaroo.'[37]

But while some Aborigines were pushed in towards the towns others went willingly in the same direction. Curiosity enticed many as did the possibilities for gathering food and tobacco by scavenging, begging, casual labour and prostitution. The larger towns were able to supply a considerable amount of food for people who were accustomed to making use of almost everything edible in their environment. The outskirts of the pioneer towns became convenient locations for clans to meet and hold ceremonies, battles, corroborees and initiations. They could draw on both the town and neighbouring bush for food and were safer from attack than in the hinterland. It seems probable that clans frequently changed the venue of regular gatherings to take advantage of the towns and even altered ceremonial calendars to coincide with such European occasions as the distribution of blankets to Aborigines on Queen Victoria's birthday, 24 May. E. J. Eyre observed the movement of South Australian clans in towards Adelaide in the 1840s. He wrote that:

> Large towns are frequently the centre of meeting for many, and very distant tribes. The facility of obtaining scraps by begging, small rewards for trifling jobs of work, donations from the charitable, and a variety of broken victuals, offal etc enable them to collect in large numbers, and indulge to the uttermost their curiosity in observing the novelties around them, in meeting strange tribes, and joining them either in war or festivity, in procuring tools, clothes etc to carry back and barter in their own districts ... Thus, Adelaide is nearly always occupied by tribes from one part or another of the country: on an average, it will support probably six hundred in the way I have described, though occasionally eight hundred have met there.[38]

The conviviality of fringe camps may have attracted Aborigines in from the bush. The interest was not the European settlement as such but the large Aboriginal gatherings which it made possible. As with so many other features of contact history the blacks appear to have used the Europeans and their towns for their own ends. The anthropologist W. E. H. Stanner remarked that in traditional society:

> the most prized goods of life were to be found, and were deliberately sought, in large associations. Everywhere, it seems, there was a propensity for bands to foregather as long as physical conditions allowed and sociability persisted.[39]

Complaints from townspeople all over Australia emphasised the constant activity of the fringe camps; the succession of corroborees, ceremonies and fighting. 'One night there is a marriage, another a death, and another a pitched battle', wrote a Darwin resident in 1874, 'there is always some occasion for noise and riot'.[40]

The acute problems which developed in the fringe camps – disease, malnutrition, addiction to alcohol or opium, the psychological tensions of sedentary living – were widely reported by European observers. Yet the dangers may not have been immediately apparent to the blacks who set up camp for the first time on the outskirts of

colonial towns. Campsites rarely began as permanent homes, the tran-
sition from nomadism to sedentary living often took a generation or
more. 'Townblacks' shifted camp regularly even though distances
moved were increasingly confined within a shrinking circle of territory.
Fringe dwellers continued to shift from places where kin had died in
much the same way as they had done before the white men came and
such sites may never have been re-occupied.

Though European men wore deep tracks to the blacks' camps on
their nocturnal search for sexual excitement the life of fringe-
dwelling communities continued without much interference from
the townspeople. The distance between town and camp probably
suited both the whites and the blacks. The two or three miles typically separating the two settlements allowed the Aborigines to continue with many aspects of traditional life which would have been
disrupted if they had lived closer to the Europeans. A recent study
of a part-Aboriginal community in southern inland Queensland reported the recollections of old people about their earlier life in the
camp on the outskirts of town. Despite the desperate poverty that
had characterised their situation what they remembered was 'the
warmth, lack of boredom, fewer responsibilities, having fun and
being together away from the prying eyes of whites'.[41]

One of the problems created for the blacks by the establishment
of European towns was the degree to which the traditional owners
of a town site could control the access of more distant clans to both
the town itself and the food and tobacco available there. This issue
was probably a major source of conflict all over the continent. The
'inside' clans appealed to tradition, the 'outsiders' felt that the arrival of the white men had radically altered the situation.
Moorhouse, the Protector of Aborigines in Adelaide, noted the tension between the local blacks and those coming in from the Murray
who told him they were 'intending to take over and expel Adelaide
blacks from town'. For their part the local people abused children
from the Murray clans who were going to school in Adelaide, ac-
cusing them of 'obtaining food in a territory to which they had no
hereditary right'.[42]

Conflict between Aborigines and settlers spilt over into the outskirts of a number of small pioneer townships. Blacks speared
horses and cattle and occasionally the citizens themselves close to
town and townspeople lived with high anxiety, loaded guns and
barricaded doors. In places like Maryborough, Cardwell and Port
Lincoln the fear of Aboriginal attack appeared to threaten the future of the settlements while acute anxiety about the local clans was
probably the major reason for the desertion of Gilberton in 1873.
Town blacks for their part appear to have used fringe camps as a
base for raids on sheep and cattle in rural hinterlands. After such an
excursion they returned quickly to the relative security of the town
where even the most ruthless squatters were constrained from ex-
acting revenge. 'The cunning fellows know they are safe in town'
wrote a Maryborough resident in 1867 'where it is next to impossible to catch them, and dispersing is not permissible'.[43]

In some towns the blacks became accomplished thieves and burglars combining their growing understanding of European society
with the stealth and patience of the traditional hunter. This development can best be illustrated by reference to Maryborough during the
first twenty years of its history. During the 1850s the resident
Commissioner for Crown Lands made many complaints about the
local black burglars. In 1855 he remarked that their movements were
so stealthy and they were 'such adepts in the Commission of robberies which they perpetrate during the night' that it was impossible
to detect them. The following year he noted that they were becoming 'very expert in house robberies'. They removed panes of glass to
release window catches, cut away sections of wall to loosen bolts,
put children through small openings to undo locked doors.[44] The
local paper observed some years later that black burglars behaved 'as
though they had served an apprentership in London or New York'.[45]
Food was the main objective, stores and drays the most common tar-
get. During six weeks in November–December 1855 there were
twenty six separate robberies in Maryborough which netted the local
blacks at least 1500 pounds of flour and 800 pounds of sugar as well
as meat, tea, clothes, bedding and utensils.

Yet it is likely that many blacks in fringe camps would have preferred to come to a negotiated settlement with the Europeans ensuring them of adequate food and protection from arbitrary violence. There was an incident in Rockhampton late in 1865 which had direct bearing on this question. A group of 'town blacks' demonstrated outside the home of the Police Magistrate. The local paper reported that 'they signified that peace and safety was only assured by the payment of a blackmail in the shape of flour, tobacco and white money.' It is intriguing to consider if such overtly political action was common but merely unreported or not even recognized as such by the white community. The response of the Rockhampton authorities was predictable. On hearing of the occurrence the police sergeant and two mounted troopers 'dispersed the vagabonds'.[46]

CONCLUSION

This is the first book to systematically explore the other side of the frontier, to turn Australian history, not upside down, but inside out. It establishes that it is possible to write Aboriginal history and present it to white Australians in such a way that they can understand black motives and appreciate the complexities of their tragic story. W. K. Hancock's judgement of 1930 that Aboriginal society was 'pathetically helpless'[1] when assailed by Europeans can be seen now as a travesty albeit still an influential one. Even today sympathetic whites speak of the blacks as the passive objects of European brutality or charity. Indeed many of the major themes of white history were mirrored on the other side of the frontier.

The Aboriginal response to invasion was much more positive, creative and complex than generations of white Australians have been taught to believe. The heroes of nationalist mythology had their little known black counterparts. The courage of European explorers pushing out into the interior was matched by that of the Aborigines who met them on the way and by others who travelled in towards the white men's settlements to observe and evaluate the interlopers. Epic journeys of discovery were not the preserve of white men. The explorer's fear of black savages was echoed by Aboriginal alarm about evil spirits and malignant magic. The improvisation and adaption of Europeans settling the land was paralleled by tribesmen who

grappled with a new world of experience on the fringes of white settlement. The stoical endurance of pioneer women was matched by
that of their black sisters who bore children and battled to keep them
alive in conditions of appalling adversity. All over the continent
Aborigines bled as profusely and died as bravely as white soldiers in
Australia's twentieth century wars.

In the long run black Australians will be our equals or our enemies. Unless they can identify with new and radical interpretations
of our history they will seek sustenance in the anti-colonial traditions of the third world. If they are unable to find a place of honour
in the white man's story of the past their loyalties will increasingly
dwell with the 'wretched of the earth'. But if the Aboriginal experience is to be woven into new interpretations of Australian history
changes will be necessary. We will have to deal with the blacks as
equals or they will see our sudden interest in their history as merely
another phase of our intellectual usurpation of their culture and traditions. We must give due weight to the Aboriginal perceptions of
ourselves and they will not be flattering. Aborigines have seen so
much of the dark underside of white Australia; they have lived with
it for two hundred years. Blacks believe that Europeans are hyp-
ocrites. 'You are very clever people', an old tribesman told W. E. H.
Stanner, 'very hard people, plenty humbug'.[2] In Aboriginal eyes the
whites were invaders who came preaching the virtues of private
property; people who talked much of British justice while unleashing a reign of terror and behaving like an ill-disciplined army of occupation once the invasion was effected; forcinators who pursued
black women in every fringe camp on the continent but in daylight
disowned both lovers and resulting offspring. Major figures of our
history will have to be reassessed – frontiersmen who lavished lead
on neighbouring clans; selectors who notched the handles of their
Colt revolvers as readily as they ring-barked rainforest trees; jolly
swagmen who at night became far from funny shagmen when they
staggered into blacks' camps. The high evaluation of explorers
needs amendment. They were usually dependent on the expertise of
their black guides; they followed Aboriginal paths, drank at their

wells; slept in their gunyahs and were often passed on from clan to clan by people who constantly monitored their progress through a landscape the Europeans chose to call a wilderness.

For many years white Australians have used Aboriginal words, symbols and designs to heighten their national distinctiveness and underline their separate identity. We can scarcely wonder if others judge us in this light and use our attitude to the Aboriginal historical experience as the acid test when they come to judge if white Australians have assimilated to the continent or are still colonists at heart. If we are unable to incorporate the black experience into our national heritage we will stand exposed as a people still emotionally chained to our nineteenth century British origins, ever the transplanted Europeans.

Much of Aboriginal history since 1788 is political history. Recent confrontations at Noonkanbah and Arukun are not isolated incidents but outcrops of a long range of experience reaching back to the beginnings of European settlement. The Tent Embassy of 1972 did not launch Aborigines into Australian politics but rather reminded white Australians of old truths temporarily forgotten. The questions at stake – land, ownership, development, progress – arrived with Governor Phillip and have been at the pivot of white-Aboriginal relations ever since. They are surely the most enduring issues of Australian politics and will in the long run prove to have been of much greater consequence than many questions which since the middle of last century claimed the attention of parliaments and public for a season or two.

Frontier violence was political violence. We cannot ignore it because it took place on the fringes of European settlement. Twenty thousand blacks were killed before federation. Their burial mound stands out as a landmark of awesome size on the peaceful plains of colonial history. If the bodies had been white our histories would be heavy with their story, a forest of monuments would celebrate their sacrifice. The much noted actions of rebel colonists are trifling in comparison. The Kellys and their kind, even Eureka diggers and Vinegar Hill convicts, are diminished when measured against the hundreds of clans who fought frontier settlers for well over a century. In parts of the continent the Aboriginal death toll overshadows even that of the overseas wars of the twentieth century. About 5,000 Europeans from Australia north of the Tropic of Capricorn died in the five wars between the outbreak of the Boer War and the end of the Vietnam engagement. But in a similar period – say the seventy years between the first settlement in north Queensland in 1861 and the early 1930s – as many as 10,000 blacks were killed in skirmishes with the Europeans in north Australia.

How, then, do we deal with the Aboriginal dead? White Australians frequently say 'all that' should be forgotten. But it will not be. It cannot be. Black memories are too deeply, too recently scarred. And forgetfulness is a strange prescription coming from a community which has revered the fallen warrior and emblazoned the phrase 'Lest We Forget' on monuments throughout the land. If the Aborigines are to enter our history 'on terms of most perfect equality', as Thomas Mitchell termed it, they will bring their dead with them and expect an honoured burial. So our embarrassment is compounded. Do we give up our cherished ceremonies or do we make room for the Aboriginal dead on our memorials, cenotaphs, boards of honour and even in the pantheon of national heroes? If we are to continue to celebrate the sacrifice of men and women who died for their country can we deny admission to fallen tribesmen? There is much in their story that Australians have traditionally admired. They were ever the underdogs, were always outgunned, yet frequently faced death without flinching. If they did not die for Australia as such they fell defending their homelands, their sacred sites, their way of life. What is more the blacks bled on their own soil and not half a world away furthering the strategic objectives of a distant Motherland whose influence must increasingly be seen as of transient importance in the history of the continent. Mother England has gone – the Empire too – yet black and white Australians have still to come to terms almost two hundred years after the British established their first beach-head at Sydney Cove.

NOTES

New Introduction

1 Henry Reynolds: *Frontier: Aborigines, Settlers and Land*, Allen and Unwin, Sydney 1987.
2 Henry Reynolds: *With the White People*, Penguin, Ringwood 1990.
3 Henry Reynolds: *The Other Side of the Frontier*, James Cook University of North Queensland 1981, p. 2.
4 Henry Reynolds: *Why Weren't We Told*, Viking, Ringwood 1999; and Penguin, Camberwell 2000.

5   *Subaltern Studies* I, Oxford University Press, Delhi 1981, p. vii.
6   *Subaltern Studies* III, Oxford University Press, Delhi 1984, p. viii.
7   Henry Reynolds: *The Other Side of the Frontier*, Penguin, Ringwood 1982, p. 2.
8   R. White: *The Middle Ground*, Cambridge University Press, Cambridge 1991.
9   Inga Clendinnen: *Dancing with Strangers*, Text Publishing, Melbourne 2003.
10 Henry Reynolds: *Nowhere People*, Viking, Camberwell 2005.
11 Henry Reynolds: *The Other Side of the Frontier*, 1981 edition, p. 99; 1982 edition, p. 122.
12 Keith Windschuttle: *The Fabrication of Aboriginal History*, Macleay Press, Sydney 2002.

1 Explorers and Before

1   Murray-Upper tapes, Black Oral History Collection: History Department, James Cook University.
2   G. F. Moore: *A Descriptive Vocabulary of the Language in Common Usage Amongst the Aborigines of West Australia*, London 1842, p. 108.
3   Murray-Upper tapes, Black Oral History Collection: James Cook University.
4   T. L. Mitchell: *Journal of an Expedition into the Interior of Tropical Australia*, London 1848, p. 325.
5   W. Hovell, Journal of a Journey from Lake George to Port Phillip, 1824–25, *Journal Royal Australian Historical Society*, Vol. 7, 1921, p. 371.
6   M. Doyle (ed.): *Extracts from the Letters and Journals of George Fletcher Moore*, London 1834, p. 110.
7   P. Warburton: *Journey across the Western Interior of Australia*, London, 1875 p. 252.
8   C. Smith: *The Booandick Tribe of South Australian Aborigines*, Adelaide 1880, p. 26.
9   Murray-Upper tapes, Black Oral History Collection: History Department, James Cook University.
10 W. E. Roth: *Ethnographical Studies Among the North-West-Central Queensland Aborigines*, Brisbane 1897, p. 137
11 W. E. H. Stanner: Ceremonial Economics of the Mulluk Mulluk and Madngella Tribes of the Daly River etc, *Oceania*, Vol. 4, No. 2, December 1933, p. 174.
12 N. Gunson (ed.): *Australian Reminiscences and Papers of L. E. Threlkeld* etc, 2 vols., Canberra 1974, Vol. 1, p. 48.
13 G. A. Robinson: Report of an Expedition to the Aboriginal Tribes of the Interior, March-August 1846, p. 25; G. A. Robinson Papers, Vol. 60. Mitchell Library (hereafter ML), MSS/7081.
14 G. Windsor-Earl: 'On the Aboriginal Tribes of the Northern Coast of Australia', *JRGS*, Vol. 16, 1846, p. 248.
15 D. R. Moore: The Australian & Papuan Frontier in the 1840's, unpublished mss, Australian Institute of Aboriginal Studies, p. 99.
16 J. Jardine, Somerset, to Governor Bowen, 1 March 1865 in F. J. Byerley (ed.): *Narrative of an Overland Expedition* etc, Brisbane 1867, p. 85.
17 G. Windsor-Earl, *op. cit.*, p. 248.
18 J. Oxley: *Journals of Two Expeditions*, p. 289.
19 'A Noted Blackfellow', *Adelaide Observer*, 14 June 1924.
20 Sydney 1834, p. xi.
21 T. L. Mitchell: *Three Expeditions into Eastern Australia*, 2 vols, London 1834, I, pp. 71–72.

22 A. H. Howitt: *Native Tribes of South East Australia*, London 1904, p. 695.
23 J. H. Tuckey: *An Account of a Voyage to Establish a Colony at Port Phillip* etc, London 1805, p. 168.
24 J. Oxley: *Journals of Two Expeditions*, London 1820, p. 328.
25 A. Searcey: *In Northern Seas*, Adelaide 1905, p. 23.
26 D. Roughsey: *Moon and Rainbow*, Sydney 1971, p. 13.
27 J. Morrell: *Sketch of a Residence*, Brisbane 1863, p. 14.
28 *Ibid.*, p. 15.
29 T. L. Mitchell: *Three Expeditions*, I, p. 248.
30 J. L. Stokes: *Discoveries in Australia* etc, 2 vols, London 1846, I, p. 252.
31 J. Morrell, *op. cit.*, p. 14.
32 E. J. Eyre: *Journals of Expeditions of Discovery* etc, 2 vols, London 1845, 2, p. 213.
33 J. Oxley: *Journals of Two Expeditions*, p. 171.
34 D. W. Carnegie: *Spinifex and Sand*, London 1898, pp. 239, 284.
35 C. Sturt: *Narrative of an Expedition into Central Australia*, 2 vols, London 1849, I, p. 315.
36 T. L. Mitchell: *Three Expeditions*, I, p. 129.
37 Report of the North-Western Exploring Expedition; *QVP*, 3, 1876, p. 375.
38 J. Oxley: *Journals of Two Expeditions*, p. 163.
39 J. L. Stokes: *Discoveries in Australia*, 2, p. 297.
40 J. B. Jukes: *Narrative of the Surveying Voyage of HMS Fly*, London 1847, p. 56.
41 J. Gilbert: *Diary*, ML/MSS 2587, p. 52.
42 J. F. Mann: *Eight Months With Dr. Leichhardt*, Sydney 1888, p. 30.
43 J. Gilbert: *Diary*, p. 51.
44 *Adelaide Observer*, 14 June 1924.
45 M. Labillardiere: *Voyage in Search of La Perouse, 1791–1794*, London 1800, pp. 300–301.
46 E. J. Eyre: *Journals of Expeditions* etc, 2, p. 211.
47 G. Blainey: *Triumph of the Nomads*, Melbourne 1975, p. 253.
48 E. S. Parker: *The Aborigines of Australia*, Melbourne 1854, p. 22.
49 E. Giles: *Australia Twice Traversed*, 2 vols, London 1889, 2, p. 282.
50 E. J. Eyre: *Journals of Expeditions* etc, 2, p. 216.
51 C. Sturt: *Narrative of an Expedition*, 2, p. 315.
52 T. L. Mitchell: *Journal of an Expedition*, p. 143.
53 L. Leichhardt: *Journal of an Overland Expedition*, p. 494.
54 C. Sturt: *Two Expeditions* etc, 2, p. 135.
55 *Diary & Letters of Sir C. H. Freemantle*, London 1928, p. 55.
56 G. B. Worgan: *Journal of a First Fleet Surgeon*, Sydney 1978, pp. 6–7.
57 B. Spencer: *Wanderings in Wild Australia*, 2 vols, London 1928, I, p. 239.
58 Murray-Upper tapes, Black Oral History Collection: History department, James Cook University.

2 Continuity and Change

1 Report of Protector of Aborigines, 3 June 1842, Colonial Secretary Letters Received 1842, South Australian Archives (hereafter SAA), GRG/24/6/483.
2 E. J. Eyre: *Journals of Expeditions of Discovery*, 2, p. 366.
3 J. L. Stokes: *Discoveries in Australia*, I, p. 60.
4 J. Morgan: *The Life and Adventures of William Buckley*, 2nd edition, London 1967 edited, C. E. Sayers, p. 21.
5 D. R. Moore: *Islanders and Aborigines at Cape York*, Canberra 1979, p. 143.

6   W. E. Roth: North Queensland Ethnography: Bulletin No. 5, *QVP*, 2, 1903, p. 492. See also C. W. Shurmann: *Vocabulary of the Parnkalla Language*, Adelaide 1844, pp. 72–73; L. E. Threlkeld: *An Australian Language*, Sydney 1892, Appendix D; G. F. Moore: *A Descriptive Vocabulary of the Language in Common Use Amongst the Aborigines of Western Australia*, London 1842, p. 28; W. Ridley: *Kamilaroi and Other Australian Languages*, 2nd edition, Sydney 1875, p. 17; C. G. Teichelmann: *Outlines of a Grammar, Vocabulary and Phraseology of the Aboriginal Language of South Australia*, Adelaide 1840, p. 39; E. Curr: *The Australian Race*, 3 vols, Melbourne 1883.
7   M. Eliade: *Australian Religions*, Ithaca 1973, pp. 60–61. See also: E. Kolig: 'Bi:N and Gadeja' etc, *Oceania*, 43, I, September 1972.
8   G. F. Moore: *A Descriptive Vocabulary*, p. 28.
9   Letter by 'Delta', *The Inquirer*, 11 May 1842.
10   G. Grey: *Journals of Two Expeditions of Discovery* etc, 2 vols, London 1841, 2, pp. 302–303.
11   Letter of Mr. T. Dodds, Cobham, 1 February 1839 in E. D. Cowan: 'Letters of Early Settlers', *WAHS*, 1, 1, 1927, p. 57.
12   G. Grey: *Journals of Two Expeditions*, 2, pp. 302–303.
13   F. Armstrong in *Perth Gazette*, 29 Oct. 1836.
14   G. F. Moore: *A Descriptive Vocabulary*, p. 28.
15   Diary of Dr. S. W. Viveash, 16 February 1840, Battye Library (hereafter BL) MSS, QB/VIV.
16   E. Shenton: 'Reminiscences of Perth 1830–1840', *WAHS*, 1, 1, 1927, p. 2.
17   C. Grey, *Journal of Two Expeditions*, 1, pp. 301–2.
18   E. J. Eyre: *Journals of Expeditions*, 2, p. 367.
19   E. D. Cowan: 'Letters of Early Settlers', p. 58.
20   W. E. Roth: North Queensland Ethnography Bulletin No. 5, p. 493.
21   J. Morgan: *The Life and Adventures of William Buckley*, p. 31.
22   29 October 1836.
23   Report of Protector of Aborigines, 30 June 1842, Colonial Secretary, Letters Received, SAA, GRG/24/6, p. 483.
24   Select Committee on the Native Mounted Police, *QVP*, 1861, p. 56.
25   *Ibid*, p. 57.
26   J. Morgan: *The Life of William Buckley* etc, p. 21.
27   Murray-Upper tapes, Black Oral History Collection: James Cook University.
28   6 October 1838.
29   *Perth Gazette*, 29 October 1836.
30   James Dredge to Bunting, 17 February 1840, James Dredge Notebook, La Trobe Library MSS, 421959.
31   E. D. Cowan: Letters of Early Settlers etc, p. 58.
32   Manners and Habits of the Aborigines of Western Australia, *Perth Gazette*, 29 October 1836.
33   Report of Protector of Aborigines, 30 June 1842, Colonial Secretary, Letters Received 1842, SAA, GRG/24/6/483.
34   21 July 1866.
35   E. Curr: *The Australian Race*, 1, p. 26.
36   L. E. Threlkeld: *An Australian Grammar* etc, p. xi.
37   George Frankland to Governor Arthur, 4 February 1829 in N. J. B. Plomley: *Friendly Mission*, p. 108.
38   Threlkeld's Account of Mission to the Aborigines of New South Wales, ML. MSS, Bonwick Transcripts, Box 52.
39   E. J. Eyre: *Journals of Expeditions* etc, 2, p. 240.

40 G. Taplin: *The Narrinyeri*, etc, Adelaide 1878, p. 30.
41 D. R. Moore: *Islanders and Aborigines*, pp. 199–200.
42 G. S. Lang: *The Aborigines of Australia*, Melbourne 1865, p. 28.
43 N. J. B. Plomley: *Friendly Mission*, Hobart 1966, p. 264.
44 23 May 1830.
45 Rhys Jones: 'Tasmanian Aborigines and Dogs', *Mankind*, 7, 1970, p. 270.
46 E. Curr: *The Australian Race*, 3, p. 193.
47 *Queenslander*, 20 May 1871.
48 *Ibid.*, 14 October 1871.
49 Report on Explorations in Cape York Peninsula, *QVP*, 2, 1881, p. 239.
50 D. F. Thomson: 'The Dugong Hunters of Cape York', *Journal Royal Anthropological Institute*, 64, 1934, p. 257.
51 G. Horne & G. Aiston: *Savage Life in Central Australia*, London 1928, p. 11.
52 Thomas to Robinson, 15 October 1840; Aboriginal Protectorate – Westernport; Victorian Public Records Office.
53 J. Jorgensen: 'A Shred of Autobiography', *Hobart Town Almanach and Van Diemens Land Annual*, 1838, p. 108.
54 Deposition of Thomas Grant *re* Collisons with Blacks at Portland Bay, Port Phillip Papers, 1840, NSW Col. Sec. 4/2510.
55 Mr. Newbolt in *Rockhampton Bulletin*, 5 August 1865. See also I. Henry to Col. Sec., Qld Col. Sec., 6952 of 1885, Col A/437, QSA.
56 *Sydney Gazette*, 19 May 1805.
57 C. Lumholtz: 'Among the Natives of Australia', *Journal of American Geographical Society*, 21, 1889, p. 11.
58 C. Chewings: *Back in the Stone Age*, p. 30.
59 H. S. Russell: *The Genesis of Queensland*, p. 281.
60 D. W. Moore: *Aborigines and Islanders* etc, p. 150.
61 W. Rogers: 'A Noted Blackfellow', *Adelaide Observer*, 14 June 1924.
62 K. L. Parker: *The Euahlayi Tribe*, London 1905, p. 36.
63 R. M. Berndt: 'Wuradjeri Magic and Clever Men', *Oceania*, 18, 1947–48, p. 71 and 17, 1946 47, p. 356.
64 A. K. Eckermann: Half-Caste, Out-Cast, Ph.D. thesis. University of Queensland 1977, pp. 122, 124.
65 G. A. Robinson to Col. Sec., 31 October 1831, 18 November 1831, 22 January 1835; Tas. Col. Sec. In Letters, Tasmanian State Archives (hereafter TSA), CSO/1/318.
66 G. F. Moore: *A Descriptive Vocabulary*, p. 105.
67 K. L. Parker: *The Euahlayi Tribe*, p. 39.
68 W. Tench: *Sydney's First Four Years*, introduced by L. F. Fitzhardinge, Sydney 1961, p. 227.
69 N. J. B. Plomley: *Friendly Mission*, p. 262.
70 Select Committee on the Condition of the Aborigines, New South Wales Legislative Council Votes & Proceedings (hereafter NSWLCV&P), 1845, p. 18.
71 S. Newland: 'The Parkinjees or the Aboriginal Tribes on the Darling River', *Proceedings Royal Geographical Society of Australia, South Australian Branch*, 2, 1887–88, p. 26.

3 Resistance: Motives and Objectives

1 'Shall We Admit the Blacks'? No. 2, *Port Denison Times*, 1 May 1869.
2 G. E. Loyau: *The History of Maryborough* etc, Brisbane 1897, p. 3.

3   E. Curr: *The Australian Race*, 1, pp. 100–106.

4   C. B. Dutton: Letter in *North Australian*, 13 December 1861.

5   F. H. Bauer: 'The Kartans of Kangaroo Island, South Australia' in A. P. Pilling and R. A. Waterman: *Diprotodon to Detribalization*, Michigan 1970, p. 198.

6   A. R. Radcliffe-Brown: 'Three Tribes of Western Australia', *Journal of Royal Anthropological Institute*, 43, 1913, p. 137.

7   A. R. Radcliffe-Brown: 'The Social Organization of Australian Tribes', *Oceania*, 1, 1930, p. 35.

8   N. B. Tindale: *Aboriginal Tribes of Australia*, Canberra 1974, p. 115. See also J. B. Birdsell: 'Local Group Composition Among the Australian Aborigines' etc, *Current Anthropology*, 11, 2, April 1970.

9   P. Sutton: Language Groups and Aboriginal Land Ownership, Paper delivered to Australian Institute of Aboriginal Studies Conference, Canberra, May 1980, p. 8.

10   L. Sharp: 'Ritual Life and Economics of the Yir-Yoront of Cape York Peninsula', *Oceania*, 5, 1934, p. 23.

11   J. Morrell: *Sketch of a Residence*, p. 15.

12   D. F. Thomson: 'The Hero Cult, Initiation and Totemism on Cape York', *Journal of Royal Anthropological Institute*, 63, 1933, p. 461.

13   R. M. W. Dixon: *The Dyirbal Language of North Queensland*, Cambridge 1972, p. 35.

14   The Journal of Francis Tuckfield, La Trobe Library, MSS 655, p. 176.

15   E. S. Parker to G. A. Robinson, 20 June 1839, Port Phillip Papers, 1840 No. 39/10026, New South Wales Archives, 4/2510.

16   Aborigines: Australian Colonies, *British Parliamentary Papers*, 1844, p. 282.

17   *Sydney Morning Herald*, 7 October 1843.

18   W. Ridley: Appendix in J. D. Lang: *Queensland*, London 1861, p. 439.

19   J. D. Wood: Remarks on the Aborigines, 10 April 1862, Qld. Col. Sec. 1118 of 1862, QSA.

20   D. Thomson: 'In Camp With the Stone Age Men', *Queenslander*, 22 and 29 January 1931.

21   K. L. Parker: *The Euahlayi Tribe*, p. 52.

22   W. Thomas: Brief Remarks on the Aborigines of Victoria, 1838–39, La Trobe Library, MSS 7838, p. 3.

23   *Ibid.*

24   J. D. Wood: Remarks on the Aborigines, p. 2.

25   Jacob Lowe, Select Committee on the Native Police, p. 9.

26   Journal of Mr. Lewis's Lake Eyre Expedition 1874–75, *South Australia Parliamentary Papers*, 2, 1876, p. 20. See also – C. Sturt: *Two Expeditions*, 2, p. 194 and J. Oxley: *Journals of Two Expeditions*, p. 347.

27   M. Moorhouse to A. M. Mundy, 12 July 1841, Protector of Aborigines Letterbook, 21 May 1840–6 January 1857, SAA GRG/52/7.

28   James Flinn to Thomas Scott, 21 November 1837, Papers Relating to the Aborigines, 1796–1839, NSW Archives, No. 1161.

29   M. Moorhouse to Mundy, 12 July 1841, Protector of Aborigines Letterbook, 21 May 1840–6 January 1857, SAA GRG/52/7.

30   W. L. Warner: *A Black Civilization*, New York 1958, p. 151.

31   *Kirchliche Mitteilungen* (Church News), 29 Sept. 1897.

32   R. Mansfield, Sydney 28 Nov. 1821, ML. MSS Bonwick Transcripts Box 52.

33   1 June 1833.

34   J. K. Wilson: Select Committee on Native Police, p. 74.

35 Report of Return of Mr. Petrie etc enclosed in report of Commissioner for Crown Lands, Moreton Bay, 30 May 1842; NSW Colonial Secretary in Letters, (hereafter NSW Col. Sec.) 4284 of 1842.
36 A. H. Brown: Select Committee on Native Police, p. 120.
37 *Perth Gazette*, 1 June 1833.
38 S. Simpson, Moreton Bay, *HRA*, Series 1, 24, p. 259.
39 F. F. Armstrong, Aboriginal Interpreter to Colonial Secretary, West Australia Colonial Secretary, In Letters, (hereafter WA Col. Sec.), 53, 1837.
40 J. D. Wood: Remarks on the Aborigines, p. 2.
41 Submission of Advocate General to Executive Council, 7 October 1841, Aborigines: Australian Colonies, 1844, p. 396.
42 Walker to Colonial Secretary, 3 April 1861, Qld. Col. Sec., 944 of 1861.
43 *North Australian*, 13 December 1861.
44 J. D. Wood: Remarks on the Aborigines.
45 Wiseman to Chief Commissioner of Crown Lands, 16 November 1857, Qld. Col. Sec., 4319 of 1857.
46 G. A. Robinson to Col. Sec., 30 January 1832, Tas. Col. Sec., CSO/1/318.
47 N. J. B. Plomley, *Friendly Mission*, p. 88.
48 R. Dry, Answers Given by Settlers . . . to Certain Questions etc, Tas. Col. Sec., CSO/1/323, pp. 289, 291.
49 *Queensland Times*, 15 November 1861.
50 Simpson to Col. Sec., 13 July 1842, New South Wales Colonial Secretary, In Letters, (hereafter NSW Col. Sec.), 4284 of 1842. See also W. Robertson: *Cooee Talks*, p. 142; H. S. Russell: *The Genesis of Queensland*, p. 279.
51 Extract from journal of W. Schmidt, Aborigines: Australian Colonies, p. 297.
52 *Maitland Mercury*, 5 February 1843.
53 J. D. McTaggart to Col. Sec., NSW Col. Sec., 1530 of 1858.
54 Government Resident, Port Curtis, to Col. Sec., NSW Col. Sec., 2128 of 1856.
55 Letter, W. H. Wiseman to Attorney General, Camboon, 29 April 1858; Select Committee on the Murders by the Aborigines on the Dawson River, NSW Legislative Assembly Votes and Proceedings, 2, 1858, p. 909.
56 W. H. Wiseman, Commissioner of Crown Lands, Leichhardt, to Chief Commissioner, Sydney, 28 August 1855; Letterbook of W. H. Wiseman, QSA, CCL 7/61.
57 Papers of G. A. Robinson, 57, 1845-49, ML, MSS A7078/1.
58 E. S. Parker, Quarterly Journal, 1 September-30 November 1840, Port Phillip Aboriginal Protectorate; North Western District, VPRO.
59 E. S. Parker: *The Aborigines of Australia*, Melbourne 1854.
60 E. S. Parker: Quarterly Reports, 1 March 1841 31 August 1841, Port Phillip Aboriginal Protectorate; North Western District, VPRO.
61 Quoted in A. R. Radcliffe-Brown: 'The Rainbow Serpent Myth in South-East Australia', *Oceania*, 1, 1930-31, p. 346.
62 M. Moorhouse to Col. Sec., 10 October 1849, Protector of Aborigines Letterbook, 21 May 1840-6 January 1857, SAA GRG/52/7.
63 E. J. Eyre: *Journals of Expeditions*, 2, pp. 358-359.
64 Diary, 1839. William Thomas Papers, ML. uncat. MSS 214.
65 *Port Denison Times*, 18 April 1874.
66 E. K. V.: 'Our Aborigines', *Queenslander*, 26 January 1884; An Ethnologist: 'The Australian Aborigines', *Queenslander*, 13 July 1895; W. Robertson: *Cooee Talks*, pp. 25-28; G. S. Lang: *The Aborigines of Australia*, pp. 28, 29.

67   K. L. Parker: *The Euahlayi Tribe*, pp. 48–49.
68   R. M. Berndt: Wuradjeri Magic and Clever Men, Part Two, *Oceania*, 18, 1947–48, pp. 73–74.

4 Resistance: Tactics and Traditions

1   F. Walker to Col. Sec., 1 March 1852, NSWLCV&P, 1852, p. 791.
2   Diary of C. Palmerston, *Queensland Heritage*, 1, 8, May 1968, p. 29.
3   8 December 1875.
4   F. D. Browne: Respecting the Habits and Character of the Natives, Tas. Col. Sec., CSO/1/323.
5   *Perth Gazette*, 13 April 1833.
6   *Cooktown Independent*, 19 November 1890.
7   N. J. B. Plomley: *Friendly Mission*, p. 553.
8   H. S. Russell: *The Genesis of Queensland*, p. 281.
9   Capt. Clark: Answers Given by Settlers ... (to) the Aborigines Committee, Tas. Col. Sec., CSO/1/323. See also: Police Magistrate, Bothwell to Col. Sec., Tas. Col. Sec., CSO/1/316, p. 39; A. Allingham: *Taming the Wilderness*, Townsville 1977, p. 157.
10   F. A. Dutton to Col. Sec., 1 November 1844, SA Col. Sec., GRG/24/6, p. 1249.
11   *Adelaide Observer*, 18 April 1846.
12   Capt. Clark: Answers Given by Settlers ... etc, Tas. Col. Sec., *op. cit.*
13   A. Reid, Great Swanport, 2 January 1829, Tas. Col. Sec., CSO/1/323, p. 77.
14   T. Hooper, Black Marsh to T. Anstey, 18 August 1830, Tas. Col. Sec., CSO/1/316, pp. 571–574.
15   *Ibid.*
16   *The Colonist*, 16 February 1839.
17   J. Howe: 'Outrages by the Blacks', *Hunter River Gazette*, 12 February 1842.
18   J. Campbell: *The Early Settlement of Queensland*, Brisbane 1936, p. 11; A. Hodgson, P. M. to Col. Sec., NSW Col. Sec., 9744 of 1841; Native Police Incidents ... etc by an ex-officer, *Queenslander*, 10 June 1899; Geographical Memoir of Melville Island and Port Essington, *JRGS*, 4, 1834, p. 153; M. Hartwig: The Progress of White Settlement in the Alice Springs District etc., Ph.D. Adelaide 1965, 2, p. 409.
19   11 September 1830.
20   Arthur to Sir George Murray, 12 September 1829, *HRA*, 1, 15, p. 446.
21   *Historical Records of New South Wales* (hereafter *HRNSW*), 5, p. 514.
22   Memorandum on the Means of Checking the Ravages of the Natives of Van Diemens Land; G. A. Arthur Papers, 19, ML, MSS A2179.
23   Quoted by J. E. Calder: Tasmanian Aborigines, ML, MSS A612, p. 249.
24   J. Jorgensen to T. Anstey, 24 February 1830, Tas. Col. Sec., CSO/1/320.
25   5 May 1840.
26   Reports of Mr. G. A. Robinson to Col. Sec., Tas. Col. Sec., CSO/1/318, pp. 383, 511, 513; N. J. B. Plomley: *Friendly Mission*, p. 553.
27   Select Committee on Native Mounted Police, p. 7.
28   Commissioner of Crown Lands, Moreton Bay to Col. Sec., 3 October 1843, NSW Col. Sec., 7448 of 1843 filed with 4122 of 1846.
29   21 January 1843.
30   3 June 1843.
31   Letter of Mr B. Doyle to C. M. Doyle, 19 January 1843, *Maitland Mercury*, 28 January 1843.
32   *Sydney Morning Herald*, 28 November 1848.

33   G. Caley: 'A Short Account Relative to the Proceedings in New South Wales', *HRNSW*, 6, p. 300.
34   Hunter to Portland, 2 January 1800, *HRNSW*, 4, p. 3.
35   See Tas. Col. Sec., CSO/1/316, pp. 127, 430–443.
36   Select Committee on Native Police, NSWLCV&P, 1856–57, 1, p. 1209.
37   *HRA*, 1, 25, p. 2.
38   *Cooktown Courier*, 1 January 1878.
39   *Queenslander*, 15 February 1879.
40   16 July 1830.
41   *Ibid.*, 1 June 1831.
42   Report of Aborigines Committee, 27 August 1830, Papers of Aborigines Committee, Tas. Col. Sec., CSO/1/319, also CSO/1/323, p. 77.
43   Report of the Aborigines Committee, 20 October 1831; Papers Relative to the Aboriginal Tribes in British Possessions, *BPP*, 1834, p. 158.
44   Stirling to Aberdeen, 10 July 1835, Despatches to Colonial Office, 14 September 1834–6 December 1838, Letter 53, BL.
45   R. M. Lyon, 'A Glance at the Manners and Language of the Aboriginal Inhabitants of W. Aus.', *Perth Gazette*, 30 March 1833.
46   Geographical Memoirs of Melville Island, p. 153.
47   24 June 1874.
48   E. J. Eyre: *Journals of Expeditions ... etc*, 2, 216–217.
49   *Queenslander*, 10 July 1880.
50   Robinson to La Trobe, 15 August 1841, Port Phillip Protectorate, In Letters, VPRO.
51   F. Tuckfield, Journal, pp. 95–96; Report of Assistant Protector, E. S. Parker to G. A. Robinson, 20 June 1839, Port Phillip Papers, 1840, Part 1.
52   W. H. Wiseman to Chief Commissioner, Crown Lands, 7 January 1857, NSW Col. Sec., 796 of 1857.
53   J. E. Tenison-Woods, 'A Day with the Myalls', 13 January 1882.
54   T.S.B., 'The Niggers Again', 26 June 1886.
55   C. Chewings: *Back in the Stone Age*, p. 131.
56   King to Hobart, 20 December 1804, *HRA*, 1, 5, pp. 166–167.
57   *Sydney Morning Herald*, 8 July 1842.
58   A. W. Howitt: *Native Tribes ... etc*, p. 299.
59   J. Morrell: *The Story ... etc*, p. 15.
60   14 January.
61   11 September 1880.
62   *Queenslander*, 23 February 1878.
63   *Ibid.*, 15 May 1875.
64   25 September 1875.
65   30 September 1879. See also *Queensland Parliamentary Debates*, 32, 1880, p. 306; speech by Mr Baynes, *Queenslander*, 16, 23 August 1879; *Maryborough Chronicle*, 16 March 1880; John Mathew Papers, Institute of Aboriginal Studies, MSS 950.
66   *Mudgee Guardian*, 23 July 1900.
67   *Ibid.*, 3 September 1900.
68   *Sydney Morning Herald*, 23 November 1900.
69   *Ibid.*, 29 October 1900. See also H. Reynolds, 'Jimmy Governor and Jimmie Blacksmith', *Australian Literary Studies*, 9, 1, May 1979.
70   Report in *Evening News*, cutting enclosed in NSW Archives file, Police/4/8581.
71   G. A. Robinson Papers, 60, ML, MSS A7081, p. 46.

72   B. Threadgill: *South Australian Land Exploration, 1856–1880*, Adelaide 1922, p. 58.
73   C. Rolleston, Darling Downs, 11 January 1851, Reports of Commissioners of Crown Lands on the State of the Aborigines for 1850, Colonial Office Papers, CO 201/442.
74   Rev. J. Y. Wilson, Replies to Circular Letter from Select Committee on the Condition of the Aborigines, NSWLCV&P, 2nd Session 1846, p. 14.
75   Select Committee on the Condition of the Aborigines, NSWLCV&P, 1845, p. 55.
76   I. Crawford: William Thomas and the Port Phillip Protectorate 1839–1849, M. A. Melbourne 1967, p. 22.
77   W. Hull, Select Committee on the Aborigines, *Proceedings of the Legislative Council of Victoria*, 1858–59, D8, p. 12.
78   Dredge to Bunting, 17 February 1840, James Dredge Notebook, La Trobe Library, MSS 421959, Box 16/5.
79   Murray-Upper tapes, Black Oral History Collection: James Cook University.

5 The Politics of Contact

1   E. S. Parker, Quarterly Report 1 December 1840–28 February 1841, Port Phillip Protectorate, 11, North West District, VPRO. Also Parker to Robinson, 1 January 1845; Aborigines 1842–52, NSW Col. Sec., 4/7153, NSW Archives.
2   Lonsdale to Deas Thomson, 28 October 1837, Aborigines and the Native Police, NSW Col. Sec., 4/1135. 1, NSW Archives.
3   The Journal of Francis Tuckfield, p. 299.
4   A. C. Grant: Early Station Life in Queensland, ML, MSS A858, p. 50.
5   M. J. Meggitt: *Desert People*, Sydney 1962, p. 25.
6   NSWLCV&P, 1846, p. 968.
7   NSWLCV&P, 1849, p. 18.
8   Select Committee on the Protectorate, NSWLCV&P, 1849, p. 18.
9   A. W. Howitt: *Native Tribes*, pp. 330–332.
10   Reports of Commissioners of Crown Lands for 1850 on the state of the Aborigines, Colonial Office CO 201/442, p. 239.
11   G. S. Olivey, Le Grange Bay, 14 May 1901, *West Australia Parliamentary Papers*, 2, 1901, No. 26, p. 50.
12   'Natives of Central Australia', *Journal of Royal Geographical Society of Australasia, South Australia Branch* (hereafter RGSSA), 4, 1898–1901, p. 27.
13   Hutt to Stanley, 8 April 1842, Aborigines: Australian Colonies, *BPP*, 1844, p. 413 also C. Symmons to Col. Sec., 31 December 1842, *Ibid.*, p. 418.
14   E. S. Parker, quoted in M. F. Christie: Race Relations ... in Early Victoria, p. 187.
15   'Some Aborigines I Have Known', *RGSSA*, 1894 5, pp. 43–45.
16   F. J. Gillen: 'Natives of Central Australia', p. 27. See also B. Spencer, F. J. Gillen: *Across Australia*, London 1912, p. 186; *The Native Tribes of Central Australia*, Dover edition, New York 1968, p. 8; *The Arunta*, London 1922, p. 7.
17   Government and General Order, 22 February 1796, HRNSW, 3, p. 26.
18   Government and General Order, 22 November 1801, HRNSW, 5, p. 628.
19   Moreton Bay correspondent, SMH, 12 October 1843.

20 Robinson to G. Whitcomb, 10 August 1832, Tasmanian Aborigines, ML, MSS A/612, p. 133.
21 D. R. Moore: *Islanders and Aborigines*, pp. 177, 231.
22 Papers Relative to the Affairs of South Australia, *BPP*, 1843, p. 299.
23 D. Collins: *Account of the English Colony of New South Wales, 1798–1804*, 2 vols, London 1802, 2, p. 96.
24 *Ibid.*, 2, pp. 22, 28. See also B. Bridges: 'Pemulwy: A Noble Savage', *Newsletter of the Royal Australian Historical Society*, 88, 1970, pp. 3–4.
25 *Perth Gazette*, 2, 16 March, 6 April, 4, 18, 22 May, 1 June, 13 July 1833. See also B. T. Haynes et al: *West Australian Aborigines 1622–1972*, Perth 1973, pp. 5–6.
26 A. Hasluck: 'Yagan the Patriot', *WAHS*, 7, 1961, pp. 33–48. For Dundalli see J. J. Knight: *In the Early Days*, Brisbane 1895; T. Petrie: *Reminiscences of Early Queensland*, Brisbane 1932; T. Welsby: *Collected Works*, 2 vols, Brisbane 1907.
27 C. Symmons, Protector of Aborigines, quarterly report to Col. Sec., 30 June 1841, WA Col. Sec., 95, 1841.
28 G. Taplin: *The Folklore, Manners, Customs* etc, p. 12.
29 W. Walker, Sydney, 5 December, 1821, Bonwick Transcripts ML:MSS Box 21.
30 G. F. Moore to Col. Sec., 23 October 1837, *WACSO*, 56, 1837.
31 Rev. Horton, 1822, reported in J. Bonwick: *The Last of the Tasmanians*, London 1870, p. 93.
32 Reports of Mr G. A. Robinson whilst in pursuit of the Natives, Tas. Col. Sec., CSC.
33 M. Sahlens: *Stone Age Economics*, London 1974, pp. 93–94.
34 Macquarie to Bathurst, 8 October 1814, *HRA*, 1, 8, 368.
35 Aborigines: Australian Colonies, *BPP 1844*, p. 119.
36 Quarterly Report of Protector of Aborigines, 31 March 1842, W.A. Col. Sec., 108/1842.
37 Peter Brown, York, 20 July 1840 to Col. Sec., W.A. Col. Sec., 89/1840.
38 Select Committee on the Aborigines and the Protectorate, NSWLCV&P, 1849, p. 17.
39 *HRA*, 1, 8, pp. 368–369.
40 Select Committee on the Aborigines and the Protectorate, NSWLCV&P, 1849, p. 17.
41 Marsden, Sydney, 21 November 1825, Bonwick Transcripts ML/MSS Box 53.
42 J. McLaren: *My Crowded Solitude*, Sun Books, Melbourne 1966, p. 37.
43 *Ibid.*, p. 40.
44 Hutt to Stanley, 8 April 1842, Aborigines: Australian Colonies, 1844, *BPP*, p. 412.
45 S. Simpson, Moreton Bay, 31 December 1849, Commissioners of Crown Lands Reports on the Conditions of the Aborigines for 1849, Colonial Office, CO 201/430.
46 A Lady (pseud.): *My Experiences in Australia* etc, London 1860 in I. McBride (ed.): *Records of Time Past*, Canberra 1978, p. 249.
47 J. B. Walker: *Early Tasmania*, Hobart 1902, p. 249.
48 Annual Report of the Chief Protector of Aborigines, 1841, Port Phillip Aborigines Protectorate, Box 10.
49 E. S. Parker, Statement without date, Loddon, Port Phillip Aborigines Protectorate, Box 12.

50   D. Collins: *An Account of the English Colony of New South Wales*, London 1802, pp. 328–329.
51   Robinson to La Trobe, 14 December 1839, Aborigines and the Native Police, NSW CSO/4/1135.1.
52   Report of Assistant Protector Parker, 20 June 1839, Port Phillip Papers, NSW Col. Sec., 1840, 4/2510.
53   G. S. Olivey, Inspector of Aborigines, La Grange Bay, 14 May 1901, *WAPP*, 2, 1901, No. 26, p. 50.
54   *Ibid*, p. 49.
55   *WAPP*, 2, 1902 3, No. 32, p. 18.
56   Report of Protector of Aborigines, 10 February 1842, S. A. Col. Sec., GRG/24/6.
57   E. Curr: *Recollections of Squatting in Victoria*, Melbourne 1883, p. 299.
58   Annual Report, Port Phillip Aboriginal Protectorate, 1848, Box 11.
59   3 December 1842.
60   *HRA*, 1, 8, pp. 370–371.
61   *Victorian Parliamentary Papers*, 3, 1877–1878, No. 76, p. 532.
62   Aborigines and the Native Police, NSW Col. Sec., CSO/4/1135.1.
63   Quoted in J. Bonwick: *The Last of the Tasmanians*, London 1870, p. 356.
64   Select Committee on the Native Police, QVP, 1861, p. 116.
65   *The Last of the Tasmanians*, pp. 382–384.
66   M. B. Hale: *The Aborigines of Australia*, London c. 1889, pp. 24–25.
67   G. Grey: *Journals ... , 2*, pp. 370–371.
68   Select Committee on the Aborigines and the Protectorate, NSWLCV&P, 1849, p. 17.
69   G. Taplin, *The Narrinyeri*, pp. 8, 9.
70   J. Bulmer: Some Account of the Aborigines of the Lower Murray etc., *Proceedings Royal Geographical Society of Victoria*, 1, 5, March 1888, p. 30.
71   James Gunther Lecture, ML/MSS B505.
72   Quoted in *The Mapoon Story*, 2, Sydney 1975, p. 24.
73   *Ibid.*
74   G. Taplin (ed.): *The Folklore, Manners, Customs* etc., p. 12.
75   *Journal of an Expedition*, pp. 416–417.
76   *The Examiner*, 3 December 1842.
77   *Ibid.*
78   *The Last of the Tasmanians*, p. 349.
79   Reports of J. B. Walker and G. W. Walker, ML/MSS B706.
80   Select Committee on the Aborigines and the Protectorate, NSWLCV&P, 1849, pp. 14, 27.
81   *Ibid*, p. 25.
82   Reports of the Commissioners of Crown Lands ..., Colonial Office, COL/201/442.
83   R. H. Bland to Col. Sec., 4 January 1843, Aborigines: Australian Colonies, 1844, *BPP*, p. 417.
84   G. Wyndham: Answer to Questionnaire of Immigration Committee re Aborigines, ML/MSS A/611.

6 The Pastoral Frontier

1   *Journal of an Expedition*, pp. 14, 16, 67, 69, 70.
2   Acting Sergeant J. Dunn, Burketown to Inspector of Police, Normanton, 15 May 1897, Qld Police Commissioner's File 412M, 17785 of 1897.

3   Report of Northern Protector of Aborigines, 1902, *QVP*, 2, 1903.
4   Commandant to Col. Sec., Callandoon, 1 March 1852, NSWLCV&P, 1852, p. 790.
5   P. Sutton, L. Hercus, Barnabus Roberts in oral history collection pending publication with Institute of Aboriginal Studies, Canberra.
6   'Bulleta': The Case for the Aboriginals, *Queenslander*, 12 November 1898.
7   *Queenslander*, 20 July 1895.
8   Report of Return of Mr Petrie from an excursion to the north, NSW Col. Sec., 4284 of 1842.
9   *Portland Mercury*, 5 October 1842.
10 T. F. Bride (ed): *Letters from Victorian Pioneers*, Melbourne 1969, pp. 103, 270.
11 H. C. Corfield in NSW Col. Sec., 9029 of 1850.
12 *SMH*, 5 October 1840.
13 *Adelaide Observer*, 18 April 1846. Report of a Journey to Mt. Bryan, SA Col. Sec., GRG/24/6.
14 A. MacPherson: *Mount Abundance*, London 1879, p. 32.
15 C. Eden: *My Wife and I in Queensland*, London 1872, p. 221.
16 16 April 1846.
17 *HRA*, 1, 24.
18 *A Journal of an Expedition*, p. 16.
19 J. Gormly: Exploration and Settlement on the Murray and Murrumbidgee [*sic*], *Journal and Proceedings Australian Historical Society*, 2, 2, 1966, p. 40.
20 Edward Mayne, 3 July 1843, Aborigines: Australian Colonies, *BPP*, 1844, p. 229.
21 6 January 1849.
22 D. S. MacMillan: *Bowen Downs 1863–1903*, Sydney 1963, p. 22.
23 Aborigines: Australian Colonies, *BPP*, 1844, pp. 114–116.
24 *HRA*, 1, 25, p. 2.
25 Reports from Resident Magistrate ... on Special Duty to the Murchison and Gascoyne Districts, West Australia Legislative Council Votes & Proceedings, 1882, No. 33, p. 10.
26 *Ibid.*
27 Some Aborigines I Have Known, pp. 53–54.
28 C. R. Haly, *QVP*, 1861, p. 80.
29 E. W. Palmer to A. W. Howitt, 5 August 1882, Howitt Papers, National Museum of Victoria.
30 Select Committee on the Aborigines Bill, *SAPP*, 1899, No. 77, p. 26.
31 *Ibid* pp. 113–114.
32 I. F. Kelsey, Bowen to H.E. The Governor, 22 October 1869, Qld Col. Sec., 852 of 1870.
33 A. S. Haydon, 'Slavery in Queensland', *Queenslander*, 12 April 1884.
34 A. C. Grant: Early Station Life, p. 96.
35 *Back in the Stone Age*, p. 44.
36 23 May 1885.

7 Other Frontiers

1   A. Searcy: *In Northern Seas*, Adelaide 1905, p. 10.
2   Commissioner of Crown Lands to Col. Sec., 14 January 1842, Aborigines: Australian Colonies, *BPP*, 1844. For Bass Strait see S. Murray-Smith: 'Beyond the Pale: The Island Community of Bass Strait in the Nineteenth Century', *THRA*, 20, 4, December 1973, p. 172.

3   First Discovery of Port Davey and Macquarie Harbour by Captain James Kelly 1815 16 and 1824, Tasmanian Legislative Council Votes & Proceedings, 1881, No. 75, p. 14.
4   A. C. V. Bligh: *The Golden Quest*, Sydney 1938, p. 35. See also Dispatches between the Governor and the Secretary of State, WALCV&P, 1872, No. 5.
5   C. Anderson: Aboriginal Economy and Contact Relations at Bloomfield River etc, *Newsletter Australian Institute of Aboriginal Affairs*, 12, September 1979, p. 35.
6   *Ibid.*
7   *Missionary Notes*, 15 January 1896.
8   W. H. Hovell: Remarks on a Voyage to Western Port, 7 November 1826–25 March 1827, La Trobe Library MSS CY, 8, 1/32C.
9   C. Anderson: Aboriginal Economy and Contact Relations at Bloomfield River etc, p. 35.
10 E. W. Streeter: *Pearls and Pearling Life*, London 1886, p. 158.
11 Report on the Pearl Shell Fisheries of Torres Strait, QVP, 1880, 2, p. 1165. See also Streeter, p. 166 for the north-west.
12 Editorial 'Aboriginal Murderers', 19 November 1890.
13 W. Saville-Kent: Pearl and Pearl Shell Fisheries of North Queensland, QVP, 1890, 3, p. 731.
14 21 April 1805.
15 14 May 1814.
16 E. C. Putt, Barron River, 13 July 1888.
17 Bidwell to Chief Commissioner of Crown Lands, Tenana, 14 October 1852, NSW Col. Sec., 9967 of 1852.
18 *Thirty-three Years in Tasmania and Victoria*, London 1862, p. 57.
19 27 January.
20 Etheridge correspondent of *Cleveland Bay Express*, 25 October 1873.
21 *Queenslander*, 8 December 1877.
22 A. C. Haldane, Mining Warden, Etheridge, *QVP*, 3, 1888.
23 A Day in the Life of the Blacks, *Church News*, 29, 6 June 1897, pp. 46–47.
24 M. Durack, *The Rock and the Sand*, p. 730.
25 *Church News*, 21, 3, March 1889, p. 21.
26 M. Hartwig, The Progress of White Settlement in the Alice Springs District, Ph.D., Adelaide 1965, p. 514.
27 *Church News*, 21, February 1889, p. 12.
28 *Ibid.*, 29, 8, August 1897, p. 63.
29 *Ibid.*, 26, 8, 1894.
30 Journal of W. Schmidt, 28 December 1842–6 January 1843, p. 123; Papers of J. D. Lang, Vol. 20, ML MSS A2240.
31 *Missionary Notes*, 15 August 1895, p. 72.
32 *Ibid.*, 15 November 1895, p. 72.
33 *Ibid.*, 15 December 1895, p. 104.
34 *Ibid.*, 22 June 1896, p. 44.
35 *Ibid.*
36 W. H. Wiseman in *Rockhampton Bulletin*, 21 January 1871.
37 'Live and Let Live', Cooktown 3 July, *Queenslander*, 20 July 1895.
38 'Aboriginal Territorial Organization', *Oceania*, 36, 1, September 1965, p. 17.
39 E. J. Eyre, *Journals of Expeditions*, 2, pp. 373, 445.
40 Letter 'The Nigger Nuisance', J.N.W., *Northern Territory Times*, 13 February 1874.
41 A. K. Eckermann, Half-Cast – Out Cast, Ph.D., Queensland 1977, p. 130.

42 Quarterly Report of Protector of Aborigines, 30 June 1843, SA Col. Sec., GRG/24/6 A(1843), p. 132; Quarterly Report of Aborigines Department, SA Col. Sec., GRG/24/6 A(1843), p. 812.
43 Maryborough correspondent, *Queenslander*, 23 February 1867.
44 *Moreton Bay Courier*, 3 July 1858; *Maryborough Chronicle*, 3 July 1858, 14 May 1863. A. E. Halloran, Commissioner for Crown Lands, Wide Bay to Chief Commissioner, 26 December 1856; Letterbook of Commissioner for Wide Bay and Burnett, QSA 30/11.
45 *Queenslander*, 6 March 1869.
46 *Rockhampton News*, 13 November 1865 quoted in *Queensland Times*, 23 November 1865.

Conclusion

1 W. K. Hancock, *Australia*, Jacaranda edition, Brisbane 1960, p. 20.
2 *After the Dreaming*, Sydney 1969, p. 49.

SELECT BIBLIOGRAPHY

Official Printed Sources

BRITAIN
House of Commons, Sessional Papers
1831, 19, No. 259: Van Diemen's Land. Return to an Address ... for Copies of all Correspondence between Lieutenant-Governor Arthur and His Majesty's Secretary of State for the Colonies, on the Subject of the Military Operations lately carried on against the Aboriginal Inhabitants of Van Diemens land
1831, 19, No. 261: New South Wales. Return to an Address ... dated 19 July 1831 for Copies of Instructions given by His Majesty's Secretary of State for the Colonies, for Promoting the Moral and Religious Instruction of the Aboriginal Inhabitants of New Holland or Van Diemens Land
1834, 44, No. 617: Aboriginal Tribes (North America, New South Wales, Van Diemen's Land and British Guinea)
1836, 7, No. 538: Report from the Select Committee on Aborigines (British Settlements)
1837, 7, No. 425: Report from the Select Committee on Aborigines (British Settlements)
1839, 34, No. 526: Australian Aborigines ... Copies or Extracts of Despatches Relative to the Massacre of Aborigines of Australia ...
1843, 33, No. 141: Port Essington: Copies or Extracts of Any Correspondence Relative to the Establishment of a Settlement ...
1843, 32, No. 505: Papers Relative to the Affairs of South Australia, (especially pp. 267–340)
1844, 34, No. 627: Aborigines (Australian Colonies) ... Return to an address ... for Copies or Extracts from the Despatches of the Governors of the Australian Colonies, with the Reports of the Protectors of Aborigines ... to illustrate the Condition of the Aboriginal Population of said Colonies ...
1897, 61, No. 8350: Western Australia: Correspondence Relating to the Abolition of the Aborigines Protection Board

NEW SOUTH WALES
Legislative Council, Votes and Proceedings
1838: Report from the Committee on the Aborigines Question

1839, 2: Report from the Committee on Police and Gaols
1841: Report from the Committee on Immigration with ... Replies to a Circular Letter on the Aborigines
1843: New South Wales (Aborigines). Return to an address by Dr Thomson ... comprising details of Government Expenditure on Aborigines, 1837–43, and a large collection of correspondence relating to the protectorate and the missions
1844, 1: New South Wales (Aborigines). Return to an address by Sir Thomas Mitchell ... for numbers of whites and Aborigines killed in conflicts since the settlement of the Port Phillip District
1845: Report from the Select Committee on the Condition of the Aborigines
1850, 1: The Native Police, Report of the Commandant to the Colonial Secretary
1852, 1: Letter from Mr F. Walker, Commandant, Native Police
1853, 1: Return of Murders by Aborigines in the Northern Districts
1855, 1: Report of Board of Enquiry Held at Moreton Bay regarding Commandant F. Walker Legislative Assembly: Votes and Proceedings
1856–57, 1: Report from the Select Committee on the Native Police Force
1858, 2: Report from the Select Committee on Murders by the Aborigines on the Dawson River

SOUTH AUSTRALIA
Parliamentary Papers
1857–58, 2, No. 156: Explorations of Mr S. Hack
1857–58, 2, No. 193: Northern Exploration
1858, 1, No. 25: Northern Exploration: Reports etc of Explorations ... by Babbage, Warburty, Geharty and Parry
1878, 4, No. 209: Journal of Mr Barlay's Exploration
1884, 3: Quarterly Report on the Northern Territory
1885, 4, No. 170: Report on the Pursuit of the Daly River Murderers
1888, 3, No. 53: Government Residents Report on the Northern Territory for 1887
1890, 2, No. 28: Government Residents Report on the Northern Territory for 1889
1892, 3, No. 129: Report on the Mai-Nini Murder Trial
1892, 3, No. 181: Government Residents Report on the Northern Territory for 1891
1899, 2, No. 77a: Report from the Select Committee on the Aborigines Bill
1899, 2, No. 77: Minutes of Evidence on the Aborigines Bill
1900, 3, No. 60: Justice in the Northern Territory; Letter from Mr Justice Dashwood
1901, 2, No. 45: Government Resident's Report on the Northern Territory for 1900
1913, 2, No. 26: Report from the Royal Commission on the Aborigines

TASMANIA
Legislative Council Journals and Papers
1863, No. 48: Half-Caste Islanders in Bass's Straits, Report by the Venerable Archdeacon Reibey
1881, No. 75: First Discovery of Port Davey and Macquarie Harbour by Captain James Kelly in ... 1815–16 and 1824

VICTORIA
Legislative Council: Votes and Proceedings
1858–59, No. D8: Report on the Select Committee of the Legislative Council on the Aborigines
Parliamentary Papers
1877–78, 3, No. 76: Report of the Royal Commission on the Aborigines
1882–83, 2, No. 5: Report of the Board Appointed to Inquire into and Report Upon ... the Coranderrk Aboriginal Station
1873–84: Ninth to Twentieth Reports of Board for the Protection of Aborigines in the Colony of Victoria, presented to both Houses of Parliament

QUEENSLAND
Votes and Proceedings of the Legislative Assembly
1860: Report of Select Committee on the Police
1861: Report of Select Committee on Native Police Force
1863: Papers Regarding the Dismissal of J. Donald Harris of the Native Police
1867, 1: Copies of Correspondence ... concerning the inquiry into the case of C. J. Blakeney, late Lieutenant of Native Police
1867, 1: Charges Against the Native Police under the Command of Mr Sub-Lieutenant Hill
1867, 2: Alleged Massacre of Blacks at Morinish Diggings
1872: Report of Acting Commandant of Police for 1871
1874, 2: Enquiry into the Claims of Patrick Corbett
1875, 1: Report of Commandant of Police for 1874
1876, 3: Report of the North-Western Exploring Expedition
1876, 3: Report of Expedition in Search of Gold ... in the Palmer District by Mulligan and Party
1878, 2: Report of the Aborigines Commissioners
1881, 1: Report of Explorations in Cape York Peninsula by R. L. Jack
1881, 2: Further Reports on the Progress of the Gold Prospecting Expedition in Cape York Peninsula
1883–84: Report of Police Magistrate, Thursday Island on Pearl Shell and Bêche de Mer Fisheries in Torres Strait
1885, 2: Reports of Mr Douglas's Cruise Among the Islands of Torres Strait
1886, 2: Visit of Inspection to Various Islands in the G.S.S. *Albatross*
1888, 3: Annual Reports of the Gold Fields Commissioners
1889, 3: Annual Reports of the Gold Fields Commissioners
1890, 3: Report on the Pearl and Pearl Shell Fisheries of North Queensland by W. Saville-Kent
1890, 3: Annual Report of the Government Resident at Thursday Island
1894, 2: Annual Report of Government Resident at Thursday Island
1896, 4: Report on the Aborigines of North Queensland by Mr A. Meston
1897, 2: Report on the North Queensland Aborigines and the Native Police by W. Parry Okeden
1900–1904: Annual Reports of Northern Protectorate of Aborigines
1902, 1: Report of the Southern Protector of Aboriginals
1903, 2: W. E. Roth: North Queensland Ethnography Bulletin No. 5

WESTERN AUSTRALIA
Votes and Proceedings of the Legislative Council
1871, No. 2: Information Respecting the Habits and Customs of the Aboriginal Inhabitants of Western Australia
1872, No. 5: Despatches between the Governor and the Secretary of State for the Colonies
1875–76, No. 12: Correspondence Relative to the State of Affairs on the North-West Coast
1880, No. A16: Report of the Government Resident, Roebourne on the Pearl Shell Industries of the North-West Coast
1882, No. 33: Reports from the Resident Magistrate ... in the Murchison and Gascoyne Districts
1884, No. 32: Report of a Commission to Inquire into the treatment of Aboriginal Native Prisoners of the Crown
1885, No. A15: Report of the Select Committee ... Appointed to Consider and Report Upon ... the Treatment and Condition of the Aboriginal Natives of the Colony
Parliamentary Papers of Western Australia
1901, 2, No. 26: Report on Stations Visited by the Travelling Inspector of Aborigines
1902–03, 2, No. 32: Report of the Aborigines Department
1903–04, 2, No. 32: Report of the Aborigines Department
1905, No. 5: Report of the Royal Commission on the Condition of the Natives

DOCUMENTARY COLLECTIONS
Historical Records of Australia, Series One, 1–25 and Series Three, 1–6
Historical Records of New South Wales, 1–7

Official Manuscript Sources

ARCHIVES OFFICE OF NEW SOUTH WALES
Colonial Secretary's Correspondence: In Letters (special bundles)
Aborigines, 4/7153
Aborigines 1833–35, 4/2219.1
Aborigines 1836, 4/2302.1
Aborigines 1837–39, 4/2433.1
Aborigines 1849, 4/1141
Aborigines 1849, 4/2831.1
Aborigines 1852, 4/713.2
Aborigines and the Native Police 1835–44, 4/1135.1
Aboriginal Outrages, 2/8020.4
Port Phillip Papers, 1839, 4/2471
Port Phillip Papers, 1840, Part 1, 4/2510
Port Phillip Papers, 1840, Part 2, 4/2511
Port Phillip Papers, 1841, Part 1, 4/2547
Port Phillip Papers, 1842, Part 1, 4/2588 B
Port Phillip Papers, 1842, Part 2, 4/2589 B

Port Phillip Papers, 1846, 4/2745-2
Letters Received from and about Wide Bay, 1850–57, 4/7173
Raffles Bay, 4/2060.2
Reports on the Border Police, 1843–46, 4/7203
Letters from Moreton Bay, 1843, 4/2618.1
Bathurst 1815–23, 4/1798
Bathurst 1824, 4/1800
Bathurst 1826, 4/1801
Bathurst 1824–26, 4/1799
Supreme Court Records
Papers Relating to the Aborigines, 1796–1839, 1161

MITCHELL LIBRARY
Aborigines MSS A/611
Letters from Government Officials, MSS A/664
Queensland Native Police: Answers to Questionnaire, 1856, MSS A467
Letterbook, Commissioner of Crown Land, Darling Downs 1843–48, MSS
    A1764–2
Somerset Letterbook No. 1, MSS B1414

TASMANIAN STATE ARCHIVES
Papers Relating to the Aborigines, 7578
Reports on the Murders and Other Outrages Committed by the Aborigines,
    CSO/1/316
Records Relating to the Aboriginals, CSO/1/317
Reports of Mr G. A. Robinson Whilst in Pursuit of the Natives, CSO/1/318
Papers of the Aborigines Committee, CSO/1/319
Reports of the Roving Parties, CSO/1/320
Suggestions Relative to the Capture of the Natives, CSO/1/323
Papers Relating to the Black Line, CSO/1/324

BATTYE LIBRARY, PERTH
Swan River Papers, 9, 10
Colonial Secretary: In Letters, Volumes concerned with the Aborigines
53, April, May 1837
54, June, July 1837
56, October 1837
89, 1840
95, 1841
108, 1842
173, 1848

STATE LIBRARY OF SOUTH AUSTRALIA
Governors Despatches GRG/2/6/1
Letterbook of the Government Resident, Port Lincoln 3/379
Report of Attack on Barrow Creek Telegraph Station GRG/24/6/1874 Nos. 332, 347
Colonial Secretary: In Letters, 1837–41, GRG/24/1; 1842–45, GRG/24/6
Colonial Secretary's Letterbooks, GRG/24/4/3; GRG/24/4

Protector of Aborigines Letterbook 1840–57, GRG/52/7

VICTORIAN PUBLIC RECORDS OFFICE
Records of the Port Phillip Aboriginal Protectorate, especially the boxes — Westernport, North-Western District, Mainly In-Letters, Mt Rouse

QUEENSLAND STATE ARCHIVES
New South Wales Colonial Secretary, Letters Received Relating to Moreton Bay and Queensland, 1822–1860
Microfilm copies of material from State Archives of NSW, Reels A2/1 — A2/48 including the special bundles and A2/48 which contains Commissioner of Crown Lands re Aborigines in the District, 1854 Government Resident, Moreton Bay re complaints about the Native Police 1857
Correspondence concerning the police firing on the Aborigines
Native Police: Moreton Bay 1857, Reels A2/47
Native Police Papers QSA/NMP 48/100, 48/111, 48/120
Government Resident, Moreton Bay, QSA/RES/2 and 3 48/101, 48/102
Letterbook of Commissioner for Crown Lands, Wide Bay and Burnett, 24/9/53-30/12/54, QSA/CCL/35/889 and 1/1/55-13/12/57, QSA/CCL/30/11
Letterbook of W. H. Wiseman, 5/2/55-30/5/60, QSA/CCL/7/61
Colonial Secretary: In Letters, 1860–1890, the QSA/Col/A files and the Special Bundles Relating to the Aborigines, QSA/Col/139-QSA/Col/144

JAMES COOK UNIVERSITY LIBRARY, TOWNSVILLE
Microfilm collection of the Joint Copying Project of Colonial Office Files re New South Wales, Tasmania and South Australia. Especially useful were the files: New South Wales, Original Correspondence, 1838–1849 and Queensland, Original Correspondence 1861–1900

Other Manuscript Sources

MITCHELL LIBRARY
Papers of Sir George Arthur, especially Vol. 19, Letters received 1827–28, MSS A/2179, Vol. 20, 1829–30, MSS A2180 and Vol. 28
Aborigines, 1825–37, MSS A2188, Tasmanian Aborigines, MSS A612
Papers of G. A. Robinson, especially Vol. 14
Port Phillip Protectorate, 1839–40, MSS A7035
Port Phillip Protectorate: Correspondence 54–57a and other papers, 1839–49, MSS A7075-7078-2
Port Phillip Protectorate, Official Reports, 59–61, 1841–49, MSS A7078-MSS A7082
J. D. Lang, Papers, 20, MSS 2240
W. Gardner, Productions and Resources of the Northern Districts of NSW, 2 vols, 1842–54, MSS A176/1, A176/2
William Thomas Papers, especially his journal for 1844–47, uncatalogued MSS 214/2 and 3
E. J. Eyre, Autobiographical of Residence and Exploration in Australia, 1832–39, MSS A1806

Diary of John Gilbert, 18/9/44-22/6/45, MSS A2587
Jesse Gregson Memoirs, MSS 1382
A. Le Souef, Personal Recollections of Early Victoria, MSS A2762 Reminiscences
    of Mr James Nesbit, MSS A1533
A. C. Grant, Early Station Life in Queensland, MSS A858
Telfer, Reminiscences, MSS A2376
J. Backhouse, G. Walker, Report of a Visit to the Penal Settlement, Moreton Bay,
    MSS B706
H. W. Best Diary, 20/9/62-15/4/63 MSS B515/1
Arthur Bloxham Diary, May-July 1863, MSS B515/1
Andrew Murray, Journal of an Expedition 1859–1860, MSS 736
R. B. Mitchell, Reminiscences 1855–66, MSS B575
J. Raven, Reminiscences of a Western Queensland Pioneer, MSS A2692
J. F. Stevens, Histories of Pioneers, MSS 1120

TASMANIAN STATE ARCHIVES
Van Diemens Land Company Papers, Letters and Despatches, 1828–1846,
    VDC 5/1-7

BATTYE LIBRARY, PERTH
Constance Norris, Memories of Champion Bay or Old Geraldton, Q994.12/
    GER
L. F. Clarke, West Australian Natives: My Experiences With them, PR 2766
Mr William Coffin, Oral History Tape, PR 9893
Reminiscences of Mr F. H. Townsend, PR 3497
Report of the Rev. John Smithers re the Swan River Aborigines, 1840, PR
    1785a
Extracts from the Diary of Lieut. G. F. Dashwood in Perth, September 1832, PR
    956/FC
Diary of Dr S. W. Viveash, QB/VIV
F. F. B. Wittenoom, Some Notes on his Life QB/WIT
Journals of Trevarthon C. Scholl, 1865–66 QB/SHO
L. C. Burgess: Pioneers of Nor'-West Australia, PR 40

STATE LIBRARY OF SOUTH AUSTRALIA
Letters Written by John Mudge ... whilst a trooper at Pt. Lincoln and Mt. Wedge,
    1857–60, SAA 1518
J. B. Bull Reminiscences 1835–94, SAA 950
Extracts from the Diary of Mary Thomas, SAA 1058M
Simpson Newland, The Ramingaries (Encounter Bay) Tribe of Aborigines,
    A571/A4
Resolution of the Bush Club, 9/5/1839, A546/B8

LA TROBE LIBRARY, MELBOURNE
W. Thomas, Brief Remarks on the Aborigines of Victoria, 1839, 7838Lt
Journal of Patrick Coady Buckley, 1844–1853, 6109, Box 214/7
Diary of Neil Black, typescript, September 1839-May 1840, Box 99/1
Foster Fyans Reminiscences, 1810–1842, 6940

W. H. Hovell, Remarks on a Voyage to Western Port, 7/11/26-25/3/27 CY, 8, 1/32 c
The Journal of Francis Tuckfield, 655
The Papers of James Dredge — Notebook, 421959; Letterbook, 421961 H. Meyrick, Letters to his family in England, 1840–47, 7959

OXLEY LIBRARY, BRISBANE
Archer Family Papers, including Durundur Diary, 1843–44, Some Letters Mainly from Australia, 1833–55
Diary of Captain G. Griffin at Whiteside, 1/1/47-16/5/49, OM72-42
Letter of T. W. Wells to H. C. A. Harrison, 24/10/61 OM66/2/f2
Reminiscences of Mrs Adelaide Morrison OM69/8/f1
Robert Hamilton, Diary at Mt Auburn Station, 18/11/61-3/9/62, OM68/28/Q2
Harry Anning, Thirty Years Ago, OM172/123
Archibald Meston Papers, OM64/17

Newspapers

NEW SOUTH WALES
Atlas, 1844–1845
Australian, 1824, 1840–41, 1848
Colonist, 1837–1839
Empire, 1851–52, 1855–58
Hunter River Gazette, 1841–42
Maitland Mercury, 1843–1850
Sydney Gazette, 1803–1830
Sydney Morning Herald, 1834–1850 (*Sydney Herald* before July 1842)

TASMANIA
Colonial Times, 1825–1831
Hobart Town Courier, 1827–1831
Hobart Town Gazette, 1819–1825
Launceston Advertiser, 1829–1831
The Tasmanian, 1827–1828

WESTERN AUSTRALIA
Geraldton Express, 1886–1890
Inquirer, 1840–1851
Northern Public Opinion, 1893–1898
Pilbara Goldfields News, 1897–1898
Perth Gazette, 1833–1840

SOUTH AUSTRALIA
Adelaide Examiner, 1842–1843
Adelaide Observer, 1844–1849
Port Augusta Dispatch, 1877–1880
South Australian Register, 1839–1844

Southern Australian, 1838–1840

VICTORIA
Geelong Advertiser, 1840–1844
Portland Gazette, 1845–1847
Portland Guardian, 1842–1843
Portland Mercury, 1842–1844
Port Phillip Gazette, 1838–1846
Port Phillip Herald, 1840
Port Phillip Patriot, 1841–1842

QUEENSLAND
Cairns Post, 1885–1888
Colonist, (Maryborough) 1884–1888
Cooktown Courier, 1874–1879
Cooktown Herald, 1874–1877
Cooktown Independent, 1888–1891
Darling Downs Gazette, 1858–1859
Herberton Advertiser, 1884–1885
Mackay Mercury, 1868–1880
Maryborough Chronicle, 1860–1880
Moreton Bay Courier, 1846–1862
Moreton Bay Free Press, 1852–1859
North Australian, (Brisbane) 1856–1865
Peak Downs Telegram, (Clermont) 1876
Port Denison Times, (Bowen) 1867–1883
Queenslander, 1866–1900
Queensland Guardian, 1861–1863
Queensland Times, (Ipswich) 1864–1866
Rockhampton Bulletin, 1865–1876
Wide Bay and Burnett News, 1881–1884
Wide Bay and Burnett Times, 1859–1860
Wild River Times, (Herberton) 1886–1889

NORTHERN TERRITORY
Northern Territory Times, 1873–1883, 1890–1895

MISSIONARY JOURNALS
Missionary Notes of the Australian Board of Missions, 1895–1905 *Kirchliche Mitteilungen,* (Church News) 1886–1900
Newspaper Cutting Books on the Aborigines and related topics in Oxley Library, Mitchell Library, State Library of South Australia

A number of the papers listed above were used for periods other than for those specified. But they were in such cases only consulted for a few issues at any one time. Numerous other papers were used for an issue or two but they have not been listed. Reference has been made to a few of these in the endnotes.

Research Theses

Allingham, A. J., 'Taming the Wilderness': The First Decade of Pastoral Settlement in the Kennedy District, B.A. Hons, James Cook, 1976

Beckett, J., A Study of a Mixed Blood Aboriginal Minority in the Pastoral West of New South Wales, M.A., A.N.U., 1958

Bell, D., From Moth Hunters to Black Trackers. An Interpretive Analysis of the Black and White Experience, B.A. Hons, Monash, 1975

Bickford, R. A., Traditional Economy of the Aborigines of the Murray Valley, B.A. Hons, Sydney, 1966

Biskup, P., Native Administration and Welfare in Western Australia 1897–1954, M.A., West Australia, 1960

Brayshaw, H., Aboriginal Material Culture in the Herbert-Burdekin District, Ph.D., James Cook, 1977

Bridges, B., Aboriginal and White Relations in New South Wales 1788–1855, M.A., Sydney, 1966

Blundell, V. J., Aboriginal Adaption in North West Australia, Ph.D., Wisconsin, 1975

Brown, R. B., A History of the Gilbert River Goldfield, 1869–1874, B.A. Hons, James Cook, 1974

Bury, W. R., The Foundations of the Pt McLeay Aboriginal Mission, B.A. Hons, Adelaide, 1964

Critchett, J. F., A History of the Framlingham and Lake Condah Aboriginal Stations, 1860–1918, M.A., Melbourne, 1980

Christie, M. F., Race Relations between Aborigines and Colonists in Early Victoria, 1835–86, Ph.D., Monash, 1978

Crawford, I. M., William Thomas and the Port Phillip Protectorate, M.A., Melbourne, 1967

Curthoys, A., Race and Ethnicity: A Study of the Response of British Colonists to Aborigines, Chinese and non-British Europeans in N.S.W. 1856–1881, Ph.D., Macquarie, 1973

Denholm, D., Some Aspects of Squatting in New South Wales and Queensland, 1847–1864, Ph.D., A.N.U., 1972

Desailly, B., The Mechanics of Genocide, M.A., Tasmania, 1978

Eckermann, A. K., Half-Caste, Out Caste, Ph.D., Queensland, 1977

Evans, G., Thursday Island, 1878–1914, B.A. Hons, Queensland, 1972

Evans, K., Missionary Effort Towards the Cape York Aborigines, 1886–1910, B.A. Hons, Queensland, 1969

Evans, R., European-Aboriginal Relations in Queensland, 1880–1910, B.A. Hons, Queensland, 1965

Gale, F., A Study in Assimilation: Part Aborigines in South Australia, Ph.D., Adelaide, 1956

Graves, A. A., An Anatomy of Race Relations, B.A. Hons, Adelaide, 1973

Hardley, R. G., Some of the Factors that influenced the Coastal Riverine and Insular Habits of the Aborigines of South-East Queensland and Northern New South Wales, B.A. Hons, Queensland, 1975

Harrison, B. W., The Myall Creek Massacre, B.A. Hons, New England, 1966

Hartwig, M. C., The Coniston Killings, B.A. Hons, Adelaide, 1960

Hartwig, M. C., The Progress of White Settlement in the Alice Springs District and its Effect on the Aboriginal Inhabitants, 1860–1914, Ph.D., Adelaide, 1965

Hoskin, G., Aboriginal Reserves in Queensland, B.A. Hons, Queensland, 1968

Jenkin, G., The Aborigines Friends' Association and the Ngarrindjeri People, M.A., Adelaide, 1976

Johnston, S. L., The New South Wales Government Policy Towards the Aborigines, 1880–1909, M.A., Sydney, 1970

Krastins, V., The Tiwi: A Culture Contact History of the Australian Aborigines on Bathurst and Melville Islands, 1705–1942, B.A. Hons, A.N.U., 1972

Loos, N. A., Aboriginal-European Relations in North Queensland, 1861–1897, Ph.D., James Cook, 1976

Loos, N. A., Frontier Conflict in the Bowen District, 1861–1874, M.A. Qualifying, James Cook, 1970

Milich, C., Official Attitudes to the South Australian Aborigines in the 1930s, B.A. Hons, Adelaide, 1967

Murray-Prior, J., Women Settlers and Aborigines, B.A. Hons, New England, 1973

O'Kelly, G. J., The Jesuit Mission Stations in the Northern Territory, 1882–1899, B.A. Hons, Monash, 1967

Pearson, M., The MacIntyre Valley: Field Archaeology and Ethno-history, B.A. Hons, New England, 1973

Prentis, M. D., Aborigines and Europeans in the Northern Rivers of New South Wales, 1823–1881, M.A., Macquarie, 1972

Rosewarne, S., Aborigines in Colonial Queensland, M.A., Melbourne, 1976

Rule, M., Relations between the Aborigines and Settlers in Selected Areas of the Hunter Valley, B.A. Hons, Newcastle, 1977

Russo, G. H., Bishop Salvado's Plan to Civilize and Christianize the Aborigines, 1846–1900, M.A., Western Australia, 1972

Ryan, L., The Aborigines in Tasmania, 1800–1974, Ph.D. Macquarie, 1976

Sabine, N., An Ethnohistory of the Clarence Valley, B.A. Hons, New England, 1970

Shelmerdine, S., The Port Phillip Native Police Corps as an Experiment in Aboriginal Policy and Practice, 1837–1853, B.A. Hons, Melbourne 1972

Shepherd, B. W., A History of the Pearling Industry of the North-West Coast of Australia, M.A., Western Australia, 1975

Smith, P., Yarrabah, 1892–1910, B.A. Hons, James Cook, 1981

Taylor, J. C., Race Relations in South East Queensland, B.A. Hons, Queensland, 1967

Taylor, N., The Native Mounted Police of Queensland, 1850–1900, B.A. Hons, James Cook, 1970

Walker, J. A., Aboriginal-European Relations in the Maryborough District, 1842–1903, B.A. Hons, Queensland, 1975

Willmott, J., The Pearling Industry in Western Australia, 1850–1916, B.A. Hons, Western Australia, 1975

Contemporary Books, Articles and Pamphlets

Archer, T., *Recollections of a Rambling Life*, Yokohama, 1897

Atkinson, J., *An Account of the State of Agriculture and Grazing in New South Wales*, London, 1826

Austin, R., *Journal of Assistant Surveyor R. Austin*, Perth, 1855

Backhouse, J., *A Narrative of a Visit to the Australian Colonies*, London, 1843

Balfour, H., 'On the Method Employed by the Natives of N.W. Australia in the Manufacture of Glass Spear Heads', *MAN*, 1903

Bartlett, T., *New Holland*, London, 1843

Barton, R. D., *Reminiscences of an Australian Pioneer*, Sydney, 1917

Bennett, M. M., *Christison of Lammermoor*, London, 1927

Bennett, S., *The History of Australasian Discovery and Colonization*, Sydney, 1867

Beveridge, P., *The Aborigines of Victoria and Riverina*, Melbourne, 1889

Beveridge, P., 'On the Aborigines Inhabiting the ... Lower Murray, Lower Murrumbidgee, Lower Lachlan and Lower Darling', *Journal of Royal Society of New South Wales*, 17, 1883

Bolderwood, R., *Old Melbourne Memories*, Melbourne 1884

Bond, G., *A Brief Account of the Colony of Port Jackson*, Oxford, 1806

Bonwick, J., *The Last of the Tasmanians*, London, 1870

Braim, T. H., *A History of New South Wales*, 2 vols, London, 1846

Breton, W. H., *Excursions in New South Wales, Western Australia and Van Diemens Land*, London, 1833

Bride, T. F., *Letters from Victorian Pioneers*, Melbourne, 1898

Brock, D. G., *To the Desert With Sturt*, Adelaide, 1975

Bull, J. W., *Early Experiences of Life in South Australia*, Adelaide, 1884

Bulmer, J., 'Some Account of the Aborigines of the Lower Murray, Wimmera and Maneroo', *Proceedings Royal Geographical Society of Victoria*, 1, 5, March 1888

Bunbury, H. W., *Early Days in Western Australia*, London, 1930

Byerley, F. J., *Narrative of an Overland Expedition*, Brisbane, 1867

Byrne, J. C., *Twelve Years Wanderings in the British Colonies*, 2 vols, London, 1848

Calder, J. E., *The Native Tribes of Tasmania*, Hobart, 1875

Calvert, A. F., *The Aborigines of West Australia*, London, 1894

Campbell, J., *The Early Settlement of Queensland*, Brisbane, 1936

Carnegie, D., *Spinifex and Sand*, London, 1898

Carrington, G., *Colonial Adventures and Experiences*, London, 1877

Carron, W., *Narrative of an Expedition of the late Assistant Surveyor Mr E. B. Kennedy*, Sydney, 1849

Chester, E., Early Days in Albany: Reminiscences of Mr E. Chester, *WAHS*, 1, 1931

Chewings, E., *Back in the Stone Age*, Sydney, 1936

Collins, D., *Account of the English Colony of New South Wales, 1798–1804*, 2 vols, London, 1802

Curr, E., *An Account of the Colony of Van Diemens Land*, London, 1824

Curr, E., *The Australian Race; its origin, languages, customs*, 4 vols, Melbourne, 1886–87

Curr, E., *Recollections of Squatting in Victoria*, Melbourne, 1883

Daly, D., *Digging, Squatting and Pioneering Life in the Northern Territory of South Australia*, London, 1887

Dawson, J., *Australian Aborigines; the languages and customs of several tribes of Aborigines in the Western District of Victoria*, Melbourne, 1881

Dawson, R., *The Present State of Australia*, London, 1830

De Brebant Cooper, F., *Wild Adventures in Australia and New South Wales,* London, 1857

De Satge, E. and O., *Pages from the Journal of a Queensland Squatter,* London, 1901

Doyle, M. (ed.), *Extracts from the Letters and Journals of George Fletcher Moore,* London, 1834

Dredge, J., *Brief Notices on the Aborigines of New South Wales,* Geelong, 1845

Dumont D'urville, M. J., *Voyage de la Corvette L'Astrolabe,* Paris, 1830

Eden, C., *My Wife and I in Queensland,* London, 1872

Eipper, C., *Statement of the Origin, Condition and Prospects of the German Mission to Aborigines at Moreton Bay,* Sydney, 1841

Eyre, E. J., *Journals of Expeditions of Discovery,* 2 vols, London, 1845

Fenwick, J., 'Diary of John Fenwick', *Queensland Heritage,* 2, 3, November, 1970

Finlayson, Pastor: Reminiscences, *RGSSA,* 6, 1902–06

Field, B., *Geographical Memoirs of New South Wales,* London, 1825

Flinders, M., *A Voyage to Terra Australis,* 2 vols, London, 1814

Fraser, J., *The Aborigines of New South Wales,* Sydney, 1892

Fremantle, C. H., *Diaries and Letters of Admiral Sir C. H. Fremantle,* London, 1928

Froggatt, W. W., 'Notes on the Natives of West Kimberley, North West Australia', *Proceedings of Linnean Society of New South Wales,* 3, May 1888

Giles, E., *Australia Twice Traversed,* 2 vols, London, 1889

Gillen, F. J., 'The Natives of Central Australia', *RGSSA,* 4, 1898–1901

Grant, J., *The Narrative of a Voyage of Discovery,* London, 1803

Gray, R., *Reminiscences of India and North Queensland,* London, 1913

Grey, G., *Journals of Two Expeditions of Discovery,* 2 vols, London, 1841

Gribble, J. B., *Black but Comely: Aboriginal Life in Australia,* London, 1884

Gribble, J. B., *Dark Deeds in a Sunny Land,* Perth, 1905

Hall, T., *A Short History of the Downs Blacks,* Warwick n.d.

Hale, M. B., *The Aborigines of Australia,* London, c.1889

Hawker, J. C., *Early Experiences in South Australia,* Adelaide, 1899

Haydon, G. H., *Five Years Experience in Australia Felix,* London, 1846

Haygarth, H. W., *Recollections of Bush Life in Australia,* London, 1848

Henderson, J., *Excursions and Adventures in New South Wales,* 2 vols, London, 1851

Henderson, J., *Observations on the Colonies of New South Wales and Van Diemens Land,* Calcutta, 1832

Hives, F., *The Journal of a Jackeroo,* London, 1930

Hodgkinson, C., *Australia: From Port Macquarie to Moreton Bay,* London, 1845

Hogson, C. P., *Reminiscences of Australia,* London, 1846

Horne, G & G. Aiston, *Savage Life in Central Australia,* London, 1924

Hovell, W., 'Journal of a Journey from Lake George to Port Phillip, 1824–25', *JRAHS,* 7, 1921

Howitt, A. W., *The Native Tribes of South-East Australia,* London, 1904

Howitt, R., *Impressions of Australia Felix,* London, 1845

Hull, H. M., *Experience of Forty Years in Tasmania,* London, 1859

Irwin, F. C., *The State and Position of West Australia,* London, 1835

Jack, R. L., *Northmost Australia*, 2 vols, London, 1921

Jorgensen, J., 'A Shred of Autobiography', *Hobart Town Almanach and Van Diemens Land Annual*, 1838

Journals of Several Expeditions Made in Western Australia, London, 1833

Jukes, J. B., *Narrative of the Surveying Voyage of HMS Fly*, London, 1847

Kennedy, E. B., *The Black Police of Queensland*, London, 1902

Kennedy, E. B., 'Extracts from the Journal of an Exploring Expedition into Central Australia', *JRGS*, 22, 1852

Kennedy, E. B., *Four Years in Queensland*, London, 1870

King, P. P., *Narrative of a Survey of the Inter-tropical and Western Coast of Australia*, 2 vols, London, 1827

Kirby, J., *Old Times in the Bush in Australia*, Melbourne, 1894

Knight, J. J., *In the Early Days*, Brisbane, 1895

Labillardiere, M., *Voyage in Search of La Perouse, 1791–1794*, London, 1800

Landor, E. W., *The Bushman or Life in a New Country*, London, 1847

Lang, G. S., *The Aborigines of Australia*, Melbourne, 1865

Lang, J. D., *Queensland*, London, 1861

Lindsay, D., *Journal of the Elder Scientific Exploring Expedition, 1891–2*, Adelaide, 1892

Lloyd, G. T., *Thirty-three Years in Tasmania and Victoria*, London, 1862

Loyau, G. E., *The History of Maryborough*, Brisbane, 1897

Lumholtz, C., *Among Cannibals*, London, 1889

Lumholtz, C., 'Among the Natives of Australia', *Journal of American Geographical Society*, 21, 1889

McCombie, T., *Essays on Colonization*, London, 1850

McCombie, T., *The History of the Colony of Victoria*, Melbourne, 1858

McCrae, G. C., 'The Early Settlement of the Eastern Shores of Port Phillip Bay', *Victorian Historical Magazine*, 1, 1911

MacGillivray, J., *Narrative of the Voyage of HMS Rattlesnake*, 2 vols, London, 1852

Mackaness, G. (ed.), *Fourteen Journeys Over the Blue Mountains of NSW, 1813–41*, Sydney, 1965

Mackay, R., *Recollections of Early Gippsland Goldfields*, Traralgon, 1916

MacKillop, D., 'Anthropological Notes on the Aboriginal Tribes of the Daly River, North Australia', *RGSSA*, 5, 1893

McKinlay, W., *McKinlays Journal of Exploration*, Melbourne, 1862

McLaren, J., *My Crowded Solitude*, Sun Books edition, Melbourne, 1966

MacPherson, A., *Mount Abundance*, London, 1897

Major, T., *Leaves from a Squatters Notebook*, London, 1900

Mann. J. F., *Eight Months with Dr Leichhardt*, Sydney, 1888

Mathew, J., *Eaglehawk and Crow*, London, 1899

Mathew, J., *Two Representative Tribes of Queensland*, London, 1910

Meston, A., *Geographical History of Queensland*, Brisbane, 1895

Meyrick, F. J., *Life in the Bush, 1840–47*, London, 1939

Mitchell, T. L., *Journal of an Expedition into the Interior of Tropical Australia*, London, 1848

Mitchell, T. L., *Three Expeditions into Eastern Australia*, 2 vols, London, 1834

Moore, G. F., *Diary of Ten Years Eventful Life of an Early Settler in West Australia*, London, 1884

Moore, G. F., *A Descriptive Vocabulary of the Language in Common Usage Amongst the Aborigines of West Australia*, London, 1842

Morrell, J., *Sketch of a Residence Among the Aborigines of North Queensland*, Brisbane, 1863

Morris, E. E., *A Dictionary of Austral English*, London, 1898

Morgan, J., *The Life and Adventures of William Buckley*, London 1967 edition, edited C. E. Sayers

Mudie, R., *The Picture of Australasia*, London, 1829

Newland, S., *Memoirs of Simpson Newland*, Adelaide, 1928

Newland, S., 'The Parkinjees or the Aboriginal Tribes on the Darling River', *RGSSA*, 2, 1887–88

Newland, S., 'Some Aborigines I Have Known', *RGSSA*, 1894–95

Nicolay, C. G., *The Handbook of Western Australia*, London, 1896

Ogle, N., *The Colony of Western Australia*, London, 1839

Oxley, J., *Journals of Two Expeditions into the Interior of New South Wales*, London, 1820

Palmerston, C., 'Diary of Christie Palmerston', *Queensland Heritage*, 1, 8, May 1968

Parker, E. S., *The Aborigines of Australia*, Melbourne, 1854

Parker, K. L., *The Euahlayi Tribe*, London, 1905

Petrie, T., *Reminiscences of Early Queensland*, Brisbane, 1932

Plomley, N. J. B. (ed.), *Friendly Mission: the Tasmanian Journals and Papers of George Augustus Robinson, 1829–1834*, Hobart, 1966

Pridden, W., *Australia, Its History and Present Condition*, London, 1843

Reilly, J. T., *Reminiscences of Fifty Years Residence in West Australia*, Perth, 1903

Ridley, W., *Kamilaroi and Other Australian Languages*, 2nd edition, Sydney, 1875

Robertson, W., *Cooee Talks*, Sydney, 1928

Ross, J., 'The Settler in Van Diemens Land Fourteen Years Ago', *Hobart Town Almanack*, 1836

Roth, H. L., *The Aborigines of Tasmania*, 2nd edition, Halifax, 1899

Roth, W. G., *Ethnographical Studies Among the North-West-Central Queensland Aborigines*, Brisbane, 1897

Rusden, G. W., *History of Australia*, 3 vols, London, 1883

Russell, H. S., *The Genesis of Queensland*, Sydney, 1888

Sadlier, R., *The Aborigines of Australia*, Sydney, 1883

Schurmann, C. W., *Vocabulary of the Parnkalla Language*, Adelaide, 1844

Searcey, A., *In Australian Tropics*, London, 1907

Searcey, A., *In Northern Seas*, Adelaide, 1905

Semon, R., *In the Australian Bush*, London, 1899

Shenton, E., 'Reminiscences of Perth 1830–1840', *WAHS*, 1, 1, 1927

Siebert, O., 'Sagen Und Sitten Der Dieri Und Nachbarstämme in Zentral-Australien', *Globus*, 47, 1916

Sinnett, F., *The Rush to Port Curtis*, Geelong, 1859

Smith, C., *The Booandick Tribe of South Australian Aborigines*, Adelaide, 1880

Smyth, R. B., *The Aborigines of Victoria*, 2 vols, Melbourne, 1876

Stevenson, J. B., *Seven Years in the Australian Bush*, Liverpool, 1880

Stokes, J. L., *Discoveries in Australia, 2 vols*, London, 1846

Streeter, E. W., *Pearls and Pearling Life*, London, 1886

Stuart, J. M., *Explorations Across the Continent of Australia 1861–1862*, Melbourne, 1863

Sturt, C., *Narrative of an Expedition into Central Australia*, 2 vols, London, 1849

Sturt, C., *Two Expeditions into the Interior of Southern Australia*, 2 vols, London, 1833

Sutherland, A. G., *Victoria and Its Metropolis*, Melbourne, 1888

Sutherland, G., *Pioneering Days: Across the Wilds of Queensland*, Brisbane, 1913

Taplin, G., *The Narrinyeri, their Manners and Customs*, Adelaide, 1878

Taplin, G. (ed.), *The Folklore, Manners, Customs and Languages of the South Australian Aborigines*, Adelaide, 1879

Taunton, H., *Australind*, London, 1903

Teichelmann, C. G., *Outlines of a Grammar, Vocabulary and Phraseology of the Aboriginal Language of South Australia*, Adelaide, 1840

Tench, W., *Sydney's First Four Years*, Sydney 1961 edition introduced by L. F. Fitzhardinge

Threlkeld, L. E., *An Australian Language*, Sydney, 1892

Threlkeld, L. E., *Australian Reminiscences and Papers*, edited N. Gunson, Canberra, 1974

Tuckey, J. H., *An Account of a Voyage to Establish a Colony at Port Phillip*, London, 1805

Westgarth, W., *Australia Felix*, Edinburgh, 1848

Westgarth, W., *Australia*, Edinburgh, 1861

Westgarth, W., *A Report on the Condition, Capabilities and Prospects of the Australian Aborigines*, Melbourne, 1846

Westgarth, W., *Tracks of McKinlay and Party Across Australia*, London, 1863

Walker, J. B., *Early Tasmania*, Hobart, 1902

Ward, A., *The Miracle of Mapoon*, London, 1908

Warburton, P., *Journey Across the Western Interior of Australia*, London, 1875

Welsby, T., *Collected Works*, 2 vols, Brisbane, 1907

West, J., *History of Tasmania*, 2 vols, Launceston, 1852

Widowson, H., *The Present State of Van Diemens Land*, London, 1829

Willshire, W. H., *The Aborigines of Central Australia*, Adelaide, 1891

Wilson, T. B., *Narrative of a Voyage Round the World*, London, 1835

Windsor-Earl, G., 'On the Aboriginal Tribes of the North Coast of Australia', *JRGS*, 16, 1846

Windsor-Earl, G., *Enterprise in Tropical Australia*, London, 1846

Withnell, J. G., *The Customs and Traditions of the Aboriginal Natives of North-Western Australia*, Roebourne, 1901

Wood, K. M., 'A Pioneer Pearler — Reminiscences of John Wood', *WAHS*, 2, 12

Woods, J. D. (ed.), *The Native Tribes of South Australia*, Adelaide, 1879

Worgan, G. B., *Journal of a First Fleet Surgeon*, Sydney, 1978

Young, S. B., 'Reminiscences of Mrs Susan Bundarre Young', *JRAHS*, 8, 1923

Zillman, J. H. L., *Past and Present Australian Life*, London, 1889

Recent Books, Articles

Abbie, A. A., *The Original Australians*, Wellington, 1969

Allen, J., 'The Archaeology of Nineteenth Century British Imperialism', *World Archaeology*, 5, 1, June 1973

Anderson, C., 'Aboriginal Economy and Contact Relations at Bloomfield River, North Queensland', *Australian Institute of Aboriginal Studies Newsletter*, 12, September 1979

Anell, B., 'Hunting and Trapping Methods in Australia and Oceania', *Studia Ethnographica Upsaliensa*, 18, 1960

Anderson, R. H., 'The Effect of Settlement upon the New South Wales Flora', *Proceedings, Linnean Society of New South Wales*, 66, 1941

Bach, J., 'The Political Economy of Pearl Shelling', *Economic History Review*, 14, 1, 1961

Baker, S. J., *The Australian Language*, Melbourne, 1966

Barwick, D., 'Coranderrk and Cumeroogunga' in T. Epstein (ed.), *Opportunity and Response*, London, 1972

Basedow, H., *The Australian Aboriginal*, Adelaide, 1925

Bates, D., *The Passing of the Aborigines*, London, 1938

Bauer, F. H., 'The Kartans of Kangaroo Island, South Australia', in A. Pilling and R. Waterman: *Diprotodon to Detribalization*, Michigan, 1970

Bennett, M. M., *The Australian Aborigine as a Human Being*, London, 1930

Bern, J., 'Ideology and Domination', *Oceania*, 50, 2, December 1979

Berndt, R. M. 'A Preliminary Report of Fieldwork in the Ooldea Region', *Oceania*, 13, 1942–43

Berndt, R. M., 'Surviving Influence of Mission Contact on the Daly River', *Neue Zeitschrift Fur Missionswissenschaft*, 8/2-3, 1952

Berndt, R. M., 'Wuradjeri Magic and Clever Men', *Oceania*, 17, 1946–47 and 18, 1947–48

Berndt, R. M. & C. H., *Arnhem Land: Its History and Its People*, Melbourne, 1954

Berndt, R. M. & C. H., *The First Australians*, 2nd edition, Sydney, 1967

Berndt, R. M. & C. H., *From Black to White in South Australia*, Melbourne, 1951

Berndt, R. M. & C. H., 'Some Recent Articles on Culture Contact', *Oceania*, 16, 1945–46

Berndt, R. M. & C. H., *The World of the First Australians*, Sydney, 1965

Berndt, R. M. & C. H., 'An Oenpelli Monologue', *Oceania*, 22, 1951–52

Bligh, A. C. V., *The Golden Quest*, Sydney, 1938

Birdsell, J. B., 'A Basic Demographic Unit', *Current Anthropology*, 14, 4, October 1973

Birdsell, J. B., 'Some Environmental and Cultural Factors Influencing the Structuring of Australian Aboriginal Populations', *American Naturalist*, 67, 1953

Birdsell, J. B., 'Ecology, Spacing Mechanisms and Adaptive Behaviour in Aboriginal Land Tenure', in R. G. Crocombe: *Land Tenure in the Pacific*, Melbourne, 1971

Birdsell, J. B., 'Local Group Composition Among the Australian Aborigines', *Current Anthropology*, 11, 2, April 1970

Blainey, G., *Triumph of the Nomads*, Melbourne, 1975

Black, J., *North Queensland Pioneers*, Townsville, n.d.

Blake, B. J., *The Kalkatunga Language*, Canberra, 1969

Brandl, E. J., *Australian Aboriginal Paintings in Western and Central Arnhem Land*, Canberra, 1973

Bridges, B., 'The Colonization of Australia: A Communication', *Teaching History*, November 1977

Bridges, B., The Aborigines and the Land Question in New South Wales', *JRAHS*, 56, 2, June 1970

Bridges, B., 'Pemulwy: A Noble Savage', *Newsletter of the Royal Australian Historical Society*, 88, 1970

Bridges, B., 'The Native Police Corps, Port Phillip District and Victoria 1837-53', *JRAHS*, 57, 2, June 1971

Chaloupka, G., 'Pack-bells on the rock face: Aboriginal paintings of European contact in north-western Arnhem Land', *Aboriginal History*, 3, 2, 1979

Chadwick, N., *A Descriptive Study of the Djingili Language*, Canberra, 1975

Chaseling, W., *Yulengor: Nomads of Arnhem Land*, London, 1957

Corris, P., *Aborigines and Europeans in Western Victoria*, Canberra, 1963

Coutts, P. J. et al, 'Impact of European Settlement on Aboriginal Society in Western Victoria', *Records of the Victoria Archaeological Survey*, 4, August 1977

Crawford, I. M., *The Art of the Wandjina*, Melbourne, 1968

Dixon, R. M. W., *The Dyirbal Language of North Queensland*, Cambridge, 1972

Dixon, R. M. W., *A Grammar of Yidin*, Cambridge, 1977

Docker, E. C., *Simply Human Beings*, Brisbane, 1964

Doolan, J. K., 'Aboriginal Concept of Boundary', *Oceania*, 44, 3, March 1979

Douglas, W. H., *The Aboriginal Languages of the South-West of Western Australia*, Canberra, 1968

Durack, M., *The Rock and the Sand*, Corgi edition, London, 1911

Eades, D. K., *The Dharawal and Dhurga Languages of the New South Wales South Coast*, Canberra, 1976

Eliade, M., *Australian Religions*, Ithaca, 1973

Elkin, A. P., *The Australian Aborigines*, 4th edition, Sydney, 1964

Elkin, A. P., *Aboriginal Men of High Degree*, Sydney, 1954

Elkin, A. P., 'Civilized Aborigines and Native Culture', *Oceania*, 6, December 1935

Elkin, A. P., 'Elements of Australian Aboriginal Philosophy', *Oceania*, 60, 2, December 1969

Elkin, A. P., 'Notes on the Aborigines of the Walgett District', *Mankind*, 3, 2, 1943

Elkin, A. P., 'Reaction and Interaction: A Food Gathering People and European Settlement in Australia', *American Anthropologist*, 53, 1951

Elkin, A. P., 'The Secret Life of the Australian Aborigines', *Oceania*, 3, December 1932

Evans, R. et al, *Exclusion, Exploitation and Extermination*, Sydney, 1975

Gale, F., *A Study of Assimilation: Part Aborigines in South Australia*, Adelaide, 1964

Geytenbeek, B. & H., *Gidabal Grammar and Dictionary*, Canberra, 1971

Gould, R. A., 'Subsistence Behaviour Among the Western Desert Aborigines', *Oceania*, 39, 1969

Gould, R. A., *Yiwara: Foragers of the Australian Desert*, London, 1969

Gould, R. A., 'Uses and Effects of Fire Among the Western Desert Aborigines', *Mankind*, 8, 1971

Green, N., 'Aboriginal and Settler Conflict in Western Australia, 1826–1852', *The Push from the Bush*, 3, May 1979

Gunson, N. (ed.), *Australian Reminiscences and Papers of L. E. Threlkeld*, Canberra, 1974

Haddon, A. C., *Head Hunters: Black, White and Brown*, London, 1932

Haglund, L., 'Dating Aboriginal Relics from the Contact Period', *Archaeology and Physical Anthropology in Oceania*, 11, 3, October 1976

Hale, H. M. & N. B. Tindale, 'Aborigines of Princess Charlotte Bay, North Queensland', *Records of South Australian Museum*, 5, 1933–36

Hale, H. M. & N. B. Tindale, 'Observations on Aborigines of the Flinders Ranges', *Records of the South Australian Museum*, 3, 1925–28

Hall, H. A., *A Partial Vocabulary of the Ngalooma Language*, Canberra, 1921

Hallam, S., *Fire and Hearth*, Canberra, 1975

Hamilton, A., 'Blacks and Whites: The Relationships of Change', *Arena*, 30, 1972

Hamman, J., 'The Coorong Massacre', *Flinders Journal of Politics and History*, 3, 1973

Hancock, W. K., *Australia*, Jacaranda edition, Brisbane, 1960

Hasluck, A., 'Yagan the Patriot', *WAHS*, 7, 1961

Hasluck, P., *Black Australians*, Melbourne, 1942

Haynes, B. T., *West Australian Aborigines, 1622–1972*, Perth, 1973

Hercus, L., *The Languages of Victoria*, Canberra, 1969

Hercus, L., 'Tales of Nadu-Dagali (Rib-Bone Billy)', *Aboriginal History*, 1, 1, 1977

Hiatt, B., 'The Food Quest and the Economy of the Tasmanian Aborigines', *Oceania*, 38, 2 and 3, 1968

Hiatt, L. R., 'Local Organization Among the Australian Aborigines', *Oceania*, 32, 1962

Hiatt, L. R., 'The Lost Horde', *Oceania*, 37, 1965

Hughes, I., 'A State of Open Warfare', *Lectures on North Queensland History*, second series, Townsville, 1975

Hutchison, D. E. (ed.), *Aboriginal Progress: A New Era?*, Perth, 1969

Inglis, J., 'One Hundred Years of Point Macleay, South Australia', *Mankind*, 5, 12, November 1962

Jones, R., 'The Demography of Hunters and Farmers in Tasmania', in D. J. Mulvaney and J. Golson: *Aboriginal Man and Environment in Australia*, Canberra, 1971

Jones, R., 'Tasmanian Aborigines and Dogs', *Mankind*, 7, 1970

Kelly, C., 'Some Aspects of Culture Contact in Eastern Australia', *Oceania*, 15, 1944–45

Kolig, E., 'Bi:H and Gadeja', *Oceania*, 43, 1, September 1972

Laver, P. K., 'Report of a Preliminary Ethno-historical and Archaeological Survey of Fraser Island', *University of Queensland, Occasional Papers in Anthropology*, No. 8

McBride, I. (ed.), *Records of Time Past*, Canberra, 1978

McCarthy, F. D., *Rock Art of the Cobar Pedeplain*, Canberra, 1976

McConnell, U., 'Social Organization of the Tribes of Cape York Peninsula', *Oceania*, 10, 1, 1939

McConnell, U., 'The Wik-Munkan Tribe of Cape York Peninsula', *Oceania*, 1, 1930–31

McMahon, A., 'Tasmanian Aboriginal Women as Slaves', *THRA*, 23, 2, June 1976

The Mapoon Story According to the Invaders, Sydney, 1975

Meggitt, M. J., 'The Association between Australian Aborigines and Dingoes', *American Association Advancement of Science*, Publication No. 78

Meggitt, M. J., *Desert People*, Sydney, 1962

Meggitt, M. J., 'Indigenous Forms of Government Among the Australian Aborigines' in I. Hogbin and L. R. Hiatt: *Readings in Australian and Pacific Anthropology*, Melbourne, 1966

Moore, D. R., *Islanders and Aborigines at Cape York*, Canberra, 1979

Moorwood, M. J., 'Three Rock Art Sites in Central Queensland', *University of Queensland: Occasional Papers in Anthropology*, 6, 1975

Mulvaney, D. J. & J. Golson, *Aboriginal Man and Environment in Australia*, Canberra, 1971

Mulvaney, D. J., *The Pre-history of Australia*, revised edition, Ringwood, 1975

Murray-Smith, S., 'Beyond the Pale: The Islander Communities of Bass Strait in the Nineteenth Century', *THRA*, 20, 4, December, 1973

Oates, W. & L., *Gugu-Yalanji and Wik-Munkan Language Studies*, Canberra, 1964

Petersen, N. (ed.), *Tribes and Boundaries in Australia*, Canberra, 1976

Piddington, R., 'A Note on Karadjeri Local Organization', *Oceania*, 61, 4, June 1971

Plomley, N. J. B., *A World List of the Tasmanian Aboriginal Languages*, Hobart, 1976

Radcliffe-Brown, A. R., 'Black Australia', *Australian Museum Magazine*, 4, 4, October-December 1930

Radcliffe-Brown, A. R., 'The Rainbow Serpent Myth in South-East Australia', *Oceania*, 1, 1930–31

Radcliffe-Brown, A. R., 'The Social Organization of Australian Tribes', *Oceania*, 1, 1930

Radcliffe-Brown, A. R., 'Three Tribes of Western Australia', *Journal Royal Anthropological Institute*, 43, 1913

Reay, M., 'Native Thought in Rural New South Wales', *Oceania*, 20, 1949

Reay, M., 'The Background of Alien Impact' in R. M. & C. H. Berndt (eds): *Aboriginal Man in Australia*, Sydney, 1965

Reece, L., *Dictionary of the Wailbri (Walpiri) Language of Central Australia*, Sydney, 1975

Reece, R. H. W., *Aborigines and Colonists: Aborigines and Colonial Society in NSW in the 1830's and 1840's*, Sydney, 1974

Reece, R. H. W., 'Feasts and Blankets: The History of Some Early Attempts to Establish Relations with the Aborigines of NSW, 1814–1846', *Archaeology and Physical Anthropology in Oceania*, 2, 3, October 1967

Reynolds, H., 'Jimmy Governor and Jimmie Blacksmith', *Australian Literary Studies*, 9, 1, May 1979

Reynolds, H., 'The Unrecorded Battlefields of Queensland', *Race Relations in North Queensland*, Townsville, 1978

Roughsey, D., *Moon and Rainbow*, Sydney, 1971

Rowley, C. D., 'Aborigines and Other Australians', *Oceania*, 32, 4, 1962

Rowley, C. D., *The Destruction of Aboriginal Society*, Melbourne, 1972

Rowley, C. D., *The Remote Aborigines*, Melbourne, 1972

Rowley, C. D., *Outcasts in White Australia*, Melbourne, 1972

Ryan, L., 'The Struggle for Recognition: part Aborigines in Tasmania in the Nineteenth Century', *Aboriginal History*, 1, 1, 1977

Sahlens, M., *Stone Age Economics*, London, 1974

Shaw, B. & J. Sullivan, 'They same as you and me': Encounters with the Gadia in the East Kimberley', *Aboriginal History*, 3, 2, 1979

Sharp, L., 'Steel Axes for Stone Age Australians' in E. H. Spicer (ed.), *Human Problems in Technological Change*, New York, 1952

Sharp, L., 'Ritual Life and Economics of the Yir-Yoront of Cape York Peninsula', *Oceania*, 5, 1934

Sharp, L., 'Social Organization of the Yir-Yoront of Cape York Peninsula', *Oceania*, 4, 1933–34

Spencer, B., *Native Tribes of the Northern Territory of Australia*, London, 1914

Spencer, B., *Wanderings in Wild Australia*, 2 vols, London, 1928

Spencer, B. & F. J. Gillen, *Across Australia*, London, 1912

Spencer, B. & F. J. Gillen, *The Arunta*, London, 1922

Spencer, B. & F. J. Gillen, *The Native Tribes of Central Australia*, Dover edition, New York, 1968

Stanner, W. E. H., 'Aboriginal Territorial Organization', *Oceania*, 36, 1965

Stanner, W. E. H., *After the Dreaming*, Sydney, 1969

Stanner, W. E. H., 'Ceremonial Economics of the Mulluk Mulluk and Madngella Tribes of the Daly River', *Oceania*, 4, 2, December 1933

Stanner, W. E. H., 'Continuity and Change Among the Aborigines', *Australian Journal of Science*, 21, 1958–59

Stanner, W. E. H., 'The Daly River Tribes', *Oceania*, 3, 4, June 1933

Stanner, W. E. H., 'Durmugam, a Nangiomeri', in J. B. Casagrande (ed.), *In the Company of Man*, New York, 1960

Strehlow, T. G. H., 'Aranda Phonetics', *Oceania*, 12, 1941–42

Strehlow, T. G. H., *Journey to Horseshoe Bend*, Sydney, 1969

Thomson, D. F., 'The Dugong Hunters of Cape York', *Journal Royal Anthropological Institute*, 64, 1934

Thomson, D. F., 'In Camp with Stone Age Men', *Queenslander*, 22, 29 January 1931

Thomson, D. F., 'The Hero Cult, Initiation and Totemism on Cape York', *Journal Royal Anthropological Institute*, 63, 1933

Thorpe, O., *First Catholic Mission to the Australian Aborigines*, Sydney, 1949

Threadgill, B., *South Australian Land Exploration, 1856–1880*, Adelaide, 1922

Tindale, N. B., *Aboriginal Tribes of Australia*, Canberra, 1974

Tindale, N. B., 'Ecology of Primitive Aboriginal Man in Australia', in A. Keast et al: *Biogeography and Ecology in Australia*, Hague, 1959

Tindale, N. B., 'Natives of Groote Eyland and of the West Coast of the Gulf of Carpentaria', *Records of South Australian Museum*, 2, 1925–28

Tindale, N. B., 'A Survey of the Half-Caste Problem in South Australia', *RGSSA*, 42, 1940–41

Wade-Broun, N., *Memoirs of a Queensland Pioneer*, Sandgate, 1944

Warner, W. L., *A Black Civilization*, New York, 1958

Wegner, J., 'The Aborigines of the Etheridge Shire' in H. Reynolds (ed.), *Race Relations in North Queensland*, Townsville, 1979

Willey, K., *Boss Drover*, Adelaide, 1971

Woolmington, J., *Aborigines in Colonial Society, 1788–1850*, Melbourne, 1973

Worsley, P., 'Utilization of Natural Food Resources by an Australian Aboriginal Tribe', *Acta Ethnographica*, 10, 1961

Wright, B. J., *Rock Art of the Pilbara Region*, Canberra, 1968

Oral History

Considerable use has been made of tapes in the James Cook University Oral History collection and especially material collected by Caroline Strachan. During the last few years I have read with great interest two excellent oral history collections which have not been published to this moment. They are Jay and Peter Read's *A View of the Past* and Louise Hercus and Peter Sutton's *This is What Happened*.

INDEX

Lightning Source UK Ltd.
Milton Keynes UK
17 December 2010

164496UK00002B/16/P